UNDERSTANDING ADA

UNDERSTANDING ADA*

KENNETH C. SHUMATE
Hughes Aircraft Company

HARPER & ROW, PUBLISHERS, New York
Cambridge, Hagerstown, Philadelphia, San Francisco
London, Mexico City, São Paulo, Sydney

* Ada is a registered trademark of the U.S. Government (Ada Joint Program Office).

The names of all computer programs and computers included herein are registered trademarks of their makers.

Sponsoring Editor: John Willig
Project Editor: Mary E. Kennedy
Designer: C. Linda Dingler
Production Managers: Marion Palen, Delia Tedoff
Compositor: Haddon Craftsmen
Art by: Kim Llewellyn
Cover design by: Steve Sullivan

Understanding Ada Copyright © 1984 by Harper & Row, Publishers, Inc.
Library of Congress Cataloging in Publication Data   Shumate, Kenneth C.
  Understanding Ada.
    Includes index
    I Ada (Computer program language) II Title.
QA76.73.A35S48 1983   001.64'24   83-12705
1SBN 0-06-046133-0

Contents

Preface

Ada is a computer programming language developed for the United States Department of Defense (DoD). The objective of this book is to provide a basic understanding of major language features. It is intended to be a first book on Ada.

Ada was developed for the purpose of constructing large computer programs to be used in embedded computer systems: systems such as aircraft or missiles, command and control systems, and computer-controlled radars or weapons. Such systems are typically constructed by large teams of programmers, take several years to develop, and have lifetimes spanning decades, during which time the programs are upgraded, corrected, and modified. Ada was designed to meet the requirements stated in a language specification. The specification established the necessary characteristics of a language for creating programs for embedded computer systems. The Ada design has been widely judged to be successful. The language has been adopted as a standard by the American National Standards Institute (ANSI) and is likely to see widespread commercial use outside the U.S. DoD.

This book explains the Ada language simply. To allow a simple explanation, some of the subtle or complicated features of Ada are ignored or treated lightly. The level of detail is such that it lets the technical engineering or data processing manager know "What is Ada? How does it work?" This book—its content and level of detail—is largely based on short, intensive courses that I have taught to technical managers. It contains information these people need to do their jobs. Programmers will also find the material in this book valuable as a prelude to reading more advanced texts on Ada. It is the first step on the (long) road to learning Ada.

Ada is a rich and complicated programming language—necessarily so, to address the complex problems for which it was designed. There are no authorized subsets of the language, since the DoD has decided that no single subset would have the features required by all users (although individual users can create their own subsets through coding standards or the use of language preprocessors). Furthermore, since Ada was designed as an integrated, unified language, it is difficult to remove features without disturbing the unity of the remainder of the language.

How then can Ada be made understandable, without elaborating all its features? First, I do not attempt to define a subset of the language for programmers to use to solve problems. Instead, I discuss and illustrate aspects of Ada that will develop significant insight into the nature of the language. I do not attempt to build complete programming skills. The examples are quite simple. They are intended to be easy to understand, for I believe that a *first* exposition of complex topics should use simple examples. Second, I concentrate initially on Pascal. Since Ada uses Pascal as a base language, it is possible to learn a great deal about the nature of Ada by first presenting those parts of the language that are similar in content to Pascal. Pascal was designed to be a language for the teaching of programming. It can simplify the teaching of Ada. My teaching of Ada to engineers whose primary experience was in FORTRAN and assembly language indicates that an introduction to the concepts used in Pascal and other Algol 60-like languages is a necessary prelude to understanding Ada. Third, I present the features of Ada that are enhancements to Pascal, and fourth, I present major new features and advances of Ada. After understanding part of Ada, it is easier to investigate the ways in which it goes beyond Pascal, both in minor modifications and in major extensions. The approach of teaching the Pascal-like parts of Ada separately from advanced concepts has the secondary advantage of isolating the two types of complexity in Ada. One facet of Ada's complexity is its combination of advanced and not widely known features: packages, tasks, generics, exceptions, private types, and others. Another facet is its use of features common and well accepted in the Algol 60 and Pascal class of languages, but unknown to engineers with largely FORTRAN backgrounds: enumeration types, records, pointers, strong typing, and others. Considering the two types of complexity separately makes Ada seem less big and complex.

C.A.R. Hoare, in his 1980 Turing Award lecture, was critical of the size and complexity of Ada. He felt that the language contained features that made it too complicated to use effectively. However, he did state that it was possible to prune Ada in such a way that it would be reliable, efficient, safe, and economic. It is likely that many of the early Ada applications, especially in a commercial environment, will not use Ada's advanced features. Indeed, Ada will probably first be used merely to replace languages such as FORTRAN, Pascal, Algol, "C," and BASIC. The parts of Ada that will satisfy this task are those which are rather like Pascal and which are emphasized in this book. Again, I do not attempt to define a Pascal-like subset of Ada, but instead focus on features that are similar to or are about the same level of complexity as related features in Pascal.

I hope to accomplish two goals. First, to make Ada understandable to technical managers so that they can make decisions regarding use of the language and can understand the programmer's work. Second, to provide an introduction to Ada for programmers who are interested in the language but are not yet prepared to spend the time to acquire the skills necessary to perform Ada implementations.

Each chapter begins with a statement of the chapter's objective followed by the chapter text. After the text, in chapters with language discussions, comes an exercise section, which presents a simple problem to be solved by the reader. Then follows an Ada program to solve the exercise. Each program has been compiled and, when appropriate, executed on a government-validated translator. A discussion of the program follows, in which some aspect of the problem is occasionally used to introduce new material. Each chapter ends with Keys to Understanding, a summary of important points covered in the chapter.

Although the book is self-contained, occasional reference is made to the Ada language reference manual (LRM). The edition used is:

ANSI/MIL-STD-1815A

22 JANUARY 1983

United States Department of Defense

Approved February 17, 1983

American National Standards Institute, Inc.

Part 1, "Introduction," sets the foundation for the remainder of the book. Chapter 1 provides some simple examples of Ada programs and briefly discusses Ada's place among programming languages. Chapter 2 provides more of the history of Ada than is common in language texts. This is consonant with the goal of providing programming, engineering, or other technical managers with a comprehensive introduction to the Ada community. Chapter 3, "Language Overview," is of particular importance. To understand the individual language features as they are introduced, it is necessary to first have some understanding of the overall language structure. Chapter 4, "Software Development Using Ada," addresses the beneficial changes that are likely to occur when using Ada. It will help answer the question "Why should I use Ada?"

Part 2, "Ada as Pascal," approaches Ada as a modern programming language, using Pascal as a model. You are not expected to be familiar with Pascal to understand this section. Indeed, if all beginning students of Ada were expert in Pascal, part 2 perhaps would not be necessary. Those who do know something about Pascal can read part 2 with profit to make comparisons and build their understanding of Ada upon a Pascal foundation. Chapter 5 outlines the Pascal concepts discussed in part 2. Chapters 6 to 12 are a straightforward presentation of features of Ada that are similar to Pascal. The Ada concepts discussed in these chapters are moderately well known, although notions of strong typing, enumeration types, records, and pointers will be new to many.

The real reason for writing part 2 stems from my observations while teaching Ada to technical managers. For those in the class who knew a language such as Pascal, much of Ada was merely the next logical step in language evolution. For those with backgrounds in FORTRAN, COBOL, or assembly language, Ada was too much to swallow in one bite. One approach to overcoming the problem of digesting Ada is to first teach Pascal, then "Ada as Pascal," and then full Ada. I have taught Pascal to both experienced and beginning programmers and have found that both kinds of students learn the language quite readily. An alternative to teaching Pascal is to present the Pascal-like parts of Ada before presenting the remainder of the language. That is the objective of part 2. Careful study of this part will allow you to understand many concepts that require thought but are by no means unique to Ada. You will then be better able to understand advances made by Ada, including its features for embedded computer systems. Perhaps one reason for my writing part 2 the way I did is that I admire Pascal and feel that Ada captures much of its simplicity, clarity, and elegance.

Part 3, "Ada as Ada," presents those aspects of Ada that are modifications and improvements to Pascal. For instance, Ada enforces even stricter type compatibility than Pascal, provides easy initialization of data structures, and provides for dynamic storage allocation for variable length arrays. Chapter 13 outlines the ways in which Ada has extended Pascal to produce a language suitable for creating production programs. Chapters 14 to 20 follow the exposition of chapters 6 to 12, elaborating on how Ada differs from Pascal. At the conclusion of part 3, you should understand Ada well enough so that it might serve as a replacement for languages you are currently using. However, if that were all that Ada accomplished, it would not be needed and certainly would not satisfy the requirements for which it was developed.

Ada is not Pascal; Ada is Ada. Programming style in Ada is likely to be quite different than programming style in Pascal. Design style will certainly be very different. Pascal is a language for writing single, independent programs, while Ada is a language for designing and creating large software systems— for programming in the large. Parts 2 and 3 present Ada primarily as a modern, block-structured language suitable for general-purpose programming. This introduction to the algorithmic aspects of Ada lays the foundation for those features that will allow Ada to be used for the design and creation of large software systems.

Part 4, "Advanced Features," presents features of Ada that will allow it to be used effectively to develop large, maintainable software systems. It covers aspects of Ada that extend beyond the current understanding of most technical managers and beyond the current skills and knowledge of most programming groups. Some of the features seem difficult only because they are new and call for us to think about program development in new ways. Others, perhaps, seem difficult because we have not yet learned appropriate ways to discuss the concepts. Chapters 21 to 25 cover advanced Ada features at a relatively high level but with enough detail to understand how each feature might be used and to understand some of the complexity issues.

Part 5, "All About Ada," continues a discussion begun in chapter 2 about the environment surrounding Ada development and use. It is less technical and language oriented than parts 2, 3, and 4, and could profitably be read immediately after part 1. Chapter 26 is concerned with the Ada Programming Support Environment, the APSE, which will provide the support system and software tools to develop Ada programs and to manage large-system development. Chapter 27 discusses the Ada Compiler Validation Capability, which will provide the DoD with the ability to enforce Ada standardization. Chapter 28 reviews and summarizes all earlier material by providing a brief discussion of twelve specific points. These points are intended to structure and focus information about Ada. The final chapter concludes with some personal observations and thoughts concerning the future of the language.

Because this book provides an easy introduction to Ada and a description of the environment in which it has been and is being developed, it can serve as a handbook for the technical manager. It provides information the technical manager needs to make decisions about the use of Ada or to direct Ada projects; it should also be an easy introduction to the language for the programmer who wants to begin understanding Ada.

ACKNOWLEDGEMENTS

Many people made important contributions during the preparation of this book. I particularly wish to thank those who read early versions of the manuscript for understandability: G. Anderson, B. Colborn, R. Fritz, J. Hooper, K. Nielsen, and R. Sauer. A number of reviewers made valuable comments, as did associates at Hughes Aircraft Company. ROLM and Data General were helpful in providing access to their Ada compiler. Special thanks to M. Shumate, who edited the manuscript during its development. Maureen, John, Karen, and Kelly Shumate were supportive during the entire project.

K. C. SHUMATE

San Diego
January 1984

PART 1

INTRODUCTION

Ada is the new computer programming language specified by the United States Department of Defense (DoD) for the programming of computers embedded within larger systems. Computers internal to aircraft, ships, radars, or command and control systems are used in different ways than in business or data processing applications. Computers in such embedded computer systems typically interface with human operators and external devices in real time, as events are occurring. They read signals from sensors and send commands to electrical and electromechanical devices. Commercial systems such as process control and data communications have similar characteristics. Ada will eventually be the single language for programming DoD embedded computer systems, will find similar use among the defense establishments of allies of the United States, and is certain to have widespread commercial use. In fact, the first delivered production Ada software was a payroll and inventory system for a truck manufacturer.

Part 1, "Introduction," presents some simple examples of Ada programs that show the form of the language, summarizes the history of Ada development and its technical requirements, provides an overview of the complete language, including its advanced features, and discusses how software will be developed using Ada. This introduction sets the foundation for the language-specific presentations of parts 2, 3, and 4.

1

Jumping Right In

Objective: to provide some simple examples of
Ada programs

Let's begin by looking at a small Ada procedure whose net effect is to write "Hello, World" on a standard output device.

```
procedure HELLO_WORLD is
begin
   PUT ("Hello, World");
end HELLO_WORLD;
```

HELLO_WORLD is the name of the procedure, which is an executable block of code. The executable part is delineated by **begin** and **end**; the procedure itself is delineated by **procedure** HELLO_WORLD and **end** HELLO_WORLD. We will use lowercase boldface to indicate Ada reserved words.

Here is a longer example, with comments. Note that "--" indicates that what follows is a comment (-- This is a comment).

```
procedure GRADES is
-- GRADES computes the SUM and MAXIMUM of
-- a set of grades
   GRADE, SUM, MAXIMUM, NUMBER_OF_STUDENTS : INTEGER;
```

```
begin
  GET(NUMBER_OF_STUDENTS);
  MAXIMUM := 0;
  SUM := 0;
  for LOOP_COUNT in 1 . . NUMBER_OF_STUDENTS loop
    GET(GRADE);
    SUM := SUM + GRADE;
    if GRADE > MAXIMUM then
      MAXIMUM := GRADE;
    end if;
  end loop;
  PUT ("MAXIMUM GRADE IS: "); PUT(MAXIMUM);  NEW_LINE;
  PUT ("SUM OF GRADES IS: "); PUT(SUM);        NEW_LINE;
end GRADES;
```

As you can see by the examples, Ada is a high-level language with a structure similar to other modern languages. Indeed, as will be shown in part 2, much of Ada is as easily understandable as Pascal, which was designed to be a simple language to be used in teaching programming. Ada, however, goes beyond Pascal in its ability to define new types of data objects and provides additional measures to help ensure safe programming practices. Certain language features allow more programmer errors to be caught at compile time rather than during run-time testing (or rather than not being caught at all and turning up as bugs in the system). Even further, Ada provides capabilities for concurrent programming, for error detection and handling, and for effective packaging of data and procedures. It also provides capabilities and tools for large programming teams to work effectively together on large projects. These capabilities allow Ada to meet its primary objective of being a language for embedded computer systems.

Ada's roots lie in the same foundation as many previous languages. In addition to its base language, Pascal, the design of Ada benefited from other languages derived from Pascal: Euclid, Lis, Modula, and Sue. In addition, Ada was influenced by languages such as PL/I, Algol 68, and Simula and the research languages Alphard and Clu.

Ada was designed to replace, and was somewhat influenced by, existing languages for the programming of DoD embedded computer systems, especially the DoD languages Jovial (USAF), CMS-2 (USN), Tacpol (USA), and SPL/I (USN). These languages have features and operating environments created for real-time, embedded computer system applications. Ada must provide these same facilities. Ada is also intended to replace FORTRAN in those embedded computer system applications that currently use that language.

The design of Ada focused on the primary concerns of program reliability, program maintainability, ease of use, and efficiency. Program reliability is critical, since DoD embedded computer systems typically deal with life-and-death situations in which the programs must not fail. Ada has special features to deal with reliability. Program maintainability is important since embedded computer systems typically have long lifetimes and are frequently modified. Maintainability concerns led to a language design philosophy that stressed ease of reading a program over ease of writing one. The concern for ease of use led to an attempt to make the language as simple as possible, considering the complex task for which it was designed. Efficiency is important, since in many respects Ada is competing with assembly language even more than with high-level languages, since efficient use of space and time is critical in most real-time applications. Whether Ada succeeds in these areas is still controversial. Efficiency depends upon the final quality of actual implementations. Reliability and maintainability depend partly on ease of use—on the ability of programmers to find Ada easy to understand and easy to use. It is these latter issues which are relevant to this book.

Now that we have a general idea of what Ada does, let us turn to its history: the requirements, the specification, the development, the implementation, and the support environment.

By the way, if you have not read the preface, you ought to do so. It provides important preliminary material, states the objectives of the book, and outlines its contents.

About the Exercises

Each of the technical chapters contains an exercise for the reader. The exercises are intended to be quite easy. Each illustrates some straighforward aspect of the chapter. They are provided to invite the reader to think further about using Ada in an actual problem. A solution in the form of a program fragment is satisfactory, although the program provided in the text will always be a complete program that has been compiled and, when appropriate, executed. The programs shown here were originally developed on the government validated NYU ANSI-ADA/ED translator version 1.1 (11 April 1983). Some of the solutions are shown with message output from the compiler. All the programs have also been run on the validated **ROLM** Ada compiler. The exercises are not meant simply as student problems—they are an integral part of the chapter text and will occasionally serve as the basis for discussion of new material. Even if you choose to not work the exercise, you should study the solution given and read the discussion. The format for the exercises is:

EXERCISE__N — A statement of the exercise/problem
PROGRAM__N — A complete program, completing the exercise. Some of the solutions show the complete output of the listing file from the translator.
DISCUSSION__N — A discussion of the exercise and the solution, occasionally introducing new material

Exercise__1

Write a program that will read two numbers of type **INTEGER**, add them together, and print the result.

Program__1

```
with TEXT__IO; use TEXT__IO;
procedure PROGRAM__1 is
  SUM, FIRST, SECOND : INTEGER;
  package IO is new INTEGER__IO(INTEGER); use IO;
begin
  PUT__LINE("Enter a number");
  GET(FIRST);
  PUT__LINE("Enter another number");
  GET(SECOND);
  SUM := FIRST + SECOND;
  PUT__LINE("The sum of the numbers is:"); PUT(SUM);
end PROGRAM__1;
```

```
No translation errors detected
Translation time: 36 seconds
Binding time: 3.1 seconds
Begin Ada execution
```

```
Enter a number              6
Enter another number        5
The sum of the numbers is:   11
```

Execution complete
Execution time: 8 seconds
I-code statements executed: 55

Discussion—1

Now that we are concerned with a real program rather than a single procedure or program fragment, we have a little more work to do. First of all, the Language Reference Manual (LRM) does not specify what constitutes a "main" program. It is implementation dependent. In Ada/Ed, the main program can be called MAIN, or a main program can be specified as a compiler option, or if there is only a single parameterless procedure it is the main program by default. Here we are using the default that we have only one procedure, so it is the main program.

The next thing we must be concerned with is the specification of the context for compilation of the program. The **with** clause specifies that our program is compiled with the library package TEXT_IO. TEXT_IO provides the mechanism for output of strings (PUT for strings) and also provides the capability (called generic packages) for output of numeric types.

Generic packages will be covered briefly in chapter 3 and then more extensively in chapter 23. Now all you need to know is that we must create an instance of a generic program (an "instantiation") by the clause

```
package IO is new INTEGER_IO(INTEGER); use IO;
```

Now that the preliminaries have been taken care of, we are ready to discuss our simple program.

It simply gets the two numbers from the standard input device, a terminal, a batch job input, or whatever else is specified, adds them together, and puts the result out to the standard output. The spacing and formatting are quite simplistic. The intent is that major using communities have the ability to define their own input/output capabilities and implement them using Ada features. The language does define some standard input and output using the Ada package. There is a capability for rudimentary formatting, but the default values for spacing and so on are usually satisfactory and we will use them. We will have little more to say about input and output in Ada.

KEY TO UNDERSTANDING

▶ For small programs, Ada has a great deal of similarity to other high-level languages.

2

History of Ada

Objective: to present the history of Ada's development, including the need for a common language, the specification of language requirements, and the constant review of the language design

Embedded computer systems are systems incorporated (embedded) into larger systems like ships, airplanes, radar, command and control systems, automated factories, and robots. The host systems have primary functions other than computing. Because this class of application is quite distinct from scientific computing or business data processing, embedded computer software is often strikingly different from software for scientific or business applications. Typical embedded computer applications must interface with external devices, reading signals from sensors and signaling commands to electrical and electromechanical devices. Control signals as well as data are output. Often, multiple processors are used to simultaneously handle different aspects of a task. In addition, the programs tend to be large (50,000 to 100,000 or more lines of code), long lived, and quite volatile (major changes are frequent), and personnel turnover is rapid. Finally, reliability is a key issue: people's lives often depend on these systems, which are typically used for fighting wars. These characteristics emphasize maintainability and require special facilities for multitasking, machine-level access, and reliability.

2.1 *REQUIREMENT FOR A COMMON LANGUAGE*

In the early 1970s studies revealed that there was a serious cost problem in the development and use of DoD computer systems, and that most of the cost was related to embedded computer systems. Figure 2-1 shows how the DoD spent $3 billion for software in 1973. Of particular interest is that the majority of the costs were not incurred for developing new systems but rather for maintaining old ones. Later studies revealed that over 200 models of computers and over 450 general-purpose programming languages and dialects were being used for embedded computer systems. Most of the software was being written in assembly language; those projects using high-order languages still used a high proportion of assembly language to overcome deficiencies and accomplish functions not amenable to high-level implementation. Such lack of commonality and use of assembly language makes the development of new software difficult and creates even more serious problems for software maintenance.

The lack of language commonality and stability caused a number of problems. First was the cost of developing translators and support environments for a number of different languages—not just the original cost, but the maintenance of all the duplicated support software over the twenty or more years of system life. Second was the extra cost incurred during system development of dealing with a sequence of new, unproven software tools. Such a

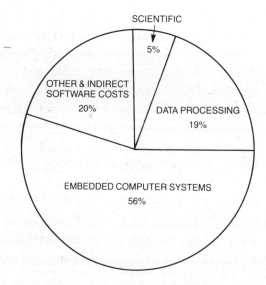

Figure 2-1   Annual DoD Software Costs

situation often leads to schedule slips and a less suitable product. Third was the difficulty and expense of maintaining system software by other than the original developers. This factor not only increases cost but can adversely affect operational readiness because of the time it takes to repair programming errors and make necessary system enhancements. Fourth was the requirement to retrain programmers. Since each DoD service and the commercial world all used different languages, some retraining was usually required when programmers moved from one community to another.

Each of the military departments was concerned with the language proliferation and related problems and began efforts separately to study the feasibility of common languages. To coordinate these efforts, the DoD established the High-Order Language Working Group (HOLWG) in 1975. The HOLWG consisted of representatives from DoD and other government agencies. It was charged with the mission to formulate requirements, evaluate existing languages, and implement a minimal set of languages for DoD use. A policy framework was established by DoD Directive 5000.29, *Management of Computer Resources in Major Defense Systems*. The directive specifically required the use of a high-order programming language (HOL) selected from the approved languages listed in DoD Instruction 5000.31:

- CMS-2
- SPL/I
- Tacpol
- J3 Jovial
- J73 Jovial
- ANSI COBOL
- ANSI FORTRAN

To formulate the capabilities a new language would have to fulfill, the HOLWG then developed a series of requirements documents:

- Strawman   (April 1975)
- Woodenman   (August 1975)
- Tinman   (January 1976)
- Ironman   (January 1977)
- Revised Ironman   (July 1977)
- Steelman   (June 1978)

These documents (extensively reviewed by government, industry, and the academic community) represent stepwise refinement of the language requirements, which culminated in *Department of Defense Requirements for High Order Computer Programming Languages: "Steelman."* In 1976 several languages were evaluated against Tinman requirements:

- Jovial, SPL/I, Tacpol, CMS-2   -- used for DoD embedded
    -- computer systems
- CORAL-66, LIS, Pearl, RTL-2, HAL/S   -- used for process control and
    -- similar applications
- Euclid, Moral, ECL, Simula-67   -- used for research
- COBOL, FORTRAN, Pascal, Algol, PL/I   -- used for general
    -- applications

There were three important conclusions from these evaluations: that no language was suitable in its current state, that one language would be a desirable and achievable goal, and that development should be started from a suitable base, such as Pascal, PL/I, or Algol 68.

2.2 CHARACTERISTICS OF STEELMAN

The Steelman document established the requirements for a language for programming DoD embedded computer systems. Ada was later designed from these requirements, although it does not meet every specification and in some ways goes beyond the stated requirements. Although Ada has evolved in many ways from its initial specification, it is still valuable to look at the original requirements to better understand what the language is attempting to accomplish.

This section highlights the major features that influenced Ada language design. The principal technical requirements established in Steelman were that the language developed must

- Be suitable for embedded computer applications
- Be appropriate for software for long-lived systems
- Be suitable as a common language
- Not impose execution costs due to unneeded generality
- Provide a base for development, maintenance, and support environment
- Exemplify good language design

Meeting these requirements sometimes involves trade-offs among opposing goals. For instance, the common language and the embedded computer application requirements, which imply that the language be of some complexity and generality, must be weighed against the requirement to not impose execution costs.

Steelman also established eight criteria for the design of the language. The following summary descriptions adopt much of the exact phrasing of the Steelman.

Generality. The language shall provide generality only to the extent necessary to satisfy the needs of embedded computer applications.

Reliability. The language should aid the design and development of reliable programs; be designed to avoid error-prone features; maximize automatic detection of programming errors; require some redundant, but not duplicative, specifications in programs.

Maintainability. The language should promote ease of program maintenance; emphasize program readability (that is, clarity, understandability, and modifiability of programs); encourage user documentation of programs; require explicit specification of programmer decisions.

Efficiency. The language design should aid the production of efficient object programs.

Simplicity. The language should not contain unnecessary complexity; should have a consistent semantic structure that minimizes the number of underlying concepts; should be as small as possible consistent with the needs of the intended applications; should have few special cases and should be composed from features that are individually simple in their semantics.

Implementability. The language shall be composed from features that are understood and can be implemented.

Machine independence. The design of the language should strive for machine independence; shall attempt to avoid features whose semantics depend on characteristics of the object machine or of the object machine operating system; there shall be a facility for defining those portions of programs that are dependent on the object machine configuration.

Complete definition. The language shall be completely and unambiguously defined.

Steelman specifies a number of language features involving types and type definitions: strong typing; definition of new types, including enumeration types and specification of subtype constraints; arithmetic types and operations; and the ability to make type conversions. Composite types are specified as arrays, with subarray operations allowed, and records, including variant records with tag fields. Steelman calls for usual features of languages such as expressions, operations, variables and constants, procedures and functions, and classical control structures, including explicit transfer of control (the GO TO). It also requires the language to provide for encapsulated definitions, including multiple explicit instantiations (or instances) of an encapsulation. The language must also have real-time features such as the capability to define parallel processes sharing resources, exception handling, low-level input-output related to physical channels and devices, and machine-level representation of language elements. An early goal of the language effort, even preceding the specification of the Ada Programming Support Environment, was that the language work in the context of, and in cooperation with, a set of software tools and support packages.

Steelman laid the foundation for the language; Ada was the result.

2.3 *THE DEVELOPMENT OF ADA*

As the final language requirements specification was being drafted, the government proceeded to select contractors to design the common language, then frequently called "DoD-1." A request for proposal (RFP) was released in April 1977, with the intent of selecting several contractors to provide competing preliminary designs. It was also intended that the design for the common language should be based upon Algol 68, Pascal, or PL/I. Most of the seventeen proposals received were based on Pascal. The four winning contractors, Cii-Honeywell Bull, Intermetrics, SofTech, and SRI International, all proposed to use Pascal as the starting point for their designs. The parallel language design efforts began in August 1977. To prevent the reviewers from knowing which company produced a design, the design documents were color-coded: Honeywell (Green), Intermetrics (Red), SofTech (Blue), and SRI (Yellow). The designs were reviewed by a wide variety of teams from the military, industrial, and research communities. In fact, throughout the course of language development the designs were regularly exposed to comment. After the preliminary designs were evaluated, Green and Red contractors were selected to develop complete designs. In May 1979 the HOLWG chose Ada as the name of the DoD common language and completed the final evaluations of the Green and Red languages. (The HOLWG had never fully accepted the name DoD-1 because it limited the language's range of application.)

Green, designed by the Cii-Honeywell Bull team led by Jean D. Ichbiah, was selected as the foundation of the DoD common language. In June 1979 the Preliminary Ada Reference Manual was distributed to over 10,000 individuals. Preliminary Ada was the basis for a series of five courses taught by Jean Ichbiah, other members of the design team, and language reviewers. An evaluation phase followed in which DoD and industry programmers used preliminary Ada to program a number of sample applications. Existing applications ranging from data processing programs to real-time processes were reprogrammed in Ada. Although a number of issues were raised, Ada was found suitable for all the applications. Over 100 different organizations participated in this test and evaluation phase, and the over 900 language issue reports they submitted provided a basis for improving the language. Revisions to the language followed, resulting in a new version of July 1980. The Ada design was formally accepted by HOLWG on August 25, 1980, and presented at an "Ada Debut" on September 4 and 5, 1980. It was adopted as a military standard, MIL-STD-1815, on December 10, 1980, and later submitted for standardization by the American National Standards Institute (ANSI). Some revision and clarification resulted in a July 1982 version, and a January 1983 version which was accepted as an ANSI standard in February 1983. There is currently an organization responsible for further Ada activity, the Ada Joint Program Office (AJPO).

The development of the Ada Programming Support Environment (APSE)—a collection of integrated software tools to assist in Ada programming—is concurrent with the language's implementation. A series of requirements documents, Sandman, Pebbleman, and Stoneman, defined a Kernel APSE (KAPSE) and a Minimal APSE (MAPSE), including an Ada compiler. The complete APSE results from the addition of user tools. APSE provides a common interface between the user and Ada; MAPSE is intended to be portable among a wide variety of host machines and operating systems.

Concurrent with the first production-quality DoD compilers is the Ada Compiler Validation Capability (ACVC). The ACVC will be used to enforce standards (and to ensure that only conforming compilers use the trademarked name Ada). The ACVC consists of approximately 1700 tests (both valid and invalid Ada programs) that must be properly processed for a compiler to be validated. In addition, automated test tools and an Ada Implementer's Guide are designed to assist compiler writers in creating conforming implementations.

The DoD common language was named Ada in honor of the world's first programmer, Countess Augusta Ada Lovelace. Ada, the daughter of the poet Lord Byron, was the friend and confidante of Charles Babbage, who is widely regarded as the father of the computer. He invented, in the mid 1800s, a never fully working analytical engine that had many computerlike characteristics. In notes to a paper about Babbage's ideas, Ada gave a set of numbered operations to solve a mathematical problem. This was essentially a program for the analytical engine and included the concept of repetition. She also wrote other analyses on how to use the Babbage engine to perform computations. These writings are considered to be the first computer programs.

Ada is here now. Compilers have been developed, the DoD has required Ada to be used as the programming language on certain systems, and it is beginning to be used for commercial applications. Universities are teaching it to undergraduates, and many public and in-plant courses are being taught. It is likely that Ada will soon be as widely recognized as Pascal.

KEYS TO UNDERSTANDING

► Software for embedded computer systems is expensive. Much of the expense is in software maintenance.

► Extensive analysis preceded the decision to develop a common DoD programming language.

► Preliminary Ada was developed based on Steelman, a language requirements specification.

► Ada underwent thorough review, test, and evaluation—by government, industry, and academia—prior to acceptance.

3

Language Overview*

Objective: to present an overview of all of Ada,
including its advanced features

Before presenting the details of Ada, it is important to understand the language's overall approach and structure. This overview discusses all of Ada, including its advanced features. After reading this overview, you should understand the capabilities of the language and how it differs from nonreal-time languages. You will then be prepared to begin a more detailed investigation of language features. You may not be able to understand everything discussed in this chapter on the first reading. That is not its purpose. It is intended to give you a brief general understanding of the language in order to place the later detailed discussions into a proper context. A number of Ada-specific terms are introduced. A glossary is provided as appendix A.

There are two parts to the overview. The first is a preliminary overview to place Ada in the spectrum of general-purpose programming languages and briefly introduce major features; the second is a longer discussion of Ada's major advances over most other languages.

3.1 PRELIMINARY OVERVIEW

There are three ways of looking at Ada:

*The material in this chapter has been adapted from the author's Portfolio 12-01-09, "The Programming Language Ada." Copyright 1982 AUERBACH Pub. Inc. Computer Programming Management.

1. Ada as a programming language, which includes identifiers, data objects, arrays, assignment statements, and control over flow of execution.
2. Ada as a modern programming language, which includes block structure, strong typing and type declarations, record data structures, and pointer data types.
3. Ada as a programming language for embedded computer systems, which includes advanced features for encapsulation, multitasking, and exception handling.

The following sections discuss Ada from each of these viewpoints.

3.1.1 *Ada as a Programming Language*

Here is a simple Ada procedure.

```
procedure MAKE_FIRST_BIG (FIRST, SECOND : in out INTEGER) is
   TEMP : INTEGER; -- Local variable
begin
  if FIRST < SECOND then
    TEMP     := FIRST;
    FIRST    := SECOND;
    SECOND   := TEMP;
  end if;
end MAKE_FIRST_BIG;
```

The reserved word **procedure** introduces the procedure specification (that is, its name and parameter list). The parameter mode is **in out,** which means that variable values can be passed between the procedure and its caller. The parameters are of type INTEGER. All variables must be declared. The "--" introduces a comment, which is terminated by the end of line. The **begin-end** pair blocks off the executable part of the procedure. The **if-end if** pair defines the statements under the control of the **if** statement.

Ada provides for constant values; for character, integer, floating, and fixed-point variables with initialization; for function subprograms as well as procedures; for arrays (with variable bounds); and for the control constructs of **if-then-elsif-else, case,** and **loop** under the control of **while** or **for.** Control constructs are summarized in figure 3-1. Input/output is defined as part of the

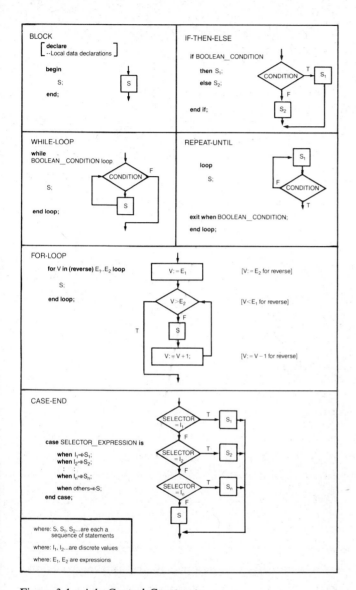

Figure 3-1   Ada Control Constructs

standard environment, and separate compilation of subprograms is supported.

3.1.2 *Ada as a Modern Programming Language*

Since Ada is based on Pascal, it provides many of the same capabilities. For
example, Ada provides the capability to nest procedures.

```
procedure MAKE_FIRST_BIG (FIRST, SECOND : in out INTEGER) is
   -- SWAP is a local procedure
   procedure SWAP (LEFT, RIGHT : in out INTEGER) is
     TEMP : INTEGER;
   begin
     TEMP    := RIGHT;
     RIGHT   := LEFT;
     LEFT    := TEMP;
   end SWAP;
begin -- MAKE_FIRST_BIG
   if FIRST < SECOND then
     SWAP (FIRST, SECOND);
   end if;
end MAKE_FIRST_BIG;
```

A feature Ada has that Pascal does not is the ability to initialize variables. The
initialization occurs when the variable is declared. For example,

```
I : INTEGER := 0;
```

The initialization can occur dynamically within a procedure. In the procedure
SWAP we could have had

```
TEMP : INTEGER := RIGHT;
```

Then the assignment,

```
TEMP := RIGHT;
```

would not have been required.

Ada follows Pascal in providing a data structure called a record to group together objects of different types. The following record has a variable called MONTH, of type MONTH__NAME. MONTH__NAME is a user-defined type called an enumeration type. MONTH may be assigned the values JAN, FEB, and so on, enumerated in the list.

```
type MONTH__NAME is  (JAN, FEB, MAR, APR, MAY, JUN, JUL, AUG,
                      SEP, OCT, NOV, DEC);
type DATE is
  record
    DAY     : INTEGER range 1 .. 31;
    MONTH : MONTH__NAME;
    YEAR   : INTEGER range 0 .. 4000;
  end record;
BIRTHDAY : DATE;
```

BIRTHDAY is a variable that contains a DAY, a MONTH, and a YEAR. Ada allows an aggregate assignment such as

```
BIRTHDAY := (10, DEC, 1815); -- Ada's birthday
```

which is equivalent to the assignment statements

```
BIRTHDAY.DAY     := 10;
BIRTHDAY.MONTH  := DEC;
BIRTHDAY.YEAR    := 1815;
```

Ada uses access variables (also called pointer or reference variables) to *point* at an object in memory. Figure 3-2 shows pointers.

Ada is a strongly typed language. It requires that variables have a type determinable at compile time and that each operator have statically defined types upon which it can operate. The compiler ensures that each variable is used in a manner consistent with its type. An integer, for example, cannot be

```
type VEHICLE is (SHIP, CAR, PLANE);
type POINTER is access VEHICLE;
P_1, P_2, P_3 : POINTER;
```

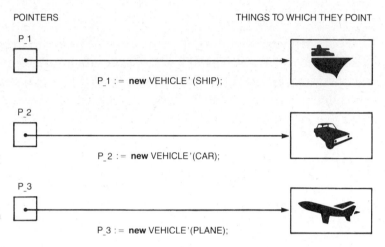

Figure 3-2   Access Types

divided by a real variable and cannot be compared or assigned to a character or pointer variable. Ada does allow mechanisms to perform such operations, but they are not allowed without explicit statements of intent by the programmer.

3.1.3 *Ada as a Programming Language for Embedded Computer Systems*

Embedded computer systems have special requirements for the effective development of large, reliable, long-lived programs. This section presents a synopsis of features in Ada that meet the requirements. Additional discussion of the advanced features is provided in section 3.2.

Potentially the most important feature of Ada is the **package** because it provides improved control over visibility of names and access to data and allows a high degree of data abstraction. It is the main structuring unit of Ada and typically encapsulates data and processes that provide access to that data. Figure 3-3 illustrates the notion of a package specification, which can be considered to be a *contract* with external users of the package, and the package body, which is the implementation. The package specification can contain

SPECIFICATION

package PACKAGE_NAME **is**

- type declarations
- variable and constant declarations
- subprogram and task specifications

private

- full declaration of private types

end PACKAGE_NAME;

- Interface specification
- Declarations are visible to users of the package and to the package body
- Private part is hidden from user-conceptually part of package body

BODY

package body PACKAGE_NAME **IS**

- subprogram bodies for all specifications in visible part
- additional type, variable, and constant declarations
- additional subprograms and tasks

begin

- may include executable statements for initialization

end PACKAGE_NAME;

- Implementation of the specification
- Additional declarations are not visible to users of the package
- May be modified without affecting code of using programs

Figure 3-3   Package Structure

type definitions, data declarations, and specification parts of subprograms or tasks.

Tasks are processes that execute in parallel, with either real or apparent concurrency. The notion of multitasking implies not only parallel execution but that the tasks cooperate in accomplishing some function, often exchanging or operating on the same data. Figure 3-4 shows the form of task declarations. Tasks can synchronize and exchange data during a *rendezvous,* which occurs when one task calls an entry in the other, and the second task is prepared to accept the entry. Ada provides extensive mechanisms for programmer control over entry calls and accepts, queueing of tasks that are waiting for a rendezvous, and task suspension and termination.

```
declare
  task T1 is -- Specification
    -- May only contain entry specifications.
  end;

  task body T1 is -- Body
    -- Implementation
    -- Contains accept statements
  end T1;


  task T2 is
    entry GET_DATA (X : out DATA_OBJECT);
  end;

  task body T2 is
    Y : DATA_OBJECT;
  begin

    . . .
    accept GET_DATA (X : out DATA_OBJECT) do
      X := Y;
    end GET_DATA;
    . . .
  end T2;
begin -- T1 and T2 become active here
       -- and operate in parallel with executable
       -- statements in the body of the block.

end;  -- Block cannot exit until T1, T2 and the
       -- block body have all completed execution.
```

Figure 3-4   Tasks

Computer programs for embedded computer systems must be capable of continuing execution despite errors or faults. An **exception** in Ada is an error, fault, or another unusual (exceptional) condition. Ada provides an explicit mechanism for identifying and handling exceptions. Names for some exceptional conditions are predeclared as part of an Ada standard environment (for example, NUMERIC_ERROR or CONSTRAINT_ERROR). Other exceptions may be defined by the programmer. The exception handler is introduced by the **exception** clause. Here is a skeleton of the exception handling process.

```
begin
   -- Statements
   -- NUMERIC_ERROR exception occurs here
   -- Remainder of block

exception

   when NUMERIC_ERROR = >
      -- Handle the exception
      -- Replaces remainder of block
end;
```

Control is transferred to exception handler

Exceptions may occur during execution of statements (for example, as in an attempted division by zero) or may explicitly be caused by use of the **raise** clause. Note that control is transferred to the exception handler, and its execution replaces the remainder of the block. Control exits the block rather than returns to the point at which the exception was raised.

Ada has other features important for development of large programs. Generic units act as templates for the creation of specific instances of general-purpose routines. For example, a general-purpose symbol table package might be created as a **generic** unit. Specific instances could be created (or, in Ada, *instantiated*) to handle integers, character strings, records, or other data objects.

Ada goes beyond Pascal in the philosophy of strong typing, by allowing the creation of new types that are identical in structure but incompatible in type with the type from which they are derived. This capability helps the compiler forbid operations on APPLES and ORANGES, even though both might be (for example) integer numbers.

Ada also has the capability to provide machine-level access in a controlled and orderly manner. For example, a task can be written as an interrupt handler. The object code can be placed starting at the memory location vectored to by the interrupt.

Ada provides extensive capabilities for controlling the order of compilation and the dependencies between packages. These facilities are part of the language definition but, of course, are closely related to the APSE. In fact, Ada blurs some old distinctions among the programming support environment, the operating environment as executive and run-time support, and the definition of the language itself.

3.1.4 *A Counter View*

There are those who feel that Ada has not met its goals. The primary contention is that Ada is too complicated: too difficult to understand, too complex, and so full of unnecessary features that effective compilers will not be created. The most well known of the critiques is by C.A.R. Hoare, presented during his 1980 A.C.M. Turing Award Lecture. The response to his criticisms has generally been that Ada is a large language but is consistent and regular in its design. It is rich, as opposed to being overly complex, and contains only those features necessary to solve the problems inherent in programming large embedded computer systems.

3.2 *MAJOR ADVANCES*

Ada has a number of advanced features that go considerably beyond languages such as Pascal and PL/I. The major language extensions discussed in this section are

> packages,
> separate compilation,
> generics,
> exceptions, and
> tasks.

3.2.1 *Packages*

Encapsulation is the grouping together of related data and the procedures that operate on the data. The internal structure of the data may be hidden to create an *abstract* data type. In Ada the primary mechanism for encapsulation and data abstraction is the package. In the example of package structure in figure 3-3, the specification was shown to be a contract with the users of the package to provide certain capabilities. A separate package body provides the implementation of the contract. A package can be considered to be a *wall* surrounding the declarations and bodies. The specification provides a *hole* in the wall that gives users of the package the minimum information necessary: the interface specification.

Here is the specification of a package that provides some types and some allowable operations on objects of the given type.

```
package BLOCKS is
    type MEASURE      is new INTEGER range 0 .. INTEGER'LAST;
    type LENGTH       is new MEASURE;
    type WIDTH        is new MEASURE;
    type AREA         is new MEASURE;
    type PERIMETER    is new MEASURE;
    function "*" (L : LENGTH; W : WIDTH) return AREA;
    function BOUNDARY (L : LENGTH; W : WIDTH) return PERIMETER;
end BLOCKS;

package body BLOCKS is
    -- Contains the implementation of "*" and BOUNDARY
end BLOCKS;
```

Ada allows the programmer to distinguish among different types of objects that are conceptually distinct. The clause **new** creates distinct types. The types LENGTH, WIDTH, AREA, and PERIMETER are all different from each other. Therefore, in accordance with Ada's strong type rules, they are incompatible. Note that the range of allowable values for objects of each type is limited to positive numbers up to INTEGER'LAST, the largest integer value for a given implementation. INTEGER'LAST is an *attribute* of the type INTEGER. To permit mixed operations on objects of different types, explicit functions and operators must be provided. For example, the function BOUNDARY is provided to allow objects of types LENGTH and WIDTH to be combined to provide a value of type PERIMETER. To allow multiplication of objects of types LENGTH and WIDTH to produce an object of type AREA, the operator "*" must be explicitly defined as shown. Since "*" also retains its usual meaning, the same symbol has two meanings; it is said to be *overloaded*. The compiler determines from context which "*" to use. Overloading is not new with Ada—operators have been implicitly overloaded since the earliest languages. (Consider "*" in FORTRAN: multiplication of integers and reals are done with the same operator.) Ada allows the programmer to explicitly overload operators.

Here is an example of how the package may be used. The **with** and **use** clauses place the procedure GEOM in the proper context to access the facilities of the package BLOCKS. The **with** clause names other, separately compiled, units upon which procedure GEOM depends. The **use** clause provides direct visibility for declarations that appear in the visible parts of named packages.

```
with BLOCKS; use BLOCKS;
procedure GEOM is
   LEN  : LENGTH;
   WID  : WIDTH;
   AR   : AREA;
   PER  : PERIMETER;
begin
   . . .
   LEN  := 10;                        -- OK
   PER  := LEN;                       -- Illegal, types incompatible
   PER  := LEN/WID;                   -- Illegal, types incompatible
   AR   := LEN * WID;                 -- Uses BLOCKS."*"
   PER  := BOUNDARY(LEN, WID);        -- Uses BLOCKS.BOUNDARY
   PER  := PERIMETER(LEN);            -- Use of type name to convert
                                      -- type from LENGTH
                                      -- to PERIMETER

   LEN  := LEN * LEN;                 -- Legal, but illogical
   LEN  := LEN - LENGTH(WID);         -- Legal, but illogical
   LEN  := LEN * 10;                  -- Legal, but illogical
   . . .
end GEOM;
```

Note that the specification of new types allows certain logical errors to be discovered by the compiler. For example,

```
PER := LEN / WID;    -- Illegal. Incompatible types.
WID := AR — PER;     -- Illegal. Incompatible types.
```

are likely to be logical errors on the part of the programmer. Notice, however, that complete protection is not provided, since expressions such as

```
LEN := LEN * 10;
```

are still legal, although they may be not be reasonable. We normally would not multiply a length by a scalar value.

The example using the package BLOCKS illustrates that a package can be used to define abstract data types consisting of a set of allowable values and a set of operations on those values. The use of the clause **new,** along with the restricted range, defines a set of values more appropriate to geometric measurement than the unrestricted range of INTEGER. Further, since each type definition introduces a distinct type, LENGTH, WIDTH, AREA, and PERIMETER are different types. This is appropriate, since we wish to forbid operations such as division of one measurement by another. Operations are said to be *inherited* from INTEGER, which is the parent type of the new types LENGTH, WIDTH, AREA, and PERIMETER. Therefore, the usual arithmetic operations are available for each of the new types derived from integer. For those situations in which we do wish to allow operations mixing distinct types, our intent must be made explicit through the use of the type name in order to change the type of an operand.

The use of what is called a **private** type gives even greater control over the use of names and types. A type that is declared **private** allows the user of the package a limited range of allowable operations, namely, assignment (:=) and comparison for equality (= and /=). The following examples provide the specification and use of such a package. Note that many more operations have become illegal.

```
package PRIVATE__BLOCKS is
    type LENGTH       is private;
    type WIDTH        is private;
    type AREA         is private;
    type PERIMETER    is private;
    function "*"(L : LENGTH; W : WIDTH) return AREA;
    function BOUNDARY(L : LENGTH; W : WIDTH) return PERIMETER;
    procedure GET(L : out LENGTH);    -- Provided by package body
    procedure GET(W : out WIDTH);     -- Provided by package body
private
    -- Types described as private above must be defined here
    -- These type definitions are unavailable to users of the package
    type MEASURE      is range 0 .. INTEGER ' LAST;
    type LENGTH       is new MEASURE;
    type WIDTH        is new MEASURE;
    type AREA         is new MEASURE;
    type PERIMETER    is new MEASURE;
end PRIVATE__BLOCKS;


package body PRIVATE__BLOCKS is
-- Implements functions and procedures defined in the package specification
end PRIVATE__BLOCKS;
```

```
with PRIVATE_BLOCKS; use PRIVATE_BLOCKS;
procedure SAFE_GEOM is
   LEN_1, LEN_2 : LENGTH;
   WID : WIDTH;
   AR  : AREA;
   PER : PERIMETER;
begin
   . . .
   GET(LEN_1); GET(WID);
   LEN_2 := LEN_1;
   AR := LEN_2 * WID;
   PER := BOUNDARY(LEN_1,WID);
   -- The operations below would be legal in
   -- procedure GEOM using package BLOCKS. In SAFE_GEOM
   -- using PRIVATE_BLOCKS the operations below are illegal.
   LEN_2 := LENGTH(WID);              -- Illegal. No type conversions
                                      -- for private types
   LEN_1 := 2;                        -- Illegal. Different types
   LEN_1 := LEN_1 * LEN_2;            -- Illegal. No "*"
                                      -- for type LENGTH
   LEN_1 := 2 * LEN_2;                -- Illegal. Different types
   LEN_1 := LEN_1 - LEN_2;            -- Illegal. No " - "
                                      -- for type LENGTH

   . . .
end SAFE_GEOM;
```

The example using package PRIVATE_BLOCKS illustrates the use of the private type. Objects defined to be of type **private** have an internal representation that is hidden from the user of the package. The representation is defined in the private part of the package specification. The importance of using private types lies in the fact that since operations are not inherited from a parent type, the developer of the package has more control over those operations allowed on the type.

Ada also provides other facilities for the use of packages; the use of packages and their implications for design extend far beyond this simple example. The important idea is that packages allow for the encapsulation of related data objects and procedures and for careful control of coupling among different parts of a large software system.

3.2.2 *Separate Compilation*

Ada provides extensive capabilities for separate compilation of program units. An essential feature of separate compilation is that complete type checking is maintained across program unit boundaries. Compilation units belong to a program library, with dependence being defined by **with** and **separate** clauses.

The **with** clause names a package that is necessary for the compilation of the current program unit. That is, the program unit depends on the capabilities provided by the package. The **with** clause specifies a partial order of compilation since the package specification must be compiled prior to the compilation of the using program unit.

The **separate** clause has two uses. The first is to specify that a program unit will be provided in a separate compilation, to implement a given specification. The second use is to specify that a compilation unit is not independent but depends on the context of some previously compiled program unit.

Taken together, the **with** and **separate** clauses provide the capability for either top-down or bottom-up program development. The separate compilation capabilities have important implications for order of compilation and of the requirements for recompilation when one unit is modified.

3.2.3 *Generics*

Generics are simply templates for packages or subprograms. Such units are generic in the sense of being general versions of processes that can be modified by parameters at compilation time. The compiler *instantiates,* or creates *instances,* of the programs, modified as necessary by the parameters. Each instance of the program may be called and used exactly like an equivalent nongeneric program. Without generics, the creation of swap procedures for objects of various types might be

```
procedure SWAP (X, Y : in out INTEGER) is
   TEMP : INTEGER := X;
begin
   X := Y; Y := TEMP;
end SWAP;

procedure SWAP (X, Y : in out REAL) is
   TEMP : REAL := X;
begin
   X := Y; Y := TEMP;
end SWAP;

procedure SWAP (X, Y : in out STUFF) is
   TEMP : STUFF := X;
```

```
begin
   X := Y; Y := TEMP;
end SWAP;
```

Here is the simpler process of creating a generic routine with the type as a parameter and then multiple instantiation of procedures.

```
generic -- Generic clause
   type SWAP_TYPE is private;   -- Generic formal parameter
procedure EXCHANGE (X, Y : in out SWAP_TYPE);

procedure EXCHANGE (X, Y : in out SWAP_TYPE) is
   TEMP : SWAP_TYPE := X ;
begin
   X := Y; Y := TEMP;
end EXCHANGE;

procedure SWAP is new EXCHANGE (INTEGER);

procedure SWAP is new EXCHANGE (REAL);

procedure SWAP is new EXCHANGE (STUFF);
```

This approach is important not simply because it saves some keystrokes but rather because it helps in code reviews, testing, and maintenance. Less code must be read, and all the routines must use the same algorithm. Both testing and maintenance are simplified, as there is less code at the source level, and a change to the generic routine ensures that all related changes also occur.

3.2.4 *Exceptions*

In Ada, an **exception** is an error or other extraordinary (exceptional) occurence. Since Ada is designed for use in real-time systems, which must continue to execute when errors occur, extensive facilities are provided for exception handling. Some exceptions are predefined in the language, and the user may define still others. The exception handlers, the sections of code executed when the exception is raised, must be provided by the programmer whether the exception is predefined or user defined. If an exception is not handled, the program is aborted. Some of the predefined exceptions in the language are

```
NUMERIC_ERROR        -- For example, division by zero
CONSTRAINT_ERROR     -- For various violations of constraints
TASKING_ERROR        -- For errors in intertask communications
```

In addition, it is possible to explicitly provide for user-defined exception declarations, such as

STACK_OVERFLOW : **exception;**

It is possible to raise or cause an exception to occur, as in

```
if <condition> then
   raise STACK_OVERFLOW;
end if;
```

and it is possible to have exception handlers at the end of program blocks.

```
begin
  -- Sequence of statements
exception
  when STACK_OVERFLOW =>
    PUT ("OVERFLOW");
  when others =>
    PUT ("FATAL ERROR");
    raise;       -- Reraises the exception that caused execution
                 -- of the handler
end;
```

The exception handler replaces the remainder of the program unit in which the exception is raised. Ada has a comprehensive set of rules for how exceptions are propagated from one block to another until an exception handler is available.

3.2.5 *Tasks*

Tasking in Ada refers to multitasking, that is, concurrent execution of related processes. The concurrency may be real or apparent, depending on whether execution is on a single processor or a multiprocessing system. Tasking implies separate threads of control and often involves task synchronization and sharing of information. The mechanism for coordination between separate threads of control is the *rendezvous,* accomplished when an entry point of a task is called. The **entry** of the task is declared in a task specification, similar to a package specification. Each entry has a corresponding **accept** in the task body defining the implementation. Figure 3-5 shows the relationship of an entry, an entry call, and an accept.

In figure 3-5 there are two separate threads of control. The task FIFO has two entries: ARRIVE and DEPART. It could be considered to be a process for adding and deleting objects from a queue: objects of type VEHICLE. The block ADD_TO_QUEUE, executing concurrently with FIFO, adds a CAR to the queue by calling the ARRIVE entry. If the **accept** statement is reached prior to the entry call, task FIFO will be suspended. If the call is issued before FIFO is ready to accept the entry, the issuing block ADD_TO_QUEUE is suspended until FIFO execution reaches the **accept** statement. When the tasks are synchronized, the data in the parameter list is passed and the **do . . . end** part of the **accept** statement is executed as a single thread of control.

Ada automatically provides for queuing of entry calls. It also provides extensive mechanisms for programmers to control when and for how long tasks

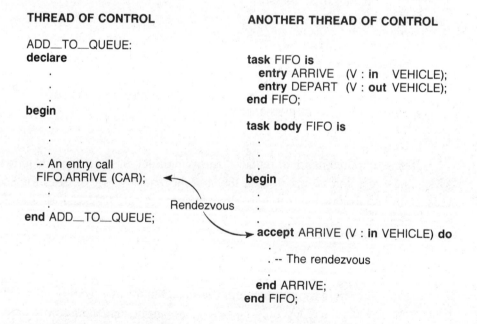

Figure 3-5   Entry Invocation

should wait under various conditions, for alternate accepts or entry calls, and for alternatives to being suspended.

3.3 *ADA SUMMARY*

Ada is generally Algol- or Pascal-like in its syntax, data structures, block structure, and definition of types. It has necessary added features to make it a production quality language for real-time embedded computer systems. Major new features are packages, tasks, separate compilation, exception handling, and generic units. The language will be used in the context of an Ada Programming Support Environment.

Exercise__3

Create a package that implements a procedure called ADD__VALUE. ADD__ VALUE takes a single INTEGER parameter of mode **in out** and adds to it an amount specified within the package. This amount is not visible to the user of the package.

Write a main procedure called USE__ADD__VALUE to call ADD__ VALUE and print the result.

Program__3

```
with TEXT__IO; use TEXT__IO;
package PROGRAM__3 is
  procedure ADD__VALUE (STUFF : in out INTEGER);
  package IO is new INTEGER__IO(INTEGER);
end;

package body PROGRAM__3 is
  VALUE : INTEGER := 6;
  use IO;

  procedure ADD__VALUE(STUFF : in out INTEGER) is
  begin
    PUT("The value of STUFF is: "); PUT(STUFF); NEW__LINE;
    STUFF := STUFF + VALUE;
  end ADD__VALUE;
```

```
begin -- package body PROGRAM__3
-- This could be used for additional initialization
  PUT("The value of VALUE is: "); PUT(VALUE); NEW__LINE;
end PROGRAM__3;


with TEXT__IO, PROGRAM__3; use TEXT__IO, PROGRAM__3;
procedure USE__ADD__VALUE is
  LOCAL__STUFF : INTEGER := 5;
  use IO;
begin
  PUT("LOCAL__STUFF is: "); PUT(LOCAL__STUFF); NEW__LINE;
  ADD__VALUE(LOCAL__STUFF);
  PUT("Now LOCAL__STUFF is: "); PUT(LOCAL__STUFF);
end USE__ADD__VALUE;
```

```
No translation errors detected
Translation time: 105 seconds
Binding time: 4.5 seconds
Begin Ada execution
The value of VALUE is:     6
LOCAL__STUFF is:           5

The value of STUFF is:     5
Now LOCAL__STUFF is:      11

Execution complete
Execution time: 13 seconds
I-code statements executed: 84
```

Discussion__3

The specification part of the package is very brief: it simply provides the interface to the **ADD__VALUE** procedure. The interface specification consists of the procedure name and the formal parameter list. The mode of the formal parameter tells the user of the package what is required and what to expect. For example, in the case of mode **in out,** a value must be provided by the user of the procedure or an uninitialized variable exception (error) will occur at run time.

An important point is that the user cannot "see" the package body. The value of 6 for VALUE and any other operations in the body are not available to the user of the package.

The **with** and **use** clauses for the procedure (which is the main program) establish the context for USE—ADD—VALUE, including the package containing ADD—VALUE. If there were no **use** clause, the package would be available and ADD—VALUE would be in scope, but it would not be immediately visible. Access would have to be by the full name PROGRAM—3.ADD—VALUE.

The execution of the procedures is straightforward. The PUT statement in the initialization part of the package body precedes the first use of the procedures in the package.

KEYS TO UNDERSTANDING

► Much of Ada can be understood as simply another high-level programming language.

► Ada has a number of features for building large, long-lived, and maintainable systems:

Packages—to encapsulate data and procedures

Tasks—for concurrent processing

Separate Compilation

Exceptions—to handle run-time errors

Generics—to ease creation of libraries

4

Software Development
Using Ada

Objective:	To describe changes likely to occur when software is developed in Ada

Ada was developed to help solve the problem of late, costly, and too frequently unreliable and difficult-to-maintain embedded computer systems software. To improve the situation the very process and methods of software development must change.

This chapter describes the changes that are likely to occur when software is developed in Ada instead of languages currently used for embedded computer systems. It focuses on

- Why software development must change
- What Ada characteristics allow change
- How software development will change
- Packages, the major influence on change

4.1 *WHY SOFTWARE DEVELOPMENT MUST CHANGE*

The reason for changing the software development process parallels the reason for using Ada as a standard language: reliability, cost, and maintainability.

DoD systems must be highly reliable; the outcome of battles and wars depends on their correct operation. Developing reliable systems is costly. A method is therefore needed to develop reliable systems at reasonable cost. This same method must result in maintainable systems, since the greatest cost in large systems is the maintenance phase of the software life cycle. But a more subtle and important point is that software maintenance has a major influence on operational capability. It is common to upgrade a system by modifying existing software. The more quickly and easily such changes can be implemented, the greater will be the capability provided to operating forces. For all these reasons Ada was needed, as were changes to the software development process.

4.2 *WHAT ADA CHARACTERISTICS ALLOW CHANGE*

Ada will change the software development process because of its standardization, its support environment, and the nature of the language itself.

The very fact that Ada is a standard language will give designers confidence that the Ada software they design and implement will have a broad spectrum of applicability. The tendency will be to design reusable and longer-lived software. At the same time standardization will lead designers to have greater confidence in their ability to reuse previously developed software. They will incorporate old software into new designs.

The Ada Programming Support Environment (APSE) will provide superior tools for software development. The editors, translators, debuggers, and management tools will increase the productivity of both individual programmers and of programming teams. Then too, the standardization of a programming environment will change people's perceptions about the creation of new tools, encouraging them to create improved support environments that can be transported from project to project.

The most important factor is the language itself. Ada is a design language and will change the way software engineers solve problems. Packages, tasks, generics, and exceptions will influence the design of programs. Of these, the most important is packages. The characteristics allowing change are summarized in figure 4-1.

The Ada package will be a major influence on design because it supports both conventional structured design and also new methods currently being developed.

- STANDARDIZATION
    - Transportability
    - Knowledge, improved skills
    - APSE
    - Components
- TOOLS
    - APSE
    - Project Control
    - Separate Compilation
- LANGUAGE FEATURES
    - Packages
    - Tasks
    - Generics
    - Exceptions

Figure 4-1   Ada Characteristics Allowing Change

Two design approaches that are closely related and are likely to become important along with Ada are *information-hiding* and *object-oriented design*. Information hiding focuses attention on major design decisions that must be made, largely related to data structures, and partitions the system into smaller elements based on the design decisions. The modules that implement the design decisions *hide* information from other modules and therefore reduce the degree of coupling or connection. This makes later changes easier to implement by decreasing the chance that a change in one module will create an error in another. Object-oriented design has a similar aim and accomplishes its purpose by focusing on the objects to be manipulated rather than on the processes to be performed. Use of either of these methods could result in a design more reliable and easier to change than one produced by more conventional methods.

Ada's ability to make effective use of information-hiding and object-oriented design is based on the language's features that allow modularity. Ada allows the problem to be partitioned into smaller problems, each small problem being solved by independent pieces of software that interact effectively with each other. A critical aspect of modularization is that *what* a program does differs from *how* it does it. This separation of specification from implementation has an important overall effect on the development methods discussed in the next section. Ada also provides for effective control over the visibility of data objects and allows the form and meaning of data structures to be abstracted from their actual physical implementation. Data abstraction and control over visibility will have considerable influence over design; they are implemented by the Ada package.

4.3 *HOW SOFTWARE DEVELOPMENT WILL CHANGE*

There are three major areas in which Ada will cause changes in the software development process:

- Design approaches and techniques
- Methods of development
- The use and reuse of software

These changes will occur because of the nature of the language itself and because of the APSE that will be provided along with it. The Ada language is intended to be used for design as well as programming; Ada's programming support environment provides powerful tools to assist the programmer and the system designer. With skill and perseverance on the part of the language implementers and those who will use the language to design and build application systems, Ada will be able to solve many software development problems.

4.3.1 *Design Approaches and Techniques*

Ada was designed to be a software engineering language, to be used for designing large software systems, for "programming in the large." This capability will change the way that computer programming systems are designed. Ada allows us to construct small, functionally cohesive modules with clearly defined interfaces. Even without any special focus on new design methodologies, different and better designs will result than if other languages were to be used for implementation. However, it is likely that along with the common introduction of Ada will come the introduction of new notions of software design.

4.3.2 *Methods of Development*

There are a number of ways in which Ada will change the methods of developing software. The basic reason for the changes is that Ada provides important capabilities as a software engineering-oriented language and hence will change our perspective on what we can do and how we should accomplish design and development of large software systems.

The first and most important of the new capabilities allowed by Ada, one that influences the entire development process, is that a single language can be used for both design and implementation of the code. This is a powerful factor. Not only does Ada offer a single set of tools and techniques, and a single set of software objects to manipulate, it allows a single, unifying set of concepts to be brought to bear on the problem. Ada is a design language. It was created to allow the design of large systems with long lifetimes. The fact that the same language, with the same tools, techniques, and concepts, can be used for both the design and the coding of a program will ease the mechanics of software production and will almost certainly change the way we think about producing software systems.

The second change in software development methods brought about by Ada will be in the area of documentation. Much current trouble with the documentation of computer programs lies in the failure to clearly define interfaces between individual pieces of software. We know how to build small reliable computer programs; what we need is to be able to piece them together into large, cohesive systems. This is the problem that Ada is designed to solve. Use of Ada constructs and features for specifying interfaces between programs will allow us to change the way we think about required documentation and will allow us to significantly alter current practice. With the interfaces clearly specified in the Ada code, less external documentation will be required.

The third change is that the system designer will have greater control over the development process. This control accrues partly from the automated management and configuration control tools provided as part of the APSE. These tools will allow the designer and the software development manager to more easily assess progress being made and to detect areas of weakness in the design—throughout the entire software development cycle. Although some sophisticated software development environments now provide many of the tools of the APSE, use of Ada and the APSE will provide a more integrated approach and will increase the number of software developers using such tools. An even more important contribution to management control is provided by Ada's ability to allow clear specification of interfaces throughout design and code. This ability will allow greater control over the specification of the design, its stepwise refinement into greater detail, and its final expression in lines of Ada code. These factors will allow for smaller design groups and consequent greater unity and cohesiveness in programs designed in Ada.

4.3.3 *The Use and Reuse of Software*

In mature programming languages it is usual to have available standard packages of software to perform common, widely used functions. For example, there are packages of statistical procedures, other mathematical procedures, graphical and plotting routines, and so on. Ada will encourage and increase the use of such packages, saving effort otherwise expended in creating special-purpose software. It will allow programmers to think at a higher level of abstraction about the problem to be solved.

Ada has special features for creating software that can be transported among machines having different characteristics. Although transportability is still not likely to be achieved easily, Ada should simplify the process. Reusing software that had been developed for similar embedded computer systems will reduce software development cost.

The very high degree of standardization of Ada will enhance both use of packages of standard software and the reuse of software created for other systems. Standardization will also make it easier to find programmers familiar with the language in which the other system is programmed. That is, no longer will programmers skilled in language ABC be trying to transport software written in language XYZ from one system to another. As the use of Ada becomes common, and more and more programmers became skilled in Ada, the use and reuse of software will be made easier.

The combination of the extensive use of standard packages, the easier transportability of software, and the common use of Ada will lead to the creation of a *software components* approach to software development. The approach should be similar to a hardware components approach. When an engineer needs a piece of hardware to serve as a shift register, or even to perform a 16-bit cyclic redundancy check, he or she does not begin to design such a device but rather looks in a catalog to determine the specifications of available products. It is likely that one exists to meet the need. The process should become the same in software. Ada will be a powerful force in helping bring into being a software components industry. Large software systems should be constructed by bringing together pieces of existing software components, with the new software being the glue that holds the components together.

4.4 *PACKAGES, THE MAJOR INFLUENCE ON CHANGE*

In discussing the nature of changes in software development, the package was noted as being a major component of the creation of change. This section explains some of the significant features of the Ada package and shows how it can control visibility and provide enhanced modularity.

The package is the primary structuring unit of Ada. Some of its features are that it

- Encapsulates data and procedures
- Allows control over visibility
- Separates specification (interface) from body (implementation)
- Allows abstraction of data structures

Figure 3-3 showed the structure of the Ada package. Of great significance is the concept of separation of the specification, constituting the interface to the package, from its implementation. This separation of the *what* from the *how*, as an inherent part of the language, eases the developers' task and should lead to clearer and more complete specification of interfaces.

There are three different ways to use packages:

- Named collections of declarations
- Groups of related subprograms
- Encapsulated data types

The first of these, use of packages to collect together declarations, is almost exactly like the use of "common" in FORTRAN. The second, groups of related subprograms, is the mechanism for implementing math or graphics packages. Of greatest interest from a design point of view is the third aspect: the notion of using the package to encapsulate data types.

A data type indicates two characteristics of data objects: a set of values (1, 2, 3, and so on) and a set of operations on those values (+, *, −, and so on). By encapsulating data and procedures in a package, Ada provides for the creation of abstract or encapsulated data types. Abstract data types are simply data types in which the creator of the type has full control over the allowable values and operations. The user of the type has no knowledge of how the type is implemented.

The three uses of packages are not disjoint; there is considerable overlap. However, it is the concepts related to encapsulation of data types that will have an effect on the way systems are designed and implemented. It is important to recognize that the new design methods are still being developed, that they are in preliminary form. The ideas have been discussed for a number of years but have not found wide application in the actual construction of software for embedded computer systems. The software community is still searching for effective ways to use object-oriented approaches and information-hiding concepts for design and to explain and teach the ideas and techniques.

The following two examples illustrate some problems that can occur in other languages and show how these problems can be solved by using an Ada package to encapsulate data and procedures.

The first example illustrates a problem existing in languages such as Algol, Pascal, or Jovial; if several nested procedures are to have access to a piece of information, the information must also be accessible to other parts of the program. This is a problem of too wide a visibility of information. The example is discussed in detail in chapter 14; here we present some basic concepts. The relevant sections of code in the figures are boxed. At this point, only the highlighted sections of code are important; it is not necessary to understand the entire example. Here is a procedure called BANK with nested procedures DEPOSIT and WITHDRAW.

```
procedure BANK is
   BALANCE : FLOAT range −1000.00 .. 10_000_000.00 := 0.0;
   NUMBER_OF_DEPOSITS : NATURAL := 0;
   NUMBER_OF_WITHDRAWALS : NATURAL := 0;

   procedure DEPOSIT (AMOUNT : in FLOAT) is
   begin
      BALANCE := BALANCE + AMOUNT;
      NUMBER_OF_DEPOSITS :=
         NUMBER_OF_DEPOSITS + 1;
   end DEPOSIT;

   procedure WITHDRAW (AMOUNT : in FLOAT) is
   begin
      BALANCE := BALANCE − AMOUNT;
      NUMBER_OF_WITHDRAWALS :=
         NUMBER_OF_WITHDRAWALS + 1;
   end WITHDRAW;
```

The information of interest is the depositor's BALANCE. Note that the maximum balance is $10,000,000.00, and the bank is willing to allow a $1000.00 overdraft. The idea is for the procedures DEPOSIT and WITHDRAW to be used to accomplish changes to the BALANCE. The procedures would also do the necessary bookkeeping for the bank. They keep track of the number of deposits and withdrawals, which are limited to the positive integers (by the Ada predefined type NATURAL) and are initialized to zero.

The main body of the procedure makes use of the capabilities of the bank.

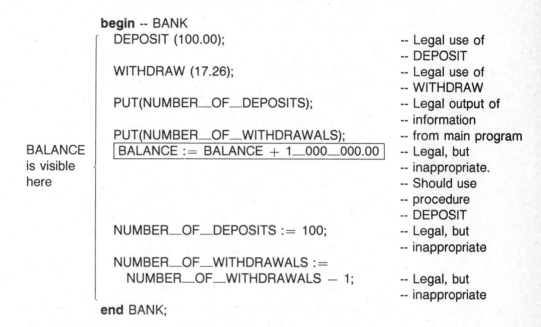

```
begin -- BANK
        DEPOSIT (100.00);                              -- Legal use of
                                                       -- DEPOSIT
        WITHDRAW (17.26);                              -- Legal use of
                                                       -- WITHDRAW
        PUT(NUMBER_OF_DEPOSITS);                       -- Legal output of
                                                       -- information
        PUT(NUMBER_OF_WITHDRAWALS);                    -- from main program
        BALANCE := BALANCE + 1_000_000.00              -- Legal, but
                                                       -- inappropriate.
BALANCE                                                -- Should use
is visible                                             -- procedure
here                                                   -- DEPOSIT

        NUMBER_OF_DEPOSITS := 100;                     -- Legal, but
                                                       -- inappropriate
        NUMBER_OF_WITHDRAWALS :=
          NUMBER_OF_WITHDRAWALS - 1;                   -- Legal, but
                                                       -- inappropriate
end BANK;
```

The example shows the use of **DEPOSIT** and **WITHDRAW** to make legitimate transactions and also shows that **BALANCE** can be modified directly by the depositor. It is as though the depositor had unrestricted freedom to change the amount of money on deposit. This is clearly not a satisfactory situation (for the bank, at any rate) for financial matters and also not a satisfactory situation for software. Such unrestricted access to variables can cause unwanted linking or coupling between different parts of a program. The strong links from one part of a program to another can make a system difficult to develop and even more difficult to change.

Here is a better bank.

```
procedure BETTER_BANK is

                    package TRANSACTIONS is
                        procedure DEPOSIT (AMOUNT : in FLOAT);
Visible to the          procedure WITHDRAW (AMOUNT : in FLOAT);
user of the package     procedure PRINT_NUMBER_OF_TRANSACTIONS;
                    end:
```

```
package body TRANSACTIONS is
    BALANCE : FLOAT range −1000.00 .. 10_000_000.00 := 0.0;
    NUMBER_OF_DEPOSITS : NATURAL := 0;
    NUMBER_OF_WITHDRAWALS : NATURAL := 0;


    procedure DEPOSIT (AMOUNT : in FLOAT) is
    begin
        BALANCE := BALANCE + AMOUNT;
        NUMBER_OF_DEPOSITS :=
            NUMBER_OF_DEPOSITS + 1;
    end DEPOSIT;


    procedure WITHDRAW (AMOUNT : in FLOAT) is
    begin
        BALANCE := BALANCE − AMOUNT;
        NUMBER_OF_WITHDRAWALS :=
            NUMBER_OF_WITHDRAWALS + 1;
    end WITHDRAW;


    procedure PRINT_NUMBER_OF_TRANSACTIONS is
    begin
        PUT(NUMBER_OF_DEPOSITS);
        PUT(NUMBER_OF_WITHDRAWALS);
    end PRINT_NUMBER_OF_TRANSACTIONS;
end TRANSACTIONS;
```

Hidden from the user of the package

The preceding example shows a better bank and a preferred software approach. Inside the bank there is a package called TRANSACTIONS with a specification which shows the capabilities for DEPOSIT and WITHDRAW. Note that the information about BALANCE does not appear in the specification of the package. The specification is the only part of the package that is visible to the outside world. It is a contract to accomplish deposits and withdrawals. Information about the BALANCE is hidden within the package body, which is the implementation of the package. Therefore, the BALANCE is not available to users of the improved bank, as it was in the first part of the example. The executable part of the procedure illustrates this point, as it shows that a depositor may freely use DEPOSIT or WITHDRAW but is thwarted by an attempt to modify the BALANCE directly.

```
          ┌ use TRANSACTIONS;
          │ begin -- BETTER__BANK
          │    DEPOSIT(100.00);
          │    WITHDRAW(17.26);
BALANCE is│    PRINT__NUMBER__OF__TRANSACTIONS;
not visible here│    BALANCE := BALANCE + 1__000__000.00;      -- Illegal
          │    NUMBER__OF__DEPOSITS := 100;                    -- Illegal
          │    NUMBER__OF__WITHDRAWALS :=
          │       NUMBER__OF__WITHDRAWALS − 1;                 -- Illegal
          └ end BETTER__BANK;
```

BETTER__BANK is sound financial practice and is also sound software design practice. External procedures (customers or depositors) cannot modify, indeed have no knowledge of (it is hidden), information inside the package. This hiding of information uncouples procedures from each other, which eases development and paves the way for easier modifications during the software maintenance phase.

The second example involves the making of copies of objects. There are often situations in which the making of copies is undesirable—keys or badges for access to work spaces, for example. Many software situations also forbid the making of copies, for example, access to files and databases. Here is a situation in which copying is undesirable but allowed by the declarations.

```
type PUBLIC__BADGE is range 0 .. 100;
MY__BADGE, COPY__BADGE, YOUR__BADGE : PUBLIC__BADGE;
. . .
. . .
ISSUE(MY__BADGE); -- Issue a valid badge
COPY__BADGE := MY__BADGE;        -- Undesirable
YOUR__BADGE := COPY__BADGE;      -- Undesirable
```

The following example encapsulates the type BADGE, and the procedures which operate on the type, within a package called BADGE__CONTROL.

```
package BADGE_CONTROL is
   type WORK_SPACE is . . . -- Something appropriate
   type BADGE is limited private;
   procedure ISSUE(B : in out BADGE);
   procedure WORK (B : in BADGE; OFFICE: out WORK_SPACE);
private
   type LEGAL_NUMBER is range 0 .. INTEGER'LAST;
   type BADGE is
      record
         NUMBER : LEGAL_NUMBER :=0;
      end record;
end;

package body BADGE_CONTROL is
   -- Implementation of ISSUE and WORK
   -- The private part of the specification is visible here
   -- The body will be provided in chapter 21

. . .
end BADGE_CONTROL;
```

Visible to user of the package

Logically invisible to the user of the package

A new feature here is that in the package specification the type of the BADGE is declared to be **limited private**. Such a declaration, a feature of Ada, forbids any operations on data objects of the type other than the operations explicitly provided for in the package. The package body BADGE_CON-TROL is the only place where objects of type BADGE may be manipulated as a record, using integer values. Specifically, it forbids assignment, or copying —the ability we wish to restrict for badges or keys. In fact, the user of the package who wishes to create and manipulate objects of type BADGE need not know or care what the internal structure of BADGE is; it is an abstract data type. There is a **private** part of the package specification that declares the structure of BADGE, but it is conceptually part of the package body. As indicated in the package BADGE_CONTROL example, the private part is not really available to the user of the package. The package body is not shown in this example, but it is the implementation of the procedures ISSUE and WORK. The idea here is that ISSUE will issue a badge, which cannot be copied, to an employee. The badge will then be used to gain access to a WORK_SPACE by using the procedure WORK.

Here is how the package can be used. Some objects are declared to be type BADGE, then ISSUE is invoked in order to obtain a valid value for MY_BADGE.

```
use BADGE_CONTROL;
procedure GO_TO_WORK is
    ┌─────────────────────────────────────────┬────────┐
    │ MY_BADGE, COPY_BADGE, YOUR_BADGE :      │ BADGE; │
    └─────────────────────────────────────────┴────────┘
    DESK : WORK_SPACE;
begin
    ISSUE(MY_BADGE);
    ISSUE(YOUR_BADGE);
    ISSUE(MY_BADGE);                              -- Will not receive a
                                                  -- new number

    ┌────────────────────────────────┐
    │ COPY_BADGE := YOUR_BADGE;       │           -- Illegal
    └────────────────────────────────┘
    if MY_BADGE = YOUR_BADGE then                 -- Illegal
  . . .
        WORK(MY_BADGE, DESK);                     -- OK. Gets a desk
        WORK(COPY_BADGE, DESK);                   -- Invalid. Does not
                                                  -- get a desk

end GO_TO_WORK;
```

Of critical importance is that the assignment or copying of one value of an object of type BADGE into another is illegal. Badges cannot be copied—the desired result. The procedure WORK can then be used to obtain a DESK. If a badge has not been formally issued, it cannot be used to obtain work space.

4.5 *SUMMARY*

The following points summarize software development using Ada.

- ADA WILL INFLUENCE
    Process of software development
    Design of large systems
    Use (and reuse) of software
- ADA HAS THE POTENTIAL TO ENHANCE
    Reliability; more nearly error-free systems
    Cost; easier testing, reuse of components
    Maintainability; easier to understand and change
- ADA'S CRITICAL CHARACTERISTICS ARE
    Standardization; transportability of programs and knowledge
    Tools; programmer's workbench
    Language features; designed for embedded systems

KEYS TO UNDERSTANDING

► Software development must change to provide less costly, more reliable, and more maintainable software.

► Ada characteristics allowing change are:

Standardization—will enhance transportability, foster improved knowledge and skills, and lead to a software components industry. The APSE will be an important part of the standardization.

Tools—The APSE tools will improve individual programmer productivity but be even more important for project control and programming team productivity.

Language features—The advanced Ada features will allow more programming in high-level languages, allow use of improved design methods, enhance uniformity of programs, encourage detection and handling of run-time errors, and result in more maintainable programs.

► Changes will occur in:

Design *techniques*—to take advantage of Ada's ability to encapsulate data and associated operations.

Methods *of development*—to take advantage of the fact that a single language can be used for both design and implementation. In addition, Ada's clear specification of interfaces could change requirements for external documentation. The APSE could cause significant change in program management and project team relationships.

Reuse *of software*—to take advantage of previously developed packages. Ada has the potential to create a software components industry.

PART 2

ADA AS PASCAL

The main base language for the design of the programming language Ada was the programming language Pascal. It is therefore instructive to begin our study of Ada by beginning with the parts of the language that are most like Pascal. Pascal was designed to be easy to learn. By investigating and learning the Pascal-like parts of Ada, we gain an easy introduction to the language and later will be able to distinguish those parts of Ada that are modifications or extensions to the base language.

To those not familiar with one of the Algol 60-based languages, Ada offers features that may seem unusual and complex, even unnecessary. However, principles of language design and current ideas of the capabilities required of a programming language dictate that these features be included. They have therefore been carried over into Ada. To those with a background of FORTRAN, COBOL, and assembly language, Ada may be perceived as creating complexity. It is, however, simply following in the footsteps of modern languages such as Pascal. By studying the Pascal-like features of Ada, we will clearly see which attributes and concepts of the language have derived from standard ideas of language design.

The following chapters present "Ada as Pascal." The purpose is to represent a large part of Ada as being firmly within the mainstream of modern programming languages. Upon completing part 2, you should have an understanding of the large part of Ada that is similar in level of complexity to Pascal. It is not necessary to understand Pascal to read these chapters. Those who do know Pascal will benefit by being able to assimilate Ada features into their knowledge of Pascal. Those who do not know Pascal will benefit by simultaneously learning classical language features as they learn a major part of Ada.

There are several things that this part of the book does not attempt to do. First, it does not present the simplest parts of Ada first. Although some concepts, such as discriminated or variant records, are quite complex to those who first encounter them, they are a feature of Pascal and hence are presented in this section. Second, there is no attempt to mimic Pascal. Rather, the intent is to present Ada features that are quite similar in terms of level of complexity. Occasionally we will make observations about Pascal to set the stage for further discussion in part 3. Last, the discussion in this part does not define a Pascal-like subset of Ada. Ada has been designed as an integrated and coherent whole. Attempts to subset the language are likely to violate the consistency of the original design and open a Pandora's box of varied and incompatible subsets. The theme of part 2 is to present the features of Ada that are related to Pascal in level of complexity.

Chapter 5 provides a very brief introduction to concepts of the language Pascal, in the same order of presentation as the Ada discussions in the following chapters. Chapters 6 to 12 present Ada as Pascal.

5

About Pascal

Objective: to briefly point out some features of
            Pascal

The programming language Pascal was developed by Niklaus Wirth to provide a language for teaching programming. It was designed to reflect the concepts of structured programming developed during the 1960s. A preliminary version of the language was developed in 1968, a first compiler was operational in 1970, and a revised version of the language was specified in a 1973 report. The language owes much to Algol 60 for having laid the basic foundation for the structuring of programs. Pascal has become very popular because of its clarity and simplicity and has been extended from its initial definition to add features necessary for the actual production of large programs by teams of programmers.

The concepts discussed in the following chapters are:

- Data, expressions, and programs: introduction to syntax and discussion of block structure and scope.
- Type definitions and strong typing: introduction to the concept of type as a data structuring mechanism.
- Control structures: selection and iteration.
- Subprograms: procedures and functions.
- Arrays: grouping of information of the same type.

- Records: grouping of information of different types.
- Pointers: indirect references to data.

Pascal is the first language to have made these concepts popular and available to a wide range of programmers. The concepts have been generally well accepted. They impose a greater structure on programs, which is likely to be of benefit in the maintenance of long-lived programs. For example, the use of the natural block structure of the language allows the nesting of procedures and hence the creation of greater modularity and privacy of data. Properly used, the block structure can lead to increased module independence and low coupling, or connectivity, between modules.

Concepts of strong typing, combined with data structures based on records and pointers, can impose order on a program's data. Increased order can reduce the time required for program debugging and make software more reliable. Use of logical control constructs such as DO-WHILE and IF-THEN-ELSE, combined with restriction of the GO TO, generally leads to improved structure and an easier-to-understand logic flow.

Some of the concepts are not easy or obvious. Many programmers have no doubt chafed over the discipline required to declare all variables, to specify their type, and to ensure that variables of different types are not mixed in expressions or assignments. But this discipline requires that the programmer carefully control design and therefore create easier-to-test and ultimately more reliable programs. The concept of combining objects of different type, which are related in a problem-specific way, into a single record is important. Some have found this concept difficult, especially when the record is allowed to have a portion (the variant part) that varies according to the value of some other field within the record. The use of pointers to reference or access data objects indirectly rather than accessing them by name has also been found difficult, particularly when pointers and records are used to build up complex data structures and when combined with recursion. Nonetheless, Pascal has introduced all these concepts to a large body of programmers, and the concepts are becoming accepted as necessary components of a modern language.

The remainder of part 2 will cover each of these concepts in essentially the level of detail and at the same level of difficulty as would a basic introduction to Pascal. The concepts presented are those of Pascal, the syntax is that of Ada.

Key to Understanding

▶ Although Pascal is a simple language, designed for teaching, it has a number of features unfamiliar to many programmers. It is useful to cover the similar Ada features first, before discussing more advanced topics.

6

Data, Expressions, and Programs

> Objective: to look at the elemental components of Ada: data, operators, and program structure

Before proceeding further, we need to look closely at tne elements of Ada. This chapter provides information on the elemental data components, the operators used to combine the data components into expressions, and the overall structure of a program. In doing all this we will also look at syntax diagrams as a mechanism to formally show the relationship among language components.

6.1 BASIC COMPONENTS

The character set used in Ada consists of uppercase letters (A .. Z), lowercase letters (a .. z), digits (0 .. 9), and a number of special characters and symbols such as

$$+ \ - \ * \ / \ () \ = \ < \ > \ >= \ <= \ /= \ <> \ << \ >> \ \& \ |$$

These symbols will be defined as we go along. Except within character strings, there is no difference between uppercase and lowercase characters. For the sake of readability, however, we will consistently use lowercase characters for Ada reserved words and uppercase characters for defined identifiers.

The reserved words in Ada that we will use in part 2 are:

abs	**constant**	**function**	**not**	**record**
access	**declare**	**goto**	**null**	**return**
all	**do**	**if**	**of**	**reverse**
and	**else**	**in**	**or**	**subtype**
array	**elsif**	**is**	**others**	**then**
begin	**end**	**loop**	**out**	**type**
body	**exit**	**mod**	**procedure**	**when**
case	**for**	**new**	**range**	**while**

In this book, reserved words will appear in boldface.

All identifiers are composed of letters, digits, and underscores; they always begin with a letter. Identifiers may not be reserved words. The language does not restrict their length except that they may not extend over a line. In this book, identifiers will be in uppercase. The following syntax diagrams define the allowable ways of constructing an identifier.

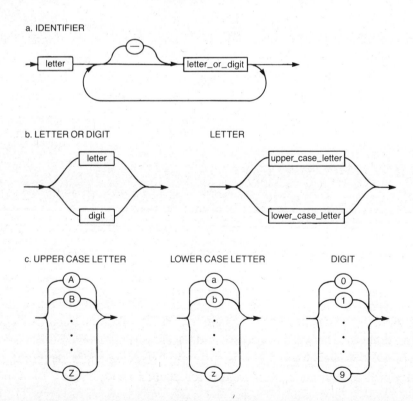

a. IDENTIFIER

b. LETTER OR DIGIT   LETTER

c. UPPER CASE LETTER   LOWER CASE LETTER   DIGIT

Each diagram defines a *phrase,* which consists of other phrases (shown boxed) and atomic elements (shown circled). The combination rules are defined by the connecting lines. A syntax diagram can be thought of as a one-way street that may be traversed in any legal way according to the rules of the road. Notice that optional paths are clearly shown as *side streets.* To construct an identifier, the diagram shows that it must begin with a letter and may consist of only one letter since there is an exit road after the letter symbol. However, it is also possible to circle repeatedly through the symbol for letter__or__digit, taking an optional side trip through the underscore (__) symbol. Notice that the rules of the road forbid two underscore symbols in a row. Some legal identifiers are

    tHis__IS__legal REAL__TIME__CLOCK PAYROLL COL__20

Some illegal identifiers are

    90__DAY__NOTE PAY_____PENALTY SINE/WAVE

Another way of showing the same relationships is through the use of Backus-Naur Form (BNF). BNF symbology defines an identifier as

```
identifier::=
    letter {[underscore] | letter__or__digit}
letter__or__digit        ::= letter | digit
letter                   ::= upper__case__letter | lower__case__letter
upper__case__letter      ::= A | B | . . . | Z
lower__case__letter      ::= a | b | . . . | z
digit                    ::= 0 | 1 | . . . | 9
```

The ::= means "is defined as." The square brackets, [ ], indicate that an item is optional. The curved brackets, { }, indicate that an item is optional and may be repeated. The vertical bar, |, is an "or" operator. In this book we will use syntax diagrams to informally discuss the relationships among language elements. The diagrams in this part do not necessarily represent the complete Ada syntax. Since our focus here is on the Pascal-like features of Ada, certain options and alternative paths are not presented. The official definition of Ada syntax is presented in appendix B in BNF notation.

Ada has numbers, or numeric literals, such as

```
1815   0   999__200   6E10        -- Integers. Note "E" for the exponent
1815.0   0.0   999.2E3   0.6E11   -- Real numbers
```

Ada also has character literals such as

```
'a' 'A' ' ' '*' '/'            -- Note apostrophe
                               -- as delimiter.
```

Ada also has character strings, such as

```
"This is a string" "May contain /*"","   -- Strings
"this is" & "one string"  "A"  "STRINGS MAY   " &
"CONTINUE ON THE NEXT LINE"
```

The double dash (--) indicates a comment. Comments continue to, and are terminated by, the end of a line. The apostrophe (') delimits a character literal, and the double quote (") delimits strings. The double quote character in a string is indicated by a pair of such characters. The "&" is the catenation (or concatenation) operator. It is used to concatenate two strings and to connect strings that extend over one line.

6.2 BASIC TYPES

This section introduces notions of type and introduces the elementary types INTEGER, FLOAT, and BOOLEAN, which are predefined in Ada.

Like Pascal and unlike FORTRAN, Ada requires the programmer to declare each variable in a program and to declare that it is of a specific type. The type defines two important characteristics of the variable being declared:

- The values that may be assigned to the variable (the values that it may contain).

- The operations that may be performed on the variable.

For example, if we define some INTEGER variables, INT__1, INT__2, and INT__3, the following assignments and operations are allowed:

```
INT__1 := 10;    -- Statements are
INT__2 := 20;    -- terminated with the semicolon.
INT__3 := INT__1 − INT__2;
INT__1 := INT__2 * INT__3;
```

However, the following assignments and operations are illegal:

```
INT__1 := "abc";            -- Illegal. Types are incompatible.
INT__2 := 'A';              -- Illegal. Types are incompatible.
INT__3 := 3.14;             -- Illegal. No implicit numeric type
                            -- conversion
INT__1 := INT__2 & INT__3;  -- Illegal operator ("&") for type
INT__1 := not INT__3;       -- Illegal unary operator ("not") for type
```

In general, Ada requires all variables to be explicitly declared. That is, there are no implicit or default declarations as in FORTRAN. The declaration specifies the type of the variable. Ada forbids the assignment of a value of one type to a variable of a different type.

In addition to integers (INTEGER), Ada provides the floating point type (FLOAT) for those values mathematically referred to as real numbers and having a floating point representation. It provides the boolean type (BOOLEAN) for variables that have only two allowable values: TRUE or FALSE. A declaration of variables using the types mentioned so far is shown below:

```
procedure DECLARATION__EXAMPLE is
-- This is the part of a procedure that contains
-- declarations of variables.
   INT__1, INT__2, INT__3                  : INTEGER;
   SIN__VAL, STD__DEV, VARIANCE            : FLOAT;
   END__OF__INPUT, INTERRUPT__PENDING      : BOOLEAN;
begin
-- This is the part of a procedure that contains
-- the executable code.
end DECLARATION__EXAMPLE;
```

The types INTEGER, FLOAT, and BOOLEAN are not reserved words but are predefined as part of the standard Ada environment. The predefined language environment is presented in appendix C. The example also shows the general structure of an Ada procedure, which has separate sections for the declaration of variables and the execution of statements.

6.3 *OPERATORS AND EXPRESSIONS*

This section introduces the syntax of expressions and the operators allowed for the types INTEGER, FLOAT, and BOOLEAN. An expression is a formula. It defines a computation and results in a value. The syntax of expressions is as follows.

expression

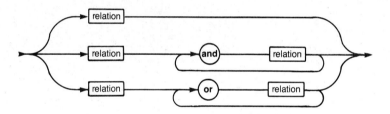

For example,

```
−15 + INT__1 * INT__2 < = 60 or not END__OF__FILE
INT__1 + INT__3
'A'
TRUE
```

An expression denotes a sequence of operations to be performed, in a specific order. It may be a relation or it may consist of "anding" or "oring" relationships. A relation is

relation

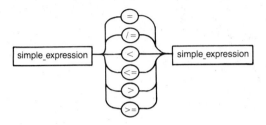

For example,

```
−15 + INT__1 * INT__2 < = 60
INT__1 + INT__3
'A'
TRUE
not END__OF__FILE
```

A relation may be a simple__expression or two simple__expressions connected by a relational__operator. A relation may also involve a determination as to whether a value lies in a specified range. Note the use of "/=" for "not equal to." The other operators have their usual mathematical meaning. A simple__expression is

simple__expression

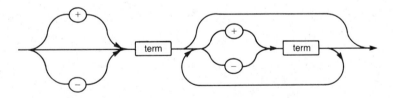

For example

```
−15 + INT__1 * INT__2
INT__1 + INT__3
'A'
TRUE
not END__OF__FILE
```

A simple_expression consists of a term. The term may be preceded by unary + or −; it may also be combined with other terms by use of adding operators. A term is

term

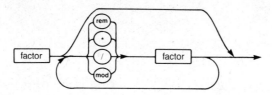

For example,

```
INT__1 * INT__2
15
'A'
TRUE
not END__OF__FILE
```

A term may simply be a factor, or it may be a number of factors combined with the usual multiplying operators: "*****" for multiplication, "**/**" for division, "**rem**" for remainder, and "**mod**" for modulo. A factor is

factor

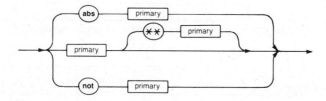

For example,

```
INT__1 ** INT__2
abs INT__1
15
'A'
TRUE
not END__OF__FILE
```

A factor may simply be a primary, optionally with **abs** or **not,** or it may be two primaries combined by the highest__precedence__operator "**" for exponentiation.

Thus far, each phrase has been defined in terms of other phrases. However, we are now ready to define primary as a relationship of (mostly) elemental components.

primary

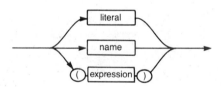

For example,

```
INT__1, INT__2, 15, 'A', TRUE, END__OF__FILE
```

A primary may be a literal such as 128 or 62.4 or 'A' or "JONES". Or it may be the name of a variable, INT__1, VARIANCE, or END__OF__FILE. It could also be any of a number of things we have not yet discussed, such as a constant or a function__call. Notice that a primary may also be a parenthesized expression. Hence the definition of expression is recursive, in that it is partially defined in terms of itself.

A simple example (having nothing to do with Ada) of a recursive definition is

letter__list

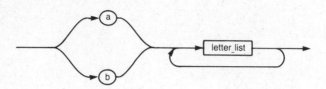

A letter__list is a string of a's and b's, of arbitrary length and order. Since letter__list is partially defined in terms of letter__list, the definition is said to be recursive. Examples of letter__lists are: aaaaa . . . , ababbab . . . , bbbbbb . . . , bababa . . . , and many other combinations.

6.3.1 *General Observations.*

Notice that the syntax diagrams are designed to reflect the precedence relationships of the operators. The separate definition of primary, factor, and term as distinct items is done to reflect the fact that in the absence of parentheses, the highest__precedence__operators are applied before the multiplying__operators, and the multiplying__operators are applied before the adding__operators.

The fact that the definition of expression is recursive makes certain aspects of the syntax appear ambiguous until the definition is complete. For example, from the highest level definition of expression, it appears as though the **and** and **or** operators cannot be combined in the same expression. In fact, in the absence of parentheses, they cannot. However, since two relations can be combined, two expressions (in parentheses) can be combined. One expression can contain **or** and the other can contain **and.** The arithmetic operators +, −, *, and / are the same for both FLOAT and INTEGER operands (terms or factors), although of course operands of two different types cannot be combined by the same operator. Since the same symbol has more than one meaning (for example, floating point or integer division), it is said to be *overloaded.* Of course, virtually all languages have similarly overloaded operators. (It is important to mention overloading here, since we will see in part 3 that it is possible in Ada for the programmer to further overload the operators.) The arithmetic operators have their usual meaning, with INTEGER division truncating, as illustrated by the following relationship

13 / 5 = 2

Both FLOAT and INTEGER may be raised to INTEGER powers, but only FLOAT values can take negative exponents.

6.3.2 *Summary*

The allowable combinations of operators (grouped by precedence) and operands used to form expressions are shown in table 6-1. Within groups, operations are performed left to right.

6.4 *PROGRAM STRUCTURE*

Within a single compilation unit the structure of an Ada program generally follows that of the classic block structure established by Algol 60 and followed by Pascal. We will use the example of a procedure as a compilation unit and suppose that it represents a complete program. The actual designation of a main program in Ada is implementation dependent, that is, not specified by the language definition. We have already seen one example of a procedure. Using a syntax diagram, it becomes

Table 6-1   OPERATORS AND OPERANDS

Group/Operator	Operand(s)	Result
Highest precedence operator:		
**	INTEGER or FLOAT	same (exponent must be INTEGER)
abs	numeric	same numeric
not	BOOLEAN	BOOLEAN
Multiplying__operator:		
*	numeric	same numeric
/	numeric	same numeric
mod	INTEGER	INTEGER
rem	INTEGER	INTEGER
Unary__operator:		
unary +	numeric	same numeric
unary −	numeric	same numeric
Adding__operator:		
+	numeric	same numeric
—	numeric	same numeric
&	string	string
Relational__operator:		
=	any	BOOLEAN
/=	any	BOOLEAN
<	numeric	BOOLEAN
<=	numeric	BOOLEAN
>	numeric	BOOLEAN
>=	numeric	BOOLEAN
Logical__operator:		
and	BOOLEAN	BOOLEAN
or	BOOLEAN	BOOLEAN

procedure

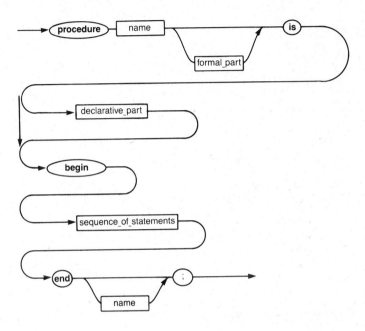

The reserved word **procedure** is followed by the name of the procedure and the reserved word **is.** The optional formal‗part states the parameter-calling specification. It will be described in chapter 9. Next comes the declarative‗part where variables and other program entities are declared. The executable part of the procedure—the statements—is bracketed by the reserved words **begin** and **end.** The repeat of the procedure name in the end clause is optional, but if included it must be identical to the name at the beginning of the procedure. The procedure is terminated by a semicolon.

Ada also allows a construct for grouping declarations and statements, called a block. Pascal also has blocks but only in connection with programs and subprograms. The syntax of a block is

block

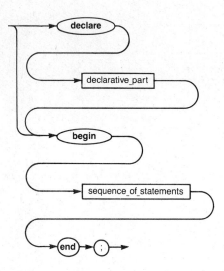

Here is a simple example of a block.

```
declare
   INT__1 : INTEGER;
begin
   INT__1 := 500;
end;
```

Notice that in both procedures and blocks, the declarations occur before the statements. Ada carefully distinguishes between declarations, which introduce new variables and other identifiers, and statements, which use and manipulate the identifiers. Declarations and statements are therefore kept separate. Either a procedure or a block can be considered to be a statement and therefore can be executed.

What is the effect of statement execution on the declarations? The first thing to occur is that the declarations are *elaborated*. Elaboration makes the identifier come into existence and assigns any initial values. Its name becomes available for use and, if appropriate, storage is allocated. Ada, unlike Pascal, allows the assignment of initial values to variables. The assignment of initial values can involve a great deal of processing.

After identifiers have been elaborated, they may be used in the executable part. Specifically, the values of the variables may be changed. What happens to the variables and the new values when we come to the end of the procedure or block? After the procedure or block has been executed, all identifiers defined in the declarative part cease to exist. The names are no longer available for use, the storage is no longer allocated, and the new values are no longer accessible. This is standard for block-structured languages. Therefore, those variables that need to exist for the life of the program must be declared at the highest level of the program and be available to all internal procedures and blocks. They are then said to be global in scope.

6.5 *THE CONCEPT OF SCOPE AND VISIBILITY*

An identifier is said to be visible in any part of a program in which it may be used. For example, a data object may be used in an assignment statement. The scope of the identifier is the part of a program in which it is potentially visible. That is, scope is the region of program text in which the identifier may have an effect. We will see in chapter 14 how Ada provides additional control over scope and visibility. A problem in languages without Ada's control mechanisms is the *invasion* of a name space due to the nesting of scopes.

For blocks and procedures, the *scope* of a declaration extends from its point of elaboration to the end of the enclosing construct, literally the **end** statement. Procedures and blocks may be nested. Among the things that may be declared in a declarative—part are subordinate procedures. Therefore, as procedures and blocks are nested deeper and deeper, more and more names are said to be in scope. Since the declaration of a procedure or the occurrence of a block does not restrict the name space, more names become visible as the nesting becomes deeper. The following example illustrates this point.

```
procedure OUTER_1 is
  A, B, C : INTEGER;

  procedure MIDDLE_1 is
    X, Y, Z : INTEGER;

    procedure INNER_1 is
      FE, FI, FO : INTEGER;
    begin -- INNER_1
    -- A, B, C, X, Y, Z, FE, FI, and FO are visible

      declare
        ME, OH, MY : INTEGER;
      begin
      -- A, B, C, X, Y, Z, FE, FI, and FO and
      -- ME, OH, MY are visible
      end;

    end INNER_1;

  begin -- MIDDLE_1
  -- A, B, C, X, Y, and Z are visible
  -- INNER_1 is visible, but FE, FI, and FO are not
  end MIDDLE_1;
begin -- OUTER_1
-- A, B, C, are visible
-- MIDDLE_1 is visible, but X, Y, Z and INNER_1 are not
end OUTER_1;
```

The procedure or block acts as a barrier to prevent *outside* scopes from looking into the procedure or block. The *inner* scopes do look outside and can see the externally declared names (including the procedure names).

If one of the externally declared names is redefined, the outer name will be hidden and only the new name will be visible. This is the only situation in which scope and visibility differ in standard block-structured languages. This is shown in the following program.

```
procedure OUTER_2 is
   A, B, C : INTEGER;

   procedure INNER_2 is
      A : INTEGER;                        -- Hides the variable A in
   begin -- INNER_2                       -- OUTER_2
      A := 100;
      B := 200;
   end INNER_2;
begin -- OUTER_2
   A := 1;
   B := 2;
   C := 3;
   INNER_2;                               -- Causes execution of INNER_2
   PUT(A); PUT(B); PUT(C);
end OUTER_2;
```

The values output by the program will be: 1   200   3. The assignment of 100 to the inner A does not affect the outer A, and the inner A is lost at the end of procedure INNER_2. On the other hand the assignment of 200 to B affects the global outer B and the value is therefore retained. In Ada, the outer instance of A can be referenced as OUTER_2.A.

The scope and visibility rules of standard block-structured languages lead to two problems:

- To give a variable life over the entire execution of the program, it must have global scope and therefore have visibility (unless hidden by internal declarations) throughout the entire program.
- Since there is no way to restrict a name space, the deeply nested procedures become cluttered with identifiers irrelevant to the function being performed. The procedure may inadvertently modify one of the variables *invading* its name space. A corollary, although less likely to create a problem, is that a procedure may inadvertently hide the name of a global variable to which it is supposed to have access.

These problems, combined with the lack of separate compilation in Pascal, create severe difficulties when developing large programming systems over a long period of time. We will see in chapters 21 and 22 that Ada provides a superior mechanism for overcoming these difficulties. The **package** provides an effective mechanism for controlling both the lifetime and visibility of variables. Combined with comprehensive separate compilation capabilities, it eases the development of large, maintainable software systems.

Exercise__6

Write a program that contains two procedures: one that adds N (passed as a parameter to the procedure), and one that subtracts N from the same globally declared data object (INTEGER).

Program__6

```
with TEXT_IO; use TEXT_IO;
procedure PROGRAM_6 is
  OBJECT : INTEGER := 0;
  package IO is new INTEGER_IO(INTEGER); use IO;

  procedure ADD_N(N : in INTEGER) is
  begin
    OBJECT := OBJECT + N;
  end ADD_N;

  procedure SUB_N(N : in INTEGER) is
  begin
    OBJECT := OBJECT - N;
  end SUB_N;
begin -- PROGRAM_6
  ADD_N(10);
  SUB_N( 5);
  OBJECT := OBJECT + 3;
  PUT(OBJECT);
end PROGRAM_6;
```

Begin Ada execution

8

Discussion__6

The creation of the program is straightforward. OBJECT must be initialized. An important point is that for OBJECT to be visible to both of the procedures, it must also be visible to the main body of the program. As previously discussed, this is undesirable. See Exercise__14 in chapter 14 for additional discussion.

KEYS TO UNDERSTANDING

▶ Ada is a strongly typed language. The type of each variable defines the values that may be assigned to the variable and the operations that may be performed on the values.

▶ Within a single compilation unit, Ada may demonstrate a classic block structure with nested subprograms and nested scope of identifiers.

7

Type Definitions
and Strong Typing

> Objective: to explain what a type is and to show that strong typing aids program reliability.

The fundamental idea of strong typing is the clear separation of data objects that are unrelated. This chapter discusses strong typing and how different types are created in Ada.

7.1 BASIC CONCEPTS

The type of an object defines the *values* that it may assume and the *operations* that are allowed on those values. The fundamental mechanism for enforcing the separation of data objects is that a value of one type may not be assigned to an object of a different type. Strong typing provides a mechanism for preventing errors by disallowing, at compile time, situations that could later cause problems during execution. For example,

```
declare
  THIS : INTEGER;
  THAT : FLOAT;
```

```
begin
  THAT := 1.0;        -- OK
  THIS := THAT;       -- Illegal
  THAT := THIS;       -- Illegal
end;
```

Or

```
declare
  MY_STUFF      : OIL;
  YOUR_STUFF    : WATER;
begin
  MY_STUFF := YOUR_STUFF; -- Illegal
end;
```

It is important to note that illegal assignments such as the preceding ones are discovered at compile time.

Although the mixing of oil and water in the last example is an obvious error, such errors occur with some frequency. The discovery of the error at compile time prevents its introduction into the run-time environment. It is costly to discover errors during testing, and the chance exists that an error might slip undetected into the operational system. The mechanism of strong typing allows the compiler to be a powerful tool in preventing programming errors.

The next mechanism for enforcing the separation of data objects is that most predefined operators may apply only to operands of a single type. That is, types may not be mixed in an expression. (In chapter 15 we will see that a programmer can explicitly define operators to allow the mixing of types in an expression.) By expression, we specifically include the concepts of relation, simple_expression, term, and factor, as defined in chapter 6. Two examples of the illegal mixing of operators and operands that use the types defined previously are

```
THIS + THAT
MY_STUFF * YOUR_STUFF
```

Refer to Table 6-1 for legal combinations of operators and operands.

There are, of course, situations where it is necessary to mix objects of different types or to assign values of one type to objects of another. Ada provides a simple mechanism for overriding the strong-type restrictions—use of the type name for an explicit type conversion between closely related types. The following statements illustrate this mechanism:

```
THIS := INTEGER(THAT);      -- Conversion with rounding
THIS := THIS + INTEGER(THAT);
THAT := THAT / FLOAT(THIS);
MY_STUFF := OIL(YOUR_STUFF);
```

As you can see, Ada does not completely forbid the use of different types in the same operation. The language requires only that the programmer be explicit in expressing an intent to do so. The intent should be explicit to allow the compiler to enforce strong typing and help in preventing errors in operational systems.

7.2 TYPES AND DECLARATIONS

So far, we have relied on the reader's general understanding of the notion of type. Now we will provide more explanation: A type establishes a set of values and a set of operations applicable to those values. For example, the values associated with INTEGER are

$$\ldots -2, -1, 0, 1, 2 \ldots$$

with a common range being $-32768 \ldots 32767$ for a 16-bit representation in two's complement. Some of the associated operations are

$$+, -, {}^*, /, >, =, <, \ldots$$

In Ada, types are defined and given a name. INTEGER is among the predefined types, but we can imagine a type definition such as

type INTEGER **is** . . .

Types are defined in the declarative part of a block or procedure, as are variables (which we've already discussed) and constants. Bringing these notions together in a single example, we have

```
declare
  type NEW__TYPE is < definition goes here > ;  -- Type declaration
  N, T : NEW__TYPE; -- Variable declaration
  INT__1 : INTEGER; -- Declaration using a predefined type
  BLOCK__SIZE : constant INTEGER := 127;    -- Declaration of an
                                            -- INTEGER constant
  CHANNEL__NUMBER : constant := 15;         -- A number
                                            -- declaration
begin
  . . .
  -- executable part of block
end;
```

The definition of **NEW__TYPE** could be an enumeration type, as shown in the next section, or a structured or access type as shown in chapters 10, 11, and 12.

It could also simply indicate a range of values as

```
type NEW__TYPE is range -100 .. 100;
```

Although the type defines a subrange of integers, it is not INTEGER. Objects of type **NEW__TYPE** are incompatible with objects of type INTEGER. Notice that a **constant** value is just that. It is constant and may not be changed. In fact, it may not appear on the left-hand side of an assignment statement. For example,

```
BLOCK__SIZE := 127; -- Illegal
```

The **CHANNEL__NUMBER** is of type *universal integer* and may be used anywhere the number 15 might be used.

7.3 ENUMERATION TYPES

Now we will see one way to define our own types. These programmer-defined types, called enumeration types, are defined by naming the type and listing (enumerating) the possible values. For example,

```
type DESSERT is (CAKE, COOKIES, ICE__CREAM);
```

is the definition of a type called DESSERT. The type characterizes the possible values of CAKE, COOKIES, and ICE__CREAM; the equality operations = and /=; and the ordering operations <, <=, >, and >=. The enumeration provides an implicit ordering of the values, with COOKIES less than ICE__CREAM, and CAKE less than COOKIES. For example,

```
declare
    SNACK, AFTER__DINNER : DESSERT;
begin
    SNACK := ICE__CREAM;                -- Assignment
    AFTER__DINNER := CAKE;
    if SNACK = AFTER__DINNER then       -- A relation
    . . .
    if SNACK <= CAKE then               -- A relation
    . . .
end;
```

The usual strong typing rules apply. Another example is

```
declare
    type APPLES      is (DELICIOUS, MCINTOSH, PIPPIN);
    type ORANGES     is (NAVEL, FLORIDA, CALIF);
    MY__STUFF        : APPLES;
    YOUR__STUFF      : ORANGES;
begin
    MY__STUFF        := PIPPIN;
    YOUR__STUFF      := DELICIOUS;       -- Illegal. Type mismatch
    YOUR__STUFF      := MY__STUFF;       -- Illegal. Type mismatch
    YOUR__STUFF      := NAVEL + CALIF:   -- Illegal. " + " not defined
                                         -- for enumeration
end;
```

Why should we bother defining enumeration types and distinguishing between them and numeric types? We do it to introduce a degree of data abstraction and to allow the compiler to help prevent logically incompatible operations. A frequent occurrence in languages such as FORTRAN is that some abstract concept, such as the days of the week, is mapped to a numeric type such as integer. Then in the programmer's mind, and in a comment if we are lucky, there is a mapping of

```
MONDAY       --> 0
TUESDAY      --> 1
    .
    .
    .
SUNDAY       --> 6
```

Then, at certain times, the integers 0 to 6 are used as a representation of the days of the week. Of course, it is possible to define variables with appropriate names and values in order to introduce some expression of intent, but this cannot always be done. Further, the danger still exists that there may be a mixing of two such mappings (such as days of the week and kinds of dessert) or of an abstract mapping and *regular* integer values. In Ada, on the other hand, we can have

```
type DAY is (MON, TUE, WED, THU, FRI, SAT, SUN);
EACH_DAY : DAY;
```

This gains for us a degree of abstraction from the physical representation of EACH_DAY and its values, as well as the protection of the strong-typing mechanism. The type DAY will appear extensively throughout the remainder of the book to illustrate the use of enumeration types. The next chapter will show how enumeration types are used in complete programs.

Although we gain an important degree of abstraction in using enumeration types, there must, of course, be an actual underlying machine representation of the values of the enumeration type. This is integer. The mapping is that which might be expected, with 0 for MON, 1 for TUE, . . . 6 for SUN. Therefore, the relational operators $<$, $>$, $<=$, $>=$ for enumeration types yield a result of the relation depending on the underlying numeric representation.

In addition to allowable operations, enumeration types have *attributes* defined for them. 'PRED and 'SUCC are attributes that serve as functions which take values as arguments and return the predecessor or successor values. Then

```
DAY'PRED(WED) = TUE
DAY'SUCC(WED) = THU
```

and for EACH—DAY = FRI,

```
DAY'PRED(EACH—DAY) = THU
DAY'SUCC(EACH—DAY) = SAT.
```

There is no predecessor of the first item in the enumeration list, nor is there a successor to the last item. Either DAY'PRED(MON) or DAY'SUCC(SUN) will result in an error; there is no wraparound from last to first.

We can now introduce the types CHARACTER and BOOLEAN. We have seen that character literals are represented as characters in single apostrophes, for example, 'A'. Character literals are allowed in enumeration types as shown:

```
type ROMAN—DIGIT is ('I', 'V', 'X', 'L', 'C', 'D', 'M');
```

The type CHARACTER is simply an enumeration type that consists of the 95 graphic characters in the ASCII character set that can be defined by character literals, plus representations of the control characters. (The detailed declaration of character is provided in appendix C, "Predefined Language Environment.")

Likewise, type BOOLEAN is a predefined enumeration type, having the simple definition

```
type BOOLEAN is (FALSE, TRUE);
```

7.4 SUBTYPES

Another feature of Ada that increases the reliability of programs is the subtype. A subtype, as any other type, characterizes a set of values and operations. However, the values of a subtype are a subset of the values characterizing the *base type* of the subtype. For example,

```
subtype PAGES        is INTEGER range 1 .. 1000;
subtype BOOK—PAGES   is INTEGER range 1 .. 400;
subtype WORK—DAY     is DAY range MON .. FRI;
subtype MONEY        is FLOAT range 0.0 .. 1—000—000.0;
```

The range introduces a constraint on the values of the base type. However, all operations are still valid, and the subtype and base type are fully compatible. The subtype declaration does not introduce a new type.

There may even be subtypes of subtypes, as the following examples show. Of course, previously existing constraints must be respected.

```
subtype SMALL__BOOK      is BOOK__PAGES range 1 .. 100;
subtype POOR             is MONEY range 0.0 .. 10.0;
subtype BANK__BALANCE    is MONEY range − 100.0 .. 100.0; -- Illegal
subtype LONG__WORK       is WORK__DAY
                            range MON .. SAT; --Illegal
```

The last two declarations are illegal since they have ranges that violate previous constraints on **MONEY** and **WORK__DAY**. The constraints must also be respected at run time, and an Ada compiler generates code to check the allowable range of values for a subtype prior to making an assignment. Using the types and subtypes just defined, we may have

```
declare
   BOOK             : PAGES;
   ADA__BOOK        : BOOK__PAGES;
   FORTRAN__BOOK : SMALL__BOOK;
begin
   FORTRAN__BOOK := 50;
   ADA__BOOK := FORTRAN__BOOK;              -- Always OK
   FORTRAN__BOOK := ADA__BOOK;              -- OK, but must have
                                            -- check at run time
   BOOK := ADA__BOOK + FORTRAN__BOOK;       -- Always OK
   BOOK := 425;                             -- OK
   ADA__BOOK := BOOK − FORTRAN__BOOK;       -- Needs run-time
end;                                        -- check
```

Notice that the last assignment will succeed and will not result in a run-time error. BOOK is 425, FORTRAN__BOOK is 50, and the result of the expression is 375. The range check does not occur until the expression has been evaluated. If FORTRAN__BOOK had had a value of 10, the value of the expression would have been 415. Since 415 is not in the allowable range of values for ADA__BOOK, a run-time error would occur and an exception would be raised.

Why should we bother to create and declare subtypes? We do so to continue the degree of data abstraction and to allow the compiler to help create programs that are secure. In fact, a well-designed Ada program will have few unrestricted variables of type INTEGER or FLOAT. Usually something is known of the nature and use of a variable that will allow the definition of a subtype with a range constraint. The limitation of the range of variables is useful during the debugging of programs, since a range violation points out that some sort of logical error has occurred. It is also valuable for operational use in that it increases program reliability while relieving the programmer from making explicit range checks. For example, suppose the proper operation of our program is critically dependent on the range of values of ADA__BOOK. If Ada did not have subtypes and automatic run-time range checks, we might well write

```
declare
    RANGE__CHECK : INTEGER;
begin
    -- INT and FORTRAN__BOOK are input values
    RANGE__CHECK := INT - FORTRAN__BOOK;
    if RANGE__CHECK > = 0 and RANGE__CHECK < = 400 then
        ADA__BOOK := RANGE__CHECK;
    else
        PUT("Attempted out of range assignment to ADA__BOOK. " &
            "No assignment made.");
    end if;
end;
```

In Ada the range checking code is generated by the compiler. If the range is not satisfied, an error indicator called an **exception** occurs. Part 4 will tell how to handle **exceptions** and accomplish the usual Ada equivalent of the **else** part of the code above.

7.5 *MEMBERSHIP TESTS*

Ada provides the membership tests **in** and **not in** to test whether a value is within a specified range. They can be used to determine if a value falls within the bounds of a subtype. For example,

```
N not in 1 .. 10;                -- Range check
TODAY in WEEKDAY;                -- Subtype check
TODAY in DAY range MON .. FRI;   -- Same subtype check
TODAY in MON .. FRI;             -- Same subtype check
RANGE__CHECK in 0 .. 400;        -- Simplify previous example
                                 -- of checks on RANGE__CHECK
```

The result of the test is BOOLEAN and can be used in the expected ways. For example,

```
if INPUT__CHAR in 'A' .. 'Z' then
   -- Upper case letter processing
else
   -- Other processing
end if;
```

Exercise__7

Write a program that defines an enumeration type and two range-restricted subtypes, one of INTEGER, the other of the previously defined enumeration type. Make legal and illegal assignments to each.

Program__7

```
procedure PROGRAM__7 is
   type US__COLOR       is (RED, WHITE, BLUE);
   subtype SKY          is US__COLOR range WHITE .. BLUE;
   subtype SHORT__INT is INTEGER range −10 .. 10;

   US__FLAG        : US__COLOR;
   PARTLY__CLOUDY  : SKY;
   TENS            : SHORT__INT;
   ANY__SIZE       : INTEGER;

begin -- PROGRAM__7

   US__FLAG  := BLUE;
   US__FLAG  := "BLUE";                       -- Illegal
      < ---------------- >
```

```
        *** Semantic Error: incompatible types for :=
PARTLY_CLOUDY := WHITE;
PARTLY_CLOUDY := RED;                   -- Out of range error
                                        -- at run time

      < -------------------- >
      *** Warning: Evaluation of expression will raise CONSTRAINT_
      ERROR
PARTLY_CLOUDY := US_FLAG;               -- Range check
                                        -- at run time

US_FLAG := PARTLY_CLOUDY;               -- Always legal


TENS         := −2;
ANY_SIZE    := 11;
TENS         := ANY_SIZE;               -- Error discovered
                                        -- at run time

ANY_SIZE    := 1;
TENS         := ANY_SIZE;               -- Range check
                                        -- at run time
ANY_SIZE    := TENS;                    -- Always legal
ANY_SIZE    := 1.0;                     -- No mixing of integer
                                        -- and real

      < -------------- >
      *** Semantic Error: incompatible types for :=
ANY_SIZE    := 'a';                     -- No mixing of integer
                                        -- and character

      < -------------- >
      *** Semantic Error: incompatible types for :=


end PROGRAM_7;


3 translation errors detected
Translation time: 29 seconds
```

Discussion_7

An attempt to make a type-incompatible assignment is discovered at compile time. Subtypes, however, are type-compatible with their base types. An out-of-range assignment generates an error at execution time. If a compiler can determine at compile time that an out-of-range situation is going to occur, it may (but does not have to) immediately generate code to raise CONSTRAINT_ ERROR. It also may provide a warning that the exception will be raised.

Keys to Understanding

▶ The fundamental idea of strong typing is that a value of one type may not be assigned to an object of a different type.

▶ Type checking is done at compile time but can prevent logical errors that could result in run-time failures.

▶ Programmers are allowed to define new types by enumerating the allowable values.

▶ Subtypes provide restricted ranges of values. The restricted ranges are supported by run-time checks.

▶ The combination of compile-time and run-time checks increases program reliability.

8

Control Structures

```
┌─────────────────────────────────────────────┐
│ Objective:  to present the basic control-flow │
│             structures of Ada                  │
└─────────────────────────────────────────────┘
```

The three basic structured programming constructs are sequence, selection, and iteration. Sequence is the usual execution of one instruction after the other. Selection implies a choice between two alternatives based on evaluation of a <condition>. Ada accomplishes selection with an **if** statement. It also provides an extended form of the **if** statement and a **case** statement to allow for multiple alternatives. Iteration is accomplished by a **loop** construct with a variety of methods of controlling exits from the loop. Ada also has an explicit transfer of control to a label. Selection and iteration (both of which include use of the sequence construct) are discussed in detail in this chapter, as is Ada's transfer mechanism.

8.1 SELECTION

The syntax of the basic **if** statement is

basic__if__statement

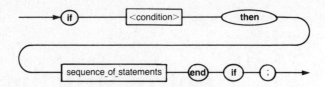

A condition is an expression that yields a value of type **BOOLEAN**. The sequence__of__statements is just that; it is executed if and only if the value of the expression is TRUE. For example,

```
if INT__1 > INT__2 then
   INT__2 := 100;
   INT__1 := 0;
end if;
```

There may be an **else** part to provide for the selection of two alternatives. The syntax for this statement is

if__then__else__statement

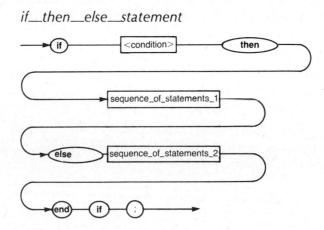

One or the other, but never both, sequence-of-statements will be executed. For example,

```
declare
   type APPAREL is (JACKET, SUIT, RAINCOAT);
   type WEATHER is (RAIN, SNOW, CLEAR);
   OUTFIT    : APPAREL;
   FORECAST  : WEATHER;
```

```
begin
  GET(FORECAST);
  if FORECAST = RAIN then
    OUTFIT := RAINCOAT;
  else
    OUTFIT := SUIT;
  end if;
end;
```

A person will wear either a raincoat or a suit, never both. Notice that the **if** statement is closed by **end** and a repeat of the **if** (**end if**). All Ada control constructs follow the structure: opening—reserved—word . . . **end** repeat—of —opening—reserved—word. Since one of the sequence—of—statements may involve selection, the statements may be nested. For example,

```
if FORECAST = RAIN then
  OUTFIT := RAINCOAT;
else
  if FORECAST = SNOW then
    OUTFIT := JACKET;
  else
    OUTFIT := SUIT;
  end if;
end if;
```

Note that in the preceding example, we could have first checked for SNOW or CLEAR. The decision is not really a nesting of choices but rather a choice of one of the three alternatives. To more clearly show this structure and prevent unnecessary nesting and indentation, Ada provides an **elsif**.

```
if FORECAST = RAIN then
  OUTFIT := RAINCOAT;
elsif FORECAST = SNOW then
  OUTFIT := JACKET;
elsif FORECAST = CLEAR then
  OUTFIT := SUIT;
end if;
```

The **elsif** may be repeated as many times as necessary to accommodate all choices, followed by a single (optional) trailing else.

Since the possible values of choices for the decision variable FORECAST are discrete and known at compile time (that is, RAIN, SNOW, CLEAR), there is an even better way to show the selection among the three alternatives: the **case** statement.

case-statement

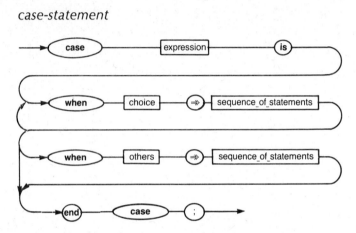

The **when** part may be repeated any number of times. The choice must be a type or subtype of INTEGER, CHARACTER, or enumeration type. It may be a simple expression, a range of values, or alternative discrete values separated by the vertical bar " | ". The value of the choice must be determinable at compile time. A choice may also be the reserved word **others** to stand for any possible choices not mentioned. For example,

```
case FORECAST is
   when RAIN      => OUTFIT := RAINCOAT;
   when SNOW      => OUTFIT := JACKET;
   when CLEAR     => OUTFIT := SUIT;
end case;
```

The choices must be mutually exclusive. The same value cannot satisfy more than one **when** clause. That is, we could not have

```
when RAIN => . . .
when RAIN | SNOW => . . .
```

The choices must also be collectively exhaustive. All possible values of the **case** selector (in the previous example, FORECAST) must be listed in the choices. For example,

```
declare
   type OPTIONS is (WORK__HARD, GOOF__OFF, PLAY);
   WHAT__TO__DO : OPTIONS;
   TODAY : DAY;
begin
   GET(TODAY);
   case TODAY is
      when MON | FRI   => WHAT__TO__DO := GOOF__OFF;
      when TUE .. THU   => WHAT__TO__DO := WORK__HARD;
      when SAT | SUN   => WHAT__TO__DO := PLAY;
        -- SAT | SUN could be replaced by others
   end case;
end;
```

The fact that the choices cover all possible alternatives must be determinable at compile time. The **case** is a natural structure for use in conjunction with enumeration types, since the list of possible values for enumeration types is usually rather small, and proper selection of the names of the enumeration items makes the code understandable.

8.2 ITERATION

The mechanism for expressing iteration or repetition is the **loop** construct.

basic__loop

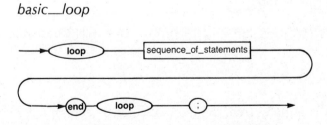

The simplest form of repetition is an endless loop:

```
loop
   -- Statements
end loop;
```

The statements in the loop body will simply be repeated over and over. That is, when execution reaches the bottom of the loop (**end loop**), control is transferred to the top of the loop (**loop**).

One of the standard structured coding constructs is referred to as the WHILE, the WHILE_DO, or the DO_WHILE loop. This structure is directly expressible in Ada:

```
while <condition> loop
   -- Statements
end loop;
```

The <condition> provides a BOOLEAN result that is evaluated prior to execution of the loop. If the result is TRUE, the statements of the loop are executed. When execution reaches **end loop,** the <condition> is reevaluated. When the <condition> is TRUE, the process repeats. When the condition is evaluated as FALSE, the loop terminates execution by transfer of control to the statement following **end loop.** Consider the following examples:

```
declare
   SEARCHING : BOOLEAN;
begin -- Find a target value using procedure LOOK_FOR
   SEARCHING := TRUE;
   while SEARCHING loop
      GET(TARGET);
      LOOK_FOR(TARGET, SEARCHING);   -- SEARCHING becomes
   end loop;                         -- false when TARGET is
end;                                 -- found
```

Since SEARCHING is initially true, the loop executes. It continues to loop until LOOK_FOR returns a value of FALSE for the variable SEARCHING. Here is another example of a **loop.**

```
declare
  TARGET_MAX : constant INTEGER := 100;
  subtype TGT_INDEX is INTEGER range 1 .. TARGET_MAX;
  TARGET_ARRAY : array (TGT_INDEX) of INTEGER;
    -- The array will be discussed in chapter 10
  I : INTEGER range 1 .. TARGET_MAX + 1;
begin
  I := 1;
  while I <= TARGET_MAX loop -- Initialize array
    TARGET_ARRAY(I) := I;
    I := I + 1;
  end loop;
  . . .
end;
```

The loop results in I taking on values from 1 to 101. TARGET_ARRAY(1) to TARGET_ARRAY(100) are assigned the value of the index I. When I becomes 101, I <= TARGET_MAX is FALSE and the loop does not execute again. The syntax diagram for the while loop is

while_loop

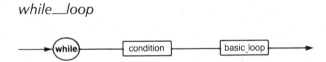

Since the condition is checked prior to execution of the basic_loop, the loop is not executed at all if the condition is initially false.

The while_loop example to perform initialization of TARGET_AR-RAY involves incrementing a variable through a specific range of values. This is so common a use for a loop that Ada provides a specific mechanism, the **for** loop, for this purpose. For example, the executable loop part of the block above could be replaced by

```
for I in 1 .. TARGET_MAX loop
  TARGET_ARRAY(I) := I;
end loop;
```

The syntax is

for__loop

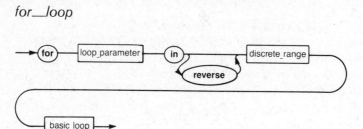

THE loop__parameter, I, takes on the values 1, 2, . . . up to the value of TARGET__MAX. The loop__parameter is implicitly declared by its appearance in the loop and automatically increments by 1. It need not be declared prior to its use. We could also have I initially take on the value of TARGET__MAX and take on values TARGET__MAX, TARGET__MAX-1, . . . 1 by adding the **reverse** clause:

```
for I in reverse 1 .. TARGET__MAX loop
   TARGET__ARRAY(I) := I;
end loop;
```

Further, since we have a defined subtype, TGT__INDEX, that defines the range of the array as 1 .. TARGET__MAX, we can use the subtype name as the discrete__range:

```
for I in TGT__INDEX loop
   TARGET__ARRAY(I) := I;
end loop;
```

We can also use attributes of the array itself to define the discrete__range:

```
for I in TARGET__ARRAY ' FIRST .. TARGET__ARRAY ' LAST loop
   TARGET__ARRAY(I) := I;
end loop;
```

and also the equivalent,

```
for I in TARGET__ARRAY ' RANGE loop
   TARGET__ARRAY(I) := I;
end loop;
```

The discrete—range need not be statically defined. For example,

```
declare
  M, N, TEMP_1, TEMP_2 : TGT_INDEX;
begin
  M := 10;
  N := 5;
  TEMP_1 := M + 2;
  TEMP_2 := M + N;
  for K in TEMP_1 .. TEMP_2 loop
    M := K + 1;
    N := M + 2;
    TARGET_ARRAY(K) := M + N;
  end loop;
end;
```

Not only can the bounds of the discrete—range be dynamically defined as shown, but the bounds can be expressions in general, not just variables. Further, the expressions are calculated only once, before the loop is executed. The use of TEMP_1 and TEMP_2 in the last example make that clear, but the following statements have the same effect.

Suppose we were in the scope of the preceding block and created the following block:

```
begin
  M := 10;
  N := 5;
  for K in M + 2 .. M + N loop
    M := K + 1;
    N := M + 2;
    TARGET_ARRAY(K) := M + N;
  end loop;
end;
```

The fact that M and N are modified within the loop does not affect the loop range of 12 .. 15. The modification of M and N within the loop is likely to result in obscure code; it is shown to illustrate that Ada does not allow such practice to change the range of the loop.

Quite frequently, the only use for the loop—parameter is to index through the loop. That is, it takes on the values in the discrete—range and has no other use or value. It has no meaning when the loop is complete.

To avoid the necessity of creating new objects that exist throughout an entire block whose only use is to control a loop, Ada implicitly declares the loop variable of the proper type at the beginning of execution of the loop. This has two beneficial aspects: it simplifies the name space within a block and it prevents any use of the final value of the loop variable after the loop is complete. The scope of the loop variable is delimited by the **for** and the **end loop.**

Further, within the loop the loop—parameter is a local constant. It cannot appear on the left-hand side of an assignment statement. This prevents modification of the loop—parameter and possible modification of the number of times the loop will be executed. It is guaranteed that the loop—parameter takes on successive values in the range, until the loop exits.

These points are illustrated in the following example.

```
declare
  TARGET_MAX : constant INTEGER := 100;
  subtype TGT_INDEX is INTEGER range 1 .. TARGET_MAX;
  TARGET_ARRAY : array (TGT_INDEX) of INTEGER;
begin
  for J in TGT_INDEX loop
    J := 5;                        -- Illegal. J is a local constant
                                   -- during each iteration

    TARGET_ ARRAY(J) := J;
  end loop;
  TARGET_ARRAY(1) := J;     -- Illegal. J does not exist here
end;
```

If the lower—bound is greater than the upper—bound, the range is considered to be null and the loop is not executed.

All examples in this section use a loop—parameter of an INTEGER type. However, the discrete—range may also be of an enumeration type, including CHARACTER. All of the following are legal:

```
for TODAY      in WED .. SAT loop
for TODAY      in WEEK_DAY loop
for ALPHABET   in 'A' .. 'Z' loop
for TODAY      in reverse TUE .. SUN loop
```

In each of the four clauses, the loop__parameter takes on each value within the discrete__range. You can picture the 'SUCC or 'PRED functions being implicitly used to obtain the next value. All rules previously discussed for INTEGER types are valid for enumeration types.

It is often useful to ensure that a loop is executed at least one time and to perform a check on a condition at the end of each iteration. Some languages provide a specific construct, often called a REPEAT__UNTIL or UNTIL loop, to control iteration in such a way. Ada allows such loop control through an **exit** clause that causes cessation of iteration. For example,

```
loop
   GET(IN__VAL);
   PROCESS(IN__VAL);
   PUT(IN__VAL);
   exit when IN__VAL < 0;
end loop;
```

The **exit when** construct has a more general use than to implement a REPEAT __UNTIL. The clause may be placed anywhere in the loop body. For example, if we did not wish to PROCESS negative values of IN__VAL, we could have

```
loop
   GET(IN__VAL);
   exit when (IN__VAL) < 0;
   PROCESS(IN__VAL);
   PUT(IN__VAL);
end loop;
```

In both of these examples, when IN__VAL is < 0 the condition becomes TRUE and the loop exits. That is, control is transferred to the statement following **end loop.**

8.3 *EXPLICIT TRANSFER OF CONTROL*

Steelman requires a mechanism for explicit transfer of control from one point in a program to another. An important rationale behind the requirement is that it facilitates mechanical translation from other languages to Ada. Ada provides a **goto** statement for transfer of control to another statement specified by a label. Ada's **goto** is restricted in scope. It must not transfer control

- out of or into a subprogram
- into a compound statement (if__statement, loop__statement, case__statement, or block)
- from one sequence__of__statements of an **if** or **case** statement, to another sequence__of__statements in the same **if** or **case**

The label is an identifier within double brackets. For example,

```
DONE := FALSE;
< <RESTART> >
  while not DONE loop
    FIRST__PROCESS (INFO, STATUS, DONE);       -- Sets DONE to
                                               -- TRUE when
                                               -- finished

    if STATUS = NOT__READY then
      goto RESTART;
    end if;
    SECOND__PROCESS (INFO, DONE);              -- Sets DONE to
                                               -- TRUE when
                                               -- finished

  end loop;
```

Ada has a sufficiently wide variety of control structures to limit the requirement for a **goto** to unusual circumstances. In fact, its use should be explicitly justified on a case-by-case basis. The scope restrictions on **goto** and labels, combined with small subprograms, make **goto** less dangerous and prone to misuse in Ada than in other languages. One of the dangers of the explicit transfer of control is not the **goto** but the label. The danger is that control may be transferred to the label from many points, without any indication in the code as to where the transfer initiated. Indeed, one wit has suggested that we should replace the "go to" with the "come from"! To control this danger, Ada provides a mechanism for restricting the scope of a label, as shown here:

```
    DONE := FALSE;
    begin
      < <RESTART> >
        while not DONE loop
          FIRST__PROCESS (INFO, STATUS, DONE);
          if STATUS = NOT__READY then
            goto RESTART;
          end if;
          SECOND__PROCESS (INFO, DONE);
        end loop;
    end;
```

Since the **begin .. end;** delimits a block, and since control may not be transferred into a block, no other **goto** can reference the label < <RESTART> >.

Exercise__8

Write a program with a scalar type of **WEEK__END** (including Friday night) with appropriate values. Use a for__loop to cycle through all values. Embed a case statement in the loop to print appropriate messages for each day of the weekend.

Program__8

```
    with TEXT__IO; use TEXT__IO;
    procedure PROGRAM__8 is
      type WEEK__END is (FRI__NIGHT, SAT, SUN);
    begin
      for I in WEEK__END loop
        case I is
          when FRI__NIGHT    => PUT__LINE("TGIF");
          when SAT           => PUT__LINE("LAWN CARE");
          when SUN           => PUT__LINE("REST");
        end case;
      end loop;
    end PROGRAM__8;

    Begin Ada execution

    TGIF
    LAWN CARE
    REST
```

Discussion__8

The loop variable "I" is implicitly declared to be of type WEEK__END. It takes on each value in the range indicated by the type WEEK__END. The case statement has an alternative provided for each value of the type WEEK__END.

Key to Understanding

▶ Ada provides control structures for selection: if__elsif__else__end__if and case__when__others__end__case.

▶ Ada provides control structures for iteration: loop__end__loop, while__loop __end__loop, for__loop__end__loop, with an exit construct of exit__when.

▶ Ada provides an explicit transfer of control, a goto, but with considerable restriction on its use.

9

Subprograms

Objective: to present subprograms

One well-established principle of programming is that a large program can be partitioned into smaller, more understandable constituent parts. Each part may, of course, be decomposed further by a series of stepwise refinements into even smaller parts. These small, functionally related blocks of processing are called subprograms; a *main* program is a block of processing whose primary function is to link the subprograms together.

Using subprograms we need write only one code that will be used many times. This is conceptually important in the development of large programs and is also valuable in terms of saving memory in an executing system.

Ada has two types of subprograms: procedures and functions. Subprograms are invoked or called as an executable sequence of statements by using their name.

A procedure can be thought of as a sequence of statements having a name, and whose name, in turn, can be used as a statement. A procedure does not return a value, although it may modify parameters. A function is similar to the mathematical notion of a function. It returns a value and can be called as a component of an expression. It may not stand alone as a statement.

As is the case with variables and constants, subprograms must be defined before they are used. In the Algol or Pascal class of languages, subprograms are defined in the declarative part of a main program, a block, or another subprogram. In chapter 21 we will see that Ada gives us another option for defining subprograms. Definition means that an interface, or calling sequence, is specified, and then the sequence of statements is listed.

9.1 *PROCEDURES*

The syntax of a procedure is

procedure__definition

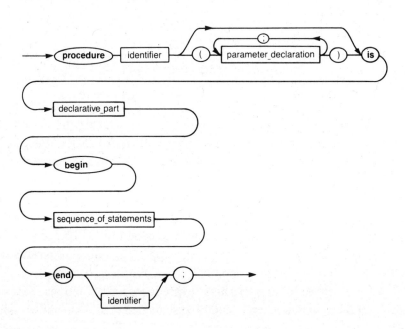

The identifier is the name by which the procedure will be called. The optional parameter__declaration list, defined below, allows parameterization of the procedure data and operation; the reserved word **is** indicates that the remainder of the definition "is" the procedure. Note that this remaining part of a procedure is similar to, and has an effect similar to, a block. In fact, Pascal calls this part of the procedure a block. Here is a procedure with no parameters:

```
procedure ADD__UP is
    IN__VAL, SUM : INTEGER;
```

```
begin
  SUM := 0;
  GET(IN_VAL);
  while INVAL >= 0 loop
    SUM := SUM + IN_VAL;
    GET(IN_VAL);
  end loop;
  PUT(SUM);
end ADD_UP;
```

The procedure is called, in the proper context, by use of its name, as:

```
begin
  . . .
  PUT("ENTER POSITIVE VALUES TO BE ADDED. "&
    "EXIT ON NEGATIVE VALUE");
  ADD_UP;

  . . .
end;
```

When this program calls ADD_UP, IN_VAL and SUM are elaborated, statements of the procedure are executed, the value of SUM is output, and the procedure exits. Control returns to the program in the statement following the call to ADD_UP. After ADD_UP is executed, the names SUM and IN_VAL are no longer in scope. The values they contain are no longer accessible.

The parameter_declaration part defines the formal parameters of the procedure, as shown:

parameter_declaration

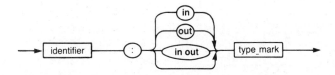

The identifier is the name of a formal parameter of the procedure. The scope of the name extends to the end of the procedure. When the procedure is called, an association is established between the formal parameter and an actual parameter in the procedure call. The types of the formal and actual parameters must be the same. Following the colon is the *mode* of the parameter, as **in, out,** or **in out.** The default mode, if none is specified, is **in.** The modes are defined as:

in   The parameter acts as a local **constant.** Its value is provided by the corresponding actual parameter.

out   The parameter acts as a local variable. However, its value may not be read in the procedure. The value of the formal parameter is assigned to the corresponding actual parameter.

in out   The parameter acts as a local variable and permits both reading and updating the corresponding actual parameter.

Parameters of **in** mode are similar to *value* parameters of Pascal in that the value of the actual parameter cannot be changed in the procedure. Ada goes even one step further: it does not allow a parameter of **in** mode to be a target of an assignment statement within the body of the procedure. The mode **in out** indicates a parameter similar to the Pascal *variable* parameter. It *must* have an initial value received from the value of the corresponding actual parameter. The value may be changed during execution of the procedure. After the procedure has completed execution, the value of the actual parameter will be the same as the changed value of the formal parameter. Mode **out** is similar to mode **in out,** except that there is no initial assignment from the actual to the formal parameter and the formal parameter may not be read in the procedure. The formal parameter must receive an assignment during execution of the procedure. The following example illustrates these points:

```
declare
   IP, OP  : FLOAT;
   IOP     : INTEGER;

   procedure SHOW (IN_VALUE        : in      FLOAT;
                   IN_OUT_VALUE    : in out  INTEGER;
                   OUT_VALUE       : out     FLOAT) is
   begin
      IN_OUT_VALUE   := IN_OUT_VALUE + 1;    -- Increment the
                                             -- input value
      OUT_VALUE      := IN_VALUE * 2.0;      -- Assign a
                                             -- value to
                                             -- OUT_VALUE
   end SHOW;
```

```
begin
   IP    := 6.0;
   IOP   := 2;
   SHOW(IP + 5.0, IOP, OP);
                              -- IP has the value 6.0
                              -- IOP has the value 3
                              -- OP has the value 22.0
end;
```

The procedure SHOW is defined in the declarative part of the block, along with some variables. The assignment to IN_OUT_VALUE takes advantage of the fact that it had an initial value and that the actual parameter will adopt the new value of the formal parameter. OUT_VALUE is assigned a value. When the procedure is called, IN_VALUE takes the value of the expression IP + 5.0. An expression is allowed as the actual parameter since the value is passed by copy to the procedure. The expression is evaluated once, and the value is then bound to the corresponding formal parameter. The actual parameters IOP and OP take on the value of the corresponding formal parameters at the end of the procedure. Note that the statement

```
IN_VALUE := 5; -- Illegal
```

is not allowed, since IN_VALUE is a local constant. The statement

```
IN_OUT_VALUE := OUT_VALUE; -- Illegal
```

is not allowed since OUT_VALUE may not be read.

Also note that the end statement terminates the procedure and causes return to the calling program. It is possible to have alternate places for termination of the procedure, indicated by the reserved word **return.** The following example illustrates the use of **return.** (We assume the existence of a SQRT function that has the expected effect.)

```
procedure FOURTH_ROOT (X : in out FLOAT;
                       VALID : out BOOLEAN) is
begin
   VALID := X > = 0.0;
   if not VALID then
      return;
   end if;
```

```
        X := SQRT(SQRT(X));
    end FOURTH_ROOT;
```

Procedures may also access global variables, within the scope rules defined in chapter 6. The following example shows nested procedures having global access and the effect of hiding the name of a global variable.

```
procedure OUTER is
    OUT_1, OUT_2, STUFF : INTEGER;

    procedure INNER(PARM_1 : in out INTEGER) is
        IN_1, STUFF : INTEGER; -- INNER.STUFF hides OUTER.STUFF
    begin -- INNER
        OUT_1  := 3;
        STUFF  := 10;
        IN_1   := 7;
        PARM_1:= PARM_1 + OUT_1 * STUFF + IN_1;
    end INNER;
begin -- OUTER
    OUT_1 := 100;
    OUT_2 := 0;
    STUFF  := 1000;
    INNER(OUT_2);
                                -- OUT_1 now has the value 3
                                -- OUT_2 now has the value 37
                                -- STUFF still has the value 1000
end OUTER;
```

The value of OUT_1 is 3, since the reference to it in procedure INNER was to the global variable. OUT_2 is 37, since that was the final value of PARM_1 $(0 + 3 * 10 + 7)$. The value of STUFF is 1000, since the assignment of 10 to STUFF in the procedure INNER was an assignment to a local variable called STUFF, similar to the assignment of 7 to IN_1. After return from INNER, the values of IN_1, STUFF (the INNER STUFF), and PARM_1 no longer exist.

9.2 FUNCTIONS

The syntax of a function is

function—definition

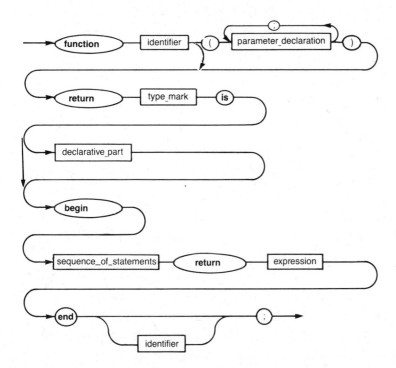

The identifier of a function is the name used in an expression that invokes the function. A function call may be used anywhere an expression can be used, including the calling sequence of a procedure or function.

The parameter—declaration is similar to that of a procedure, but the only allowable mode is **in.**

The **return** in the function specification indicates the type of the value provided by the function. The function call, its name, and its parameter list can be used in a manner similar to that of a **constant** of the type indicated by the return. Of course it cannot appear on the left-hand side of an assignment statement (except when it returns an access or pointer value), nor as an actual parameter associated with a procedure formal parameter of mode **out** or **in out.**

The remainder of the function is similar to a procedure except that it is terminated by a **return** statement. The sequence—of—statements must include at least one "**return** expression." The expression must be of the type or subtype stated in the function specification. Multiple **return** statements are allowed. A single **return** need not be at the end of the sequence—of—statements, but the function must not terminate by coming to an **end** statement.

We can rewrite the procedure FOURTH_ROOT as a function, return-ing 0 to indicate negative (invalid) entries, as shown:

```
function FOURTH_ROOT (X : FLOAT) return FLOAT is
begin
  if X < 0.0 then
    return 0.0;
  else
    return SQRT(SQRT(X));
  end if;
end FOURTH_ROOT;
```

Then the function can be used in an expression, as follows:

```
declare
  Y, Z : FLOAT;
begin
  Z := 256.0;
  Y := Z + FOURTH_ROOT(Z);
end;
```

Functions can access, even modify, global variables. That is, side effects are allowed. However, functions with side effects can be dangerous, so we will avoid using them here. It is safest to have a function access only its parameters and to modify the external environment only through the value it returns. Using functions in this way makes them more reasonable to use as a replacement for expressions. For example,

```
function ODD (X : INTEGER) return BOOLEAN is
begin
  return X mod 2 /= 0;
end ODD;
```

The function returns TRUE for odd values, FALSE for even values. It could be used in

```
declare
  IN_VAL : INTEGER;
begin
  GET(IN_VAL);
  if ODD(IN_VAL) then
    PUT(SQRT(FOURTH_ROOT(FLOAT(IN_VAL + 1))));
  else
    PUT(IN_VAL/2);
  end if;
end;
```

It would be misleading if any of the functions, ODD, SQRT, or FOURTH
_ROOT, modified global values. FLOAT also looks like a function, used to
change the type of IN_VAL + 1 to a floating point type. It is necessary since
FOURTH_ROOT required a FLOAT type as its parameter. Note the nesting
of functions and the use of the value returned by a function as a parameter. Also
observe that although FOURTH_ROOT uses SQRT, there are no conflicts.

9.3 *COMMON CHARACTERISTICS*

All functions and procedures are automatically reentrant. All functions and
procedures may be recursive as well. Although factorials are most efficiently
computed iteratively, the factorial is an easy example of a recursive function
—one that is defined in terms of itself. We first define a type with restricted
range,

```
subtype FACTORS is INTEGER range 0 .. 10;
```

and then the function:

```
function FACTORIAL(N : FACTORS) return POSITIVE is
begin
  if N = 0 then
    return 1;
  else
    return N * FACTORIAL (N-1);
  end if;
end FACTORIAL;
```

The function computes n! = n * n-1 * n-2 .. 1, with 0! defined as 1. So 4! is
4 * 3 * 2 * 1 , or 24. Note that FACTORIAL(4) results in the invocation of
FACTORIAL(3), FACTORIAL(2), FACTORIAL(1), and FACTORIAL(0).
POSITIVE is a predefined (part of the standard environment) subtype as,

```
subtype POSITIVE is INTEGER range 1 .. INTEGER'LAST;
```

where INTEGER'LAST is the largest INTEGER value for a specific implementation.

Exercise__9

Write a program to test for legal and illegal operations on the formal parameters of a procedure. Try assigning a value to a parameter with **in** mode. See what happens when **in out** or **out** mode formal parameters are not assigned values.

Program__9

```
with TEXT__IO; use TEXT__IO;
procedure PROGRAM__9 is
    T__IO, T__OUT, T__IN: INTEGER;
    package IO is new INTEGER__IO(INTEGER); use IO;

    procedure MODES  (I__IN   : in INTEGER;
                      I__IO   : in out INTEGER;
                      I__OUT : out INTEGER) is
    begin
      if I__IN > 10 then
        I__IO   := I__IN;
        I__OUT := I__IN + 1;
      end if;
    end MODES;
begin    -- PROGRAM__9
  T__IN := 20; T__IO := 100;
  MODES(T__IN, T__IO, T__OUT);
  PUT("IN, IN/OUT, OUT ARE: ");
  PUT(T__IN); PUT(T__IO); PUT(T__OUT);
  NEW__LINE;
  T__IN := 1; T__IO := 200;
  MODES(T__IN, T__IO, T__OUT);
  PUT("IN, IN/OUT, OUT ARE: ");
  PUT(T__IN); PUT(T__IO); PUT(T__OUT);
  NEW__LINE;
end PROGRAM__9;
```

Begin Ada execution

IN, IN/OUT, OUT ARE: 20 20 21
*** Exception PROGRAM__ERROR (uninitialized object) raised in MAIN-TASK PROGRAM__9 statement 25
*** No handler, task is terminated

Execution complete

Discussion_9

In procedure MODES, if we had attempted to make an assignment to I_IN, it would have resulted in an error at compile time. I_IN is a local constant and the error can be detected before execution. Similarly, we must not attempt to read (have on the right side of an assignment statement) I_OUT. It is to be used only for output and cannot be read in the procedure. This error also would be detected at compile time. During execution of PROGRAM_9, if we had not assigned a value to T_IN or T_IO, we would have had an error for an uninitialized variable when we attempted to invoke MODES. In the program shown, we successfully execute the first call to MODES by ensuring that I_OUT receives a value. On the second invocation of MODES we use a value of T_IN to cause no assignment to I_OUT. Since an **out** mode variable must receive a value in the procedure, this causes the exception PROGRAM_ERROR to be raised. (Statement 25 is the second call to MODES.)

Keys to Understanding

▶ Ada has two types of subprograms: procedures, which can act as statements, and functions, which return a value and can act as components of an expression.

▶ The direction of information flow in a procedure is given by the mode: **in, in out,** or **out.**

▶ Subprograms are automatically reentrant and may be used recursively.

10

Arrays

Objective: to present arrays

Until now we have been discussing simple, unstructured types of data that consist of single elements. The next three chapters introduce structured or composite data types and mechanisms for constructing complex data structures. We begin with the array.

10.1 *SIMPLE ARRAYS*

An array is an object. It is a composite, or collection, of other objects. An important characteristic and limitation of arrays is that all objects they contain must be of the same type.

To declare an object to be an array type, we should first define the type. A simple array type definition is

    type VECTOR **is array**(1..10) **of** INTEGER;

The name of the type is VECTOR; it is an array; its possible index values are given by the discrete range of 1..10; and it is a collection of other objects of type INTEGER. A typical declaration of objects of type VECTOR is

```
A, B, C : VECTOR;
```

The individual INTEGER objects are accessed by indexing the VECTOR objects. The name of the array is followed by a subscript or index value. We may have a program such as

```
for I in 1 .. 10 loop
   A(I) := I + 1;
end loop;             -- Assign values to the individual variables
for I in 2 .. 9 loop
   B(I) := A(I);      -- Assign some of the values to B
end loop;
   C := A;            -- Assign all the values of A to C
```

The last assignment is consistent with the Ada approach, since C and A are of the same type. Note that a statement such as

```
C := A + B; -- Illegal
```

is illegal, since the + , or addition, operator is not defined for array types. (Chapter 14 will show how to define an addition operator for arrays, thereby making this operation legal.)

Each type definition introduces a new and distinct type. It is the name of the type, not simply its structure, that is important. For example,

```
type ROW is array(1 .. 10) of INTEGER ;
X , Y : ROW;
```

These statements serve to declare objects of type ROW. We now have

```
X := Y; -- Legal
X := A; -- Illegal
```

The second assignment is illegal since X and A are of different types (despite the fact that they are both arrays of INTEGER of identical length and index values). If we wish to make them compatible, we must declare

A , X : VECTOR;

There are alternate ways of describing the discrete range. For example,

```
type LONG_VEC      is array(INTEGER range  −100 .. 100) of
                       FLOAT;
subtype INDEX      is INTEGER range −10 .. 20;
type VEC           is array(INDEX) of COLOR;
type SHOULD_WORK   is array(DAY) of BOOLEAN;
```

Note that any discrete type, including user-defined enumeration types, can be used as the index. We may then have a program such as

```
declare
   type SHOULD_WORK is array(DAY) of BOOLEAN;
   WORK_DAY  : SHOULD_WORK;
   TODAY     : DAY;
begin
   for THIS_DAY in DAY loop
     case THIS_DAY is
       when MON .. FRI  => WORK_DAY(THIS_DAY) := TRUE;
       when SAT | SUN => WORK_DAY(THIS_DAY) := FALSE;
     end case;
   end loop;
   loop
     GET(TODAY);
     if WORK_DAY(TODAY) then
       WORK;
     else
       PLAY;
     end if;
   end loop; -- Live forever (no retirement)
end;
```

10.2 *LARGER ARRAYS*

Arrays are not limited to one dimension. In fact, there are no language-defined limitations on the number of dimensions allowed in an array. For example,

```
type MATRIX is array(1 .. 5, −5 .. 9) of FLOAT;
type CUBE is array(1 .. 3, 1 .. 3, 1 .. 3) of INTEGER;
```

We may also have arrays whose components consist of arrays. For example,

```
type VECTORS__ARRAY is array(1 .. 100) of VECTOR;
```

The corresponding declaration of objects is

```
STORAGE        : MATRIX;
THREE__DIM     : CUBE;
VECTOR__LIST   : VECTORS__ARRAY;
```

Access to the component objects is given as

```
STORAGE(2, −5)
THREE__DIM(1, 2, 3)
VECTOR__LIST(50) (5) -- The 5th component of the 50th VECTOR
```

Note that since a component of VECTOR__LIST is of the type VECTOR, the following assignment is legal.

```
VECTOR__LIST(10) := A;        -- Assigns all the values of A to the 10th
                              -- component of VECTOR__LIST
```

The language definition does not limit the allowable number of dimensions or the degree to which arrays of arrays are to be permitted.

10.3 ANONYMOUS ARRAYS

It is possible to declare an array object without having first defined a specific array type. Such an object is said to be of an anonymous array type. For example,

```
ANON__ARRAY  : array(1 .. 5)   of FLOAT;
ANON__LIKE   : array(1 .. 5)   of FLOAT;
VECTOR__LIKE : array(1 .. 10)  of INTEGER;
```

However, since each declaration introduces a distinct type, such arrays are not compatible even if they are of identical structure. Nor are they compatible with arrays of a named type, even if the structure is identical. For example,

        ANON__ARRAY := ANON__LIKE; -- Illegal

and for

        type VECTOR   **is array** (1 .. 10) **of** INTEGER;
        type ROW   **is array** (1 .. 10) **of** INTEGER;
        A : VECTOR;
        X : ROW;

we have

        VECTOR__LIKE := A; -- Illegal. Different types
        VECTOR__LIKE := X; -- Illegal. Different types

Even

        BOY__TWIN, GIRL__TWIN : **array**(1 .. 5) **of** FLOAT;

results in different types.

        BOY__TWIN := GIRL__TWIN; -- Illegal. Different types

Of course, the individual components retain their type independent of the type of the array.

        ANON__ARRAY(3) := ANON__LIKE(2);   -- Legal. Both of type FLOAT
        VECTOR__LIKE(3) := A(6);   -- Legal. Both of type INTEGER

Anonymous types are useful to avoid cluttering a program declaration with type definitions that will be used only once. Use of named type declarations in such circumstances does not contribute to program clarity. However, when several arrays of the same structure are being used, and they represent the same abstract data type, a named array type should be declared and used to declare the array objects.

10.4 *STRINGS*

Ada provides a predefined one-dimensional array type called STRING. It is an array of CHARACTER, indexed by positive integers. The declaration of objects of type STRING is

```
NAME, ALT_NAME    : STRING(1 .. 7);
EMP_NAME          : STRING(1 .. 10);
```

Then we could have

```
NAME          := "AUGUSTA";
ALT_NAME      := NAME;
NAME(5)       := 'T';              -- Operation on a component of
                                   -- the array
if NAME = "AUGUTTA" then           -- True
   NAME(5) := ALT_NAME(5);
end if;
```

The sizes of the strings must be compatible. Strings must be padded or truncated before assignment.

```
NAME := "JONES";                   -- Illegal. Different types
NAME := "JONES     ";              -- Now OK. Types/sizes are com-
                                   -- patible
```

We can use the catenation operator to combine parts of strings or a string and a character.

```
NAME          := "AUG" & "USTA";
EMP_NAME      := NAME & "ADA";
NAME          := "AUGUST" & 'A';
```

We can also operate on parts of the array, called *slices*.

```
EMP_NAME(1 .. 7)    := ALT_NAME;
EMP_NAME(1 .. 6)    := "BANANA"; -- A slice of banana
EMP_NAME(7 .. 10)   := EMP_NAME(3 .. 6);
```

Exercise__10

Write a program with a procedure that (1) reads ten values into an array of
FLOAT (passed as a parameter) and (2) adds the average value to each element
of the array. It should print the average value and pass the modified array
(containing the value + the average) back to the main program. The main
program should print the array.

Program__10

```
with TEXT__IO; use TEXT__IO;
procedure PROGRAM__10 is
  type ARRAY__10 is array(1 .. 10) of FLOAT;
  A : ARRAY__10;
  package IO is new FLOAT__IO(FLOAT); use IO;


  procedure READ__10__ARRAY(P : out ARRAY__10) is
    LOCAL__P : ARRAY__10;
    SUM : FLOAT := 0.0;
    AVERAGE : FLOAT;
  begin
    for I in 1 .. 10 loop
      GET (LOCAL__P(I));
      P(I) := LOCAL__P(I);
      SUM := SUM + LOCAL__P(I);
    end loop;
    AVERAGE := SUM / 10.0;
    PUT("HERE IS THE AVERAGE VALUE: ");
    PUT(AVERAGE); NEW__LINE; NEW__LINE;
    for J in 1 .. 10 loop
      P(J) := LOCAL__P(J) + AVERAGE;
    end loop;
  end READ__10__ARRAY;
begin -- PROGRAM__10
  READ__10__ARRAY(A);
  PUT__LINE("HERE IS THE A ARRAY -- "); NEW__LINE;
  for K in 1 .. 10 loop
    PUT(A(K)); NEW__LINE;
  end loop;
end PROGRAM__10;
```

Discussion—10

This is much like a program written in any modern language. We have used the Ada initialization capability to assign zero to SUM. The array is of mode **out** since the procedure is essentially providing data to the caller.

Keys to Understanding

▶ An **array** is a composite object, a collection of other objects of the same type.
▶ Any discrete type may be used as the index of an array.
▶ There are no language-defined limitations on the number of dimensions of an array.

11

Records

Objective: to present records

A record is a composite data object that generally consists of named components of different types. The fact that it may consist of components of different types gives the record considerable flexibility and overcomes an important limitation of arrays. The record can be used to construct complex data structures. We will first consider some simple examples of records, then some data structures with records as components, and then records with variable parts.

11.1 *SIMPLE RECORDS*

We define records by declaring a record type, as shown:

```
type DATE is
  record
    DAY     : INTEGER range 1 .. 31;
    MONTH   : MONTH_NAME;
    YEAR    : INTEGER range −4000 .. 4000;
  end record;
```

Where MONTH_NAME has been defined as

```
type MONTH__NAME is (JAN, FEB, MAR, APR, MAY, JUN, JUL, AUG,
                     SEP, OCT, NOV, DEC);
```

We then declare objects of the type

```
BIRTHDAY : DATE;
```

Then we can make assignments to the components of the record BIRTHDAY.

```
BIRTHDAY.DAY    := 10;
BIRTHDAY.MONTH := DEC;
BIRTHDAY.YEAR   := 1815;
```

The notation BIRTHDAY.DAY is a specific case of the notation

```
record__name.component__name
```

which is called a *selected component.*

Each of the selected components of BIRTHDAY is a variable in its own right and may be used independently. However, since BIRTHDAY is also an object of a specific type, assignment and certain operations ($=$ and $/=$) are also applicable to it as a composite object. For example,

```
declare
   INT__1, INT__2  : INTEGER;
   ANY__DAY        : DATE;
begin
   INT__2        := 165;
   INT__1        := BIRTHDAY.YEAR + INT__2;
   ANY__DAY   := BIRTHDAY;            -- Assignment for type DATE
   if ANY__DAY = BIRTHDAY then        -- Comparison for type DATE
      ANY__DAY.YEAR := 0;
   end if;
end;
```

The assignment

```
ANY__DAY := BIRTHDAY;
```

is equivalent to the assignments

```
ANY__DAY.DAY      := BIRTHDAY.DAY;
ANY__DAY.MONTH := BIRTHDAY.MONTH;
ANY__DAY.YEAR    := BIRTHDAY.YEAR;
```

Equality is defined for records. Two records are equal if, and only if, each of their components are equal. Otherwise they are not equal.

A record may have an array as a component, as shown:

```
declare
   TOP__GRADE : constant := 4.0;
   COMPLETE    : constant := 50;
   type GRADE__ARRAY is array (1 .. COMPLETE) of FLOAT
      range 0.0 .. TOP__GRADE;
      type STUDENT__RECORD is
        record
           NAME                    : STRING(1 .. 25);
           NUMBER__OF__COURSES  : INTEGER
                                    range 0 .. COMPLETE;
           GRADEPOINTS            : GRADE__ARRAY;
        end record;
   GPA, TGP  : FLOAT range 0.0 .. TOP__GRADE * COMPLETE;
   A             : STUDENT__RECORD;
begin
   GET(A.NAME);
   GET(A.NUMBER__OF__COURSES);
   for N in 1 .. A.NUMBER__OF__COURSES loop
      GET(A.GRADE__POINTS(N));
   end loop;
   if A.NUMBER__OF__COURSES > = 1 then
      TGP := 0.0;
      for N in 1 .. A.NUMBER__OF__COURSES loop
         TGP := TGP + A.GRADE__POINTS(N);
      end loop;
      GPA := TGP / FLOAT(A.NUMBER__OF__COURSES);
      PUT(A.NAME);
      PUT(GPA);
   end if;
end;
```

The array GRADE__POINTS may be accessed by selected component notation and used in any way appropriate for an array. The record type definition must not contain an anonymous array type. It must use a named array type such as GRADE_ARRAY. Note that A.NAME is also an array, although we are usually not interested in its individual elements.

11.2 *NESTED RECORDS*

Since a record is a type, and since records can contain elements of different types (including record types), it follows that records can be nested. For example,

```
type PERSON is
  record
    NAME       : STRING(1 .. 5);
    BIRTHDAY   : DATE;
  end record;
EMPLOYEE : PERSON;
```

Then we may have

```
EMPLOYEE.NAME                := "JONES";
EMPLOYEE.BIRTHDAY.DAY        := 6;
EMPLOYEE.BIRTHDAY.MONTH      := NOV;
EMPLOYEE.BIRTHDAY.YEAR       := 1942;
```

to specify an employee record.

The power of such type definitions comes from the ability to combine types. For example, we can create an array of records to contain employee information for a company:

```
type INDEX                is range 1 .. 1000;
type EMPLOYEE_RECORDS     is array (INDEX) of PERSON;
MY_COMPANY : EMPLOYEE_RECORDS;
```

Then we can have

```
MY_COMPANY(100) := EMPLOYEE; -- Defined above
```

After the assignment, the one-hundredth employee is JONES. If JONES becomes SMITH,

MY__COMPANY(100).NAME := "SMITH";

accomplishes the change.

Many other combinations of records, arrays, and other types are possible and can be used to meet practical problems for the definition of data structures for both real-time or batch applications.

11.3 *DISCRIMINATED RECORDS*

Often it is desirable to have a record partially fixed in form and type and partially variable in form and type. That is, a structure and type that can vary depending on the values in the fixed part of the record. Such a situation calls for a record type with a variant part specifying alternate lists of components; this is called a discriminated record type. In addition to the record definitions previously introduced, there are two new parts to a discriminated record:

- the discriminant, which defines which of the variant parts will be referenced and
- the variant part, which defines the components for the discriminant.

For example,

```
type ITEM is (BOOK, TAPE);
type FILE__CARD (NEW__BUY : ITEM := BOOK) is -- NEW__BUY is
                                            -- the discriminant
   record
     COST : FLOAT; -- This component is always present
     case NEW__BUY is
       when BOOK =>
         AUTHOR           : STRING (1 .. 15);
       when TAPE =>
         TIME__TO__PLAY   : INTEGER range 1 .. 60;
     end case;
   end record;
```

NEW__BUY is the discriminant, the value of which determines whether the last part of the record contains a STRING or an INTEGER. NEW__BUY can take on only the values specified by the type ITEM , that is, BOOK or TAPE. We have provided a default initial value of BOOK. The variant parts of the

record are defined by the case-type construct within the record. Then if NEW_
BUY has the value BOOK, the record looks like this:

```
record
   COST    : FLOAT;
   AUTHOR : STRING(1 .. 15);
end record;
```

If NEW_BUY has the value TAPE, the record looks like this:

```
record
   COST         : FLOAT;
   TIME_TO_PLAY : INTEGER range 1 .. 60;
end record;
```

The discriminated record allows us to combine the two different but similar
records into a single file of library items, rather than separate files of books and
tape recordings.

We next define an object of the type FILE_CARD.

```
LIBRARY_ITEM : FILE_CARD;
```

Now LIBRARY_ITEM can be a record of either structure just shown, depending on the value of NEW_BUY. NEW_BUY can be assigned a new
value only by an aggregate assignment, which also provides values for the
remaining items in the record.

This is an aggregate assignment:

```
LIBRARY_ITEM := (BOOK, 12.95, "SHAKESPEARE    ");
```

The values are assigned to the record variables in the order in which they
appear in the aggregate assignment; hence the effect is that

```
NEW_BUY = BOOK,
COST = 12.95,
AUTHOR = "SHAKESPEARE    ".
```

There is no TIME_TO_PLAY for this LIBRARY_ITEM. Once the discriminant is defined, the other values may be changed by the usual selected
component notation, as shown:

```
LIBRARY__ITEM.COST      := 21.99;
LIBRARY__ITEM.AUTHOR  := "ARCHIMEDES      ";
LIBRARY__ITEM.TIME__TO__PLAY -- Illegal
```

The value of the discriminant cannot be changed by itself.

```
LIBRARY__ITEM.NEW__BUY : = TAPE; -- Illegal
```

But it can be changed if all the values are changed, consistent with the new variant part of the record. Hence,

```
LIBRARY__ITEM := (TAPE, 8.95, 45);              -- OK
LIBRARY__ITEM := (TAPE, 8.95, "BACH        "); -- Illegal
```

The last attempted assignment is not allowed. Since the record discriminant is TAPE, the last value must be an **INTEGER range** 1 .. 60, not a STRING.

Note that since the discriminant is assigned an initial value, and since the discriminant can be changed only by an aggregate assignment including appropriately typed variables for the variant part, the values for the variant part are always consistent with the types of the record components. For our example, the integer values of TIME__TO__PLAY can never be mixed with the string representation of AUTHOR. Pascal has variant records with the same structure as Ada, but its compilers tend to be careless about type-checking associated with changes in the discriminant variable. Ada is safer.

Records are important for building up complex and useful data structures. We can also define data structures that provide storage in a dynamic way, in accordance with the needs of the program during execution. To accomplish this, one of the components of the record must be a pointer variable, which can reference or access other variables. The next chapter discusses pointer variables.

Exercise__11

Write a program that declares an employee record containing an employee name, number, and a department number to which the employee is assigned. Assign values to the components of the record using both individual assignment and aggregate assignment. Print the results with both positional and named notation.

Program__11

```
with TEXT__IO; use TEXT__IO;
procedure PROGRAM__11 is
   subtype E__NUMBERS is INTEGER range   0 .. 9999;
   subtype D__NUMBERS is INTEGER range 1000 .. 9999;
   type EMPLOYEE is
     record
       NAME                    : STRING (1 .. 8);
       EMPLOYEE__NUMBER   : E__NUMBERS;
       DEPT__NUMBER        : D__NUMBERS;
     end record;
   PROGRAMMER : EMPLOYEE;
   package IO is new INTEGER__IO(INTEGER); use IO;
begin
   PROGRAMMER.NAME                    := "JOHN    ";
   PROGRAMMER.EMPLOYEE__NUMBER := 17;
   PROGRAMMER.DEPT__NUMBER        := 1234;
   PUT("Name is: ");
   PUT(PROGRAMMER.NAME);                          NEW__LINE;
   PUT("Employee number is: ");
   PUT(PROGRAMMER.EMPLOYEE__NUMBER);         NEW__LINE;
   PUT("Department number is: ");
   PUT(PROGRAMMER.DEPT__NUMBER);               NEW__LINE;

   PROGRAMMER := ("KAREN    ", 15, 4567);      NEW__LINE;
   PUT("Name is: ");
   PUT(PROGRAMMER.NAME);                          NEW__LINE;
   PUT("Employee number is: ");
   PUT(PROGRAMMER.EMPLOYEE__NUMBER);         NEW__LINE;
   PUT("Department number is: ");
   PUT(PROGRAMMER.DEPT__NUMBER);               NEW__LINE;

   PROGRAMMER := (NAME => "KELLY    ",
   EMPLOYEE__NUMBER => 12,
   DEPT__NUMBER => 8910);                        NEW__LINE;
   PUT("Name is: ");
   PUT(PROGRAMMER.NAME);                          NEW__LINE;
   PUT("Employee number is: ");
   PUT(PROGRAMMER.EMPLOYEE__NUMBER);         NEW__LINE;
   PUT("Department number is: ");
   PUT(PROGRAMMER.DEPT__NUMBER);               NEW__LINE;
end PROGRAM__11;
```

Begin Ada execution

Name is: JOHN
Employee number is: 17
Department number is: 1234

Name is: KAREN
Employee number is: 15
Department number is: 4567

Name is: KELLY
Employee number is: 12
Department number is: 8910

Execution complete

Discussion_11

Subtype definitions are used here to constrain the allowable values for employee and department number. The use of a defined subtype is not required for a record definition but is usually good practice. A declaration in the record such as

EMPLOYEE_NUMBER : INTEGER **range** 0 .. 9999; -- Legal

is legal. The three types of assignment shown are all equivalent in effect.

KEYS TO UNDERSTANDING

▶ A **record** is a composite object consisting of named components (objects) that may be of different types.
▶ Records may contain composite objects, including other records.
▶ Records may have variant parts, depending on the value of a discriminant.

12

Pointers

Objective: to present access types, or pointers

The usual way to access a data object is through its name. To modify the value of a variable, the name is placed on the left of an assignment operator. It then assumes the value of the expression on the right-hand side. Data structures created using the names of objects, including arrays and records, have a fixed or static form. It is often useful to have more complicated data structures, especially ones that can grow or shrink as requirements change and that allow the expression of variable relationships among data.

To allow for the construction of such data structures, Ada provides a mechanism for providing access to an object other than by a name. It provides a pointer to an object, as in:

The object has a type but does not have a name. The pointer has a name and, of course, a type. A simple declaration of a pointer is

type INT_POINTER **is access** INTEGER;

Now we can create an instance of the pointer:

```
        INT__P : INT__POINTER;
```

Objects of type **INT__POINTER** may point only to integers. Therefore, the type of the pointer is closely bound to the type of the object to which it points. Now, **INT__P** is not very interesting yet. It does not point to any integer. In fact, it has an initial value of **null**, denoting that it does not point to anything. Since **INT__P** is a variable, it can be accessed through its name. The usual rules of strong typing hold, and **INT__P** can be used in expressions and assignments with other objects of the same type.

The pointer gets a value other than null through the use of an allocator, the clause **new**:

```
        INT__P := new INTEGER;
```

The allocator does two things: it creates an object of the appropriate type, and it provides an access value that designates the object. Although we normally want to be at a higher level of abstraction than thinking about the computer memory, it may be useful to think of the value of the pointer (the access value) as a memory address that is the address of the object designated.

Now **INT__P** has a value, but the object to which it points does not. There are two ways for an object to get a value. First, we could have given it a value when we created or allocated the object:

```
        INT__P := new INTEGER ' (500);
```

The form is **new** followed by a *qualified expression* (type' (expression)) to provide a value. The second method of providing a value to a referenced object is with the assignment statement.

The way to change an object's value is to use an assignment statement, using **all** to denote that we intend to assign a value to the object pointed to by **INT__P**:

```
        INT__P.all := 123;
```

This can be read as "Assign 123 to the object pointed to by **INT__P**." Now the object has a value of 123 rather than 500. It is important to differentiate between pointers and the objects to which they point. The following figures help make that distinction.

Figure 12-1 provides some type and pointer definitions and illustrates the creation of objects that are accessible by the pointers. Figure 12-2(a) illustrates the assignment of one pointer to another. The net result of the assignment is that P__1 points to the same object that P__2 points to. The objects themselves are not changed. Note that the ship in Figure 12-2(a) is *lost* unless some other pointer is able to reference it. It is automatically dereferenced. Figure 12-2(b) tells a different story. The assignment of the object being referenced to another object being referenced leaves the pointers as they were, but changes the value of the object. The assignment of figure 12-2(b) may be stated as "the object pointed to by P__1 is assigned the value of the object pointed to by P__2."

The only operations allowed are type-compatible assignment and comparison for equality. Arithmetic is not allowed. For example,

```
if P__1 = P__2 then . . .           -- Legal
P__1                  := P__2 + P__1;   -- Illegal. No arithmetic allowed.
P__1                  := 128;           -- Illegal. Types incompatible.
INT__P                := P__1;          -- Illegal. Types incompatible.
```

```
type VEHICLE is (SHIP, CAR, PLANE);
type POINTER is access VEHICLE;
P_1, P_2, P_3 : POINTER;
```

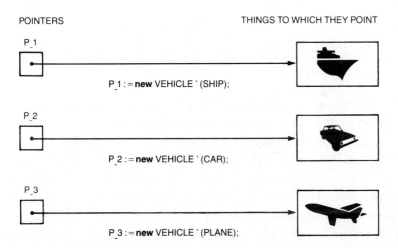

POINTERS   THINGS TO WHICH THEY POINT

P_1

P_1 := **new** VEHICLE ' (SHIP);

P_2

P_2 := **new** VEHICLE ' (CAR);

P_3

P_3 := **new** VEHICLE ' (PLANE);

Figure 12-1   Access Types

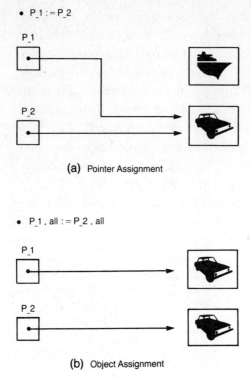

- P_1 := P_2

P_1

P_2

(a) Pointer Assignment

- P_1 . all := P_2 . all

P_1

P_2

(b) Object Assignment

Figure 12-2   Access Type Assignment

The primary use of access-type variables is not for the simple cases illustrated thus far. The importance of access variables is to create linked data structures of the types illustrated in figure 12-3. Such data structures have considerable flexibility in both organization and size: they can grow or contract to meet changing requirements. To create such structures, it is necessary to create a record object that has components to contain the value of interest to the application and components to contain the pointers to the next instance of the record. The following example illustrates the simple case of the linked list.

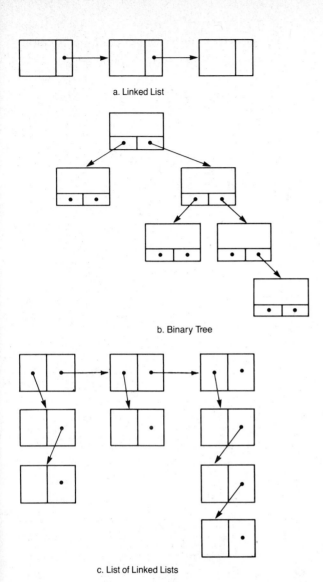

a. Linked List

b. Binary Tree

c. List of Linked Lists

Figure 12-3   Linked Data Structures

Let's say we wish to create a type called LIST, which contains a value field and a pointer field. The pointer field must be of a type that points to objects of type LIST. Since this is a circular definition of LIST (containing a reference to LIST before it is completely defined), we must begin with an incomplete type specification:

```
declare
   type VEHICLE is (SHIP, CAR, PLANE);
   type LIST; -- Incomplete type specification
   type LINK is access LIST;
   type LIST is
      record
         THING  : VEHICLE;
         NEXT   : LINK;
      end record;
   P, BASE : LINK; -- Initial value of null
begin -- See figure 12-4.
   for I in SHIP .. PLANE loop
      P          := new LIST ' (I, null);
      P.NEXT  := BASE;
      BASE     := P;
   end loop;
end;
```

Having given the incomplete definition of LIST, we can define LINK, then complete the definition of LIST. Note that the specification part of the block does not declare any objects of type LIST. The variables P and BASE are pointers that can only reference or access objects (yet to be created) of type LIST.

The executable part of the block creates objects of type LIST and places them in the linked list. The list to be created is a last-in-first-out (LIFO) queue. The pointer BASE will always point to the base, or last item to be entered into the queue. This item would normally be the first item to be removed from the queue. Figure 12-4 illustrates the creation of the list. On the first iteration, SHIP is created and pointed to by both P and BASE.   P. NEXT is null, or points to nothing at all. On the second iteration, CAR is created, with P pointing to

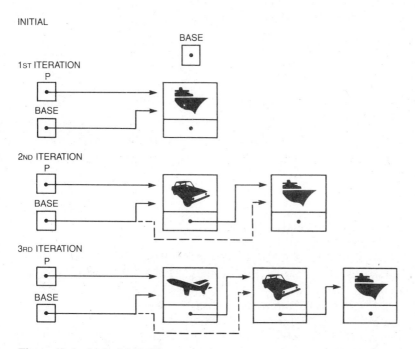

Figure 12-4   Linked List Diagram

it. **P.NEXT** points to the SHIP, and then BASE is made to point to CAR rather than SHIP. PLANE is similarly added to the list on the third iteration.

Note that the selected component notation is used to identify parts of the record, as in any other record reference. The notation for reference to the entire record uses **all**, as in our earlier example. The assignments

```
P          := BASE.NEXT;          -- Selected component
BASE.all   := P.all;              -- Use of all
```

would result in two **CARS** and one **SHIP**. Both cars point to the ship.

Access variables may point to any other type of objects: arrays, discriminated records, even other access types. To provide for nonlinear structures, such as a binary tree or a list of lists, two or more access variables may be established as components of a record; they are free to point in a variety of directions. The algorithms using pointers to create and manipulate these more complex data structures can be difficult to understand at first, but they are elegant and simple in their power to accomplish a great deal of processing with small amounts of code. Both Ada and the Algol-like languages, including Pascal, share this power and complexity.

Exercise__12

Write a program that declares a record with an employee number and a pointer to a record of the same type. Declare a pointer to the record type and an object of the record type. Create a "linked list" of length two. Differentiate between assignments to the declared object and the objects created dynamically.

Program__12

```
with TEXT__IO; use TEXT__IO;
procedure PROGRAM__12 is
  type NUMBER__RANGE is range 0 .. 1000;
  package IO is new INTEGER__IO (NUMBER__RANGE); use IO;
  type N__RECORD;
  type N__POINTER is access N__RECORD;
  type N__RECORD is
    record
      NUMBER : NUMBER__RANGE;
      NEXT     : N__POINTER;
    end record;
  P : N__POINTER;
  N : N__RECORD;
begin -- PROGRAM__12
  P := new N__RECORD'(100, null);
  P := new N__RECORD'(101, P );
  P.NUMBER := 102;
  N.NUMBER := 200;
  N := (201, P );
  N := (201, P.NEXT);
  P.all := (103, null);
  PUT("Here is number in N: "); PUT(N.NUMBER); NEW__LINE;
  PUT("Here is number pointed to by P: "); PUT(P.NUMBER);
  NEW__LINE;
end PROGRAM__12;
```

Begin Ada execution

Here is number in N: 201
Here is number pointed to by P: 103

Discussion__12

The declarations of N and P have quite different effects. For N, storage for a record is allocated—for both a number and a pointer. For P, storage is only allocated for a pointer that will (later) reference (or point, or provide access to) a record. The first assignment to P creates a record for employee 100. The creation of the record object is caused by the allocator new. The use of the qualified expression

N__RECORD ' (100, **null**)

assigns an initial value to the record. P points to the record just created.

The next assignment creates a record for employee 101. This record also references (points to) the previous record. Next we change 101 to 102 in the record pointed to by P. The pointer P is itself unchanged. The next assignment is superficially similar, but now N itself is changed. The next three assignments demonstrate the difference. We use an aggregate assignment to change N to employee 201 and make it point to employee 102 (the record for employee 102). Then we make N point to employee 100. The assignment N.NEXT := P.NEXT would have the same effect. This assignment is complicated to state in words. It is "The access component of N is made to reference the same object pointed to by the access component of the object pointed to by P" (!). Finally, we make an aggregate assignment to the record pointed to by P. The following seven pictures show the effect of the seven assignments.

1. P := **new** N__RECORD' (100, **null**);

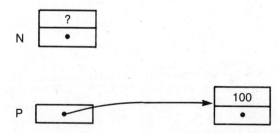

2. P := **new** N__RECORD' (101, P);

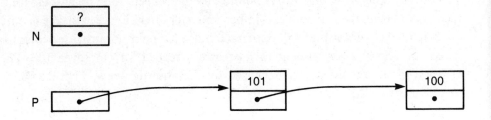

3. P.NUMBER := 102;

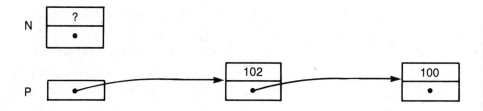

4. N.NUMBER := 200;

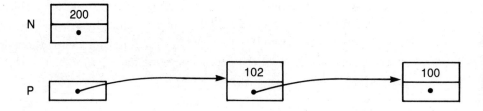

5. N := (201, P);

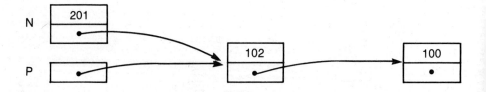

6. N := (201, P.NEXT);

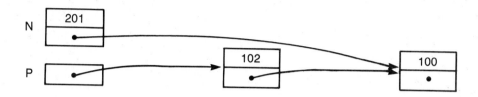

7. P.all := (103, **null**);

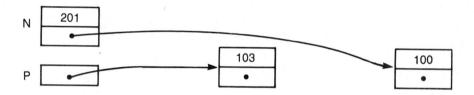

KEYS TO UNDERSTANDING

► Access types point to objects of interest.
► It is important to distinguish between the pointer and the thing that is being pointed to.
► Pointers may be used to create complex and flexible data structures.

PART 3

ADA AS ADA

To meet its design objectives, Ada had to improve on its base language, Pascal, in two ways: modifications and major advances. The purpose of part 3 is to discuss those aspects and features of Ada that are modifications to the foundation laid by Pascal. Some of the modifications increase the complexity of the language by adding additional features, but the general complexity of its concepts remains low.

One language feature is briefly introduced that has the potential for creating a considerable difference in the way a programmer approaches the solution to a problem: the **package**. The Ada package offers potential for restricting visibility of subprograms in a more effective way than does Pascal, and offers the opportunity for new ways of encapsulating data and associated procedures. It is a major advance over Pascal and an advanced feature of Ada. The full capabilities of the package and its likely influence on design will be discussed in part 4. In part 3 we will only introduce the notion of the package and illustrate some of its capabilities.

There are a number of aspects of Ada that we do not discuss at all since they are not needed for a general understanding of the language. For example, except in the exercises, we have not discussed the complex interaction between input-output, derived types (chapter 15), and generic instantiation (chapter 23). (When a new type is established, new input__output procedures must be created to provide a new GET and PUT.) As another example, it is occasionally necessary to communicate information to the compiler, such as a suggestion to optimize for time or space, or to suppress automatic range checking. We do not discuss such *pragmas* further, but a list of language-defined pragmas is provided as appendix D. We also do not discuss Ada's mechanisms for *representation specifications*, the methods for machine-level control. An example of a representation specification is the placing of a task or a vector to a task (chapter 25) that will serve as an interrupt handler at a specific location in memory. We will leave these topics for more advanced discussions of the language.

Chapter 13 points out in a general way some of Ada's improvements over Pascal, while chapters 14 to 20 discuss specific issues. The discussion in these chapters follows the order of presentation of chapters 6 to 12.

13

About Ada

Objective: to highlight some of the advances Ada provides over Pascal capabilities

Ada has been designed to satisfy a language specification to meet the requirements for the development of software for embedded computer systems. Pascal was designed as a teaching language. It does not have the features necessary to be a production language for large systems. Although Ada used Pascal as a starting point, it has added a number of important features and improvements. The improvements to Pascal fall into four categories:

- Ada corrects Pascal's weaknesses. For example, it removes the Pascal restriction against dynamic array sizes.
- Ada changes Pascal's syntax. For example, it modifies the form of the procedure declaration and adds the requirement that each control construct (for example, **if**) have a corresponding closing construct (for example, **end if**). These changes make Ada more readable than Pascal.
- Ada increases safety. For example, it increases the number of modes (**in, out, in out**) for subprogram parameters and requires that all choices in a case statement be defined.
- Ada extends Pascal's capabilities. For example, it specifies precision for floating point numbers to enhance portability, allows finer distinctions in type defini-

tion through the use of derived types, and increases the programmer's ability to control the scope of names through the use of packages.

Even though Ada goes considerably beyond the Pascal definition, it shares many of Pascal's characteristics. To the extent that we will consider it in part 3, Ada is concise, compact, learnable, readable, and an effective general-purpose language. It is not necessary to learn Ada's advanced features before using it for some programming. Ada is potentially the language of choice for the instruction of beginning programmers.

KEYS TO UNDERSTANDING

► Ada corrects some Pascal weaknesses, uses a more readable syntax, and enhances safety and portability of programs.
► Ada makes these improvements while remaining a small, learnable language for general purpose programming.

14

Data, Expressions, and Programs

Objective: to emphasize Ada's features for control over the scope of names and to introduce the concept of overloading of operators

Ada has a number of major additions to Pascal in regard to the way the language is structured and in its expressions. The largest change to the Pascal approach is the manner in which Ada allows control over the scope of names. The following sections discuss the topics in the same order as in chapter 6.

14.1 BASIC COMPONENTS

The additional reserved words that we will use in the remainder of part 3 are

delta	**rem**
digits	**renames**
package	**use**
private	**xor**

The identifier definition introduced in section 6.1 allowed the underscore character. The use of an underscore improves readability by allowing multiword identifiers. Ada also provides an extended capability for specification of numbers. Numbers may be expressed in any base from 2 to 16 inclusive, by enclosing the digits between # and preceding the #digits# by the base.

```
2#1101#            -- Base 2, decimal value is 13
8#15#              -- Base 8, decimal value is 13
16#D#              -- Base 16, decimal value is 13
8#06#E2            -- Decimal equivalent is 6 * 64, not 6 * 100
2#1101.101#        -- A based real number with decimal
                   -- equivalent of 13 + 1/2 + 1/8
```

The number 123E-2 becomes 1.23 in Pascal but is illegal in Ada since it confuses the distinction between **INTEGER** and **FLOAT**. Even 12300E-2 is illegal. However, 12300.0E-2 is legal. The value is 123.00, and there is no implicit change to 123 as an **INTEGER**.

14.2 BASIC TYPES

Ada extends the declaration of types to include additional specific information about the programmer's intent regarding the use of the type. Such increased specification enhances portability. For example,

```
type FLEXIBLE_INTEGER is range −33000 .. 33000;
```

All implementations of Ada must have a predefined type called **INTEGER** but may also have **LONG_INTEGER** and **SHORT_INTEGER** to provide a greater or lesser range of values. On a 16-bit machine an **INTEGER** might be defined as a 16-bit word with possible values −32768 to +32767. Hence, **FLEXIBLE_INTEGER** would have to be a **LONG_INTEGER**. However, the designers of a compiler for a 60-bit machine architecture might specify an **INTEGER** as 60 bits and be able to handle **FLEXIBLE_INTEGER**. If we had defined

```
subtype INFLEXIBLE_INTEGER is INTEGER range −33000 .. 33000;
```

then **INFLEXIBLE_INTEGER** would work on the 60-bit architecture but not on the 16-bit architecture. The subtype declaration requires that the compiler use an INTEGER to hold the values. The declaration of FLEXI-BLE__INTEGER, providing only the range of required values without specifying INTEGER or LONG__INTEGER, allows the compiler to select whichever integer type is appropriate. Of course if only a 16-bit integer is available, the compiler will reject either declaration as impossible to implement (since the range of values is too large to be contained in a 16-bit word).

Real numbers consist of floating-point types and fixed-point types. We will be concerned almost exclusively with floating point. All implementations must have the predefined type FLOAT and may also have other predefined types such as LONG__FLOAT and SHORT__FLOAT. Similar to the discussion for integers, if we define

    type REAL **is digits** 10;

we achieve greater portability than if we were to define REAL in terms of FLOAT or LONG__FLOAT. The declaration given ensures that the type REAL will have at least 10 decimal digits of precision, if it can be implemented at all. In general, programs should avoid using the predefined types. We have used, and will continue to use, predefined types for simplicity of exposition. Production programs should have user-defined types such as REAL and FLEXIBLE__INTEGER in order to closely represent the program's requirements and to enhance portability.

There are no predefined fixed-point types. They are declared by providing a range and an absolute error:

    type FIXED   **is delta** 0.125 **range** 0.0 .. 1024.0;
    type WATER__TEMP   **is delta** 0.5 **range** 0.0 .. 100.0;

The LRM goes into considerable detail about the exact specification of real numbers: their representation and precision.

14.3 *OPERATORS AND EXPRESSIONS*

Ada differs in several ways from Pascal in the area of operators and expressions: it has several new operators not available in either standard Pascal or the usual extensions to Pascal, and it provides a capability for *overloading* operators.

Overloading is simply the use of the same name for different purposes. It provides additional or different meanings for the standard operators. We will first discuss overloading, then the new operators.

14.3.1 *Operator Overloading*

Several types of overloading are permitted in Ada. Chapter 17 will discuss overloading of subprogram names; here we will discuss overloading of operators.

Overloading of operators is of particular interest since it allows a very natural use of infix operators to manipulate other than scalar objects. For example, the infix operator "+" in A + B can be defined such that A and B need not be numbers but can be complex composite data structures. Without the operator-overloading capability, we would be forced to define a function such as ADD(A, B) to accomplish such an operation. Overloading is potentially dangerous, since the operators could be redefined in misleading ways. For example, there is nothing in the language to prevent a programmer from defining "+" to result in multiplication of values. (Of course, subprogram names can also be misleading; ADD could be a misnomer for a function that multiplied two numbers.) However, the language designers felt that the positive aspects of overloading were so important in contributing to program readability that it should be allowed.

All Ada operators with the exception of "/=" may be overloaded. When "=" is defined by a user, "/=" is implicitly defined as the reverse case. The six classes of operators, given in order of precedence (logical__operator is lowest), are:

logical__operator	::=	**and** | **or** | **xor**
relational__operator	::=	= | /= | < | <= | > | >=
binary__adding__operator	::=	+ | − | **&**
unary__adding__operator	::=	+ | −
multiplying__operator	::=	* | / | **mod** | **rem**
highest__precedence__operator	::=	** | **abs** | **not**

A frequent arithmetic requirement is the manipulation of vectors and matrices. Overloading "+" and "*" can be used for the natural extension of these operations to vectors.

The following declarations and operations show vector manipulation without operator overloading.

```
declare
  type INDEX      is range 1 .. 10;
  type VECTOR    is array (INDEX) of INTEGER;
  VEC, TOR, RESULT  : VECTOR;
  ANSWER            : INTEGER;
begin
  . . .
  -- Fill VEC and TOR with values.
  . . .
  for I in INDEX loop
    RESULT(I) := VEC(I) + TOR(I);
  end loop; -- Vector addition
  ANSWER := 0;
  for I in INDEX loop
    ANSWER := ANSWER + VEC(I) * TOR(I)
  end loop; -- Inner product vector multiplication
end;
```

Here is the subprogram that redefines the "+" operator for **VECTOR** operations:

```
function "+" (V, T : VECTOR) return VECTOR is
  LOC_VEC : VECTOR;
begin
  for I in INDEX loop
    LOC_VEC(I) := V(I) + T(I);
  end loop;
  return LOC_VEC;
end "+"; -- For VECTOR addition
```

Note that there is no ambiguity in the addition operator used inside the function definition, since V(I) and T(I) are of type INTEGER. Therefore, V(I) + T(I) uses the standard addition operator. If clarification were necessary or desired, it would be possible to write **STANDARD.** "+" (V(I), T(I)), in order to emphasize the use of the standard operator definition.

The corresponding function definition for the "*" operator is

```
function "*" (V, T : VECTOR) return INTEGER is
  LOC_INT : INTEGER := 0;
```

```
      begin
        for I in INDEX loop
          LOC_INT := LOC_INT + V(I) * T(I);
        end loop;
      return LOC_INT;
      end "*"; -- For VECTOR inner product
```

Note that LOC_INT is initialized to 0. A useful feature of Ada is the initialization of variables at their declaration.

Now that we've defined the overloaded operator, we can write the previous example as

```
      declare
        type INDEX      is range 1 .. 10;
        type VECTOR  is array (INDEX) of INTEGER;
        VEC, TOR, RESULT  : VECTOR;
        ANSWER             : INTEGER;

        function "+" (V, T : VECTOR) return VECTOR is
          LOC_VEC : VECTOR;
        begin
          for I in INDEX loop
            LOC_VEC(I) := V(I) + T(I);
          end loop;
          return LOC_VEC;
        end "+"; -- For VECTOR addition

        function "*" (V,T : VECTOR) return INTEGER is
          LOC_INT : INTEGER := 0;
        begin
          for I in INDEX loop
            LOC_INT := LOC_INT + V(I) * T(I);
          end loop;
          return LOC_INT;
        end "*"; -- For VECTOR inner product
      begin
        . . .
        -- Fill VEC and TOR with values.
        . . .
        RESULT  := VEC + TOR;
        ANSWER := VEC * TOR;
      end;
```

If we were to perform the operations in the example only once, we would not bother to overload the operators. This mechanism is used primarily to provide mathematical packages in which the type definitions and the operator definition are made available to user programs. We could have defined the types and operators in a package called VECTOR__OPS. (Ada packages will be discussed later in this chapter.) Using the package VECTOR__OPS with the overloaded operators, our previous example would simply be

```
declare
   VEC, TOR, RESULT  : VECTOR;
   ANSWER            : INTEGER;
begin
   . . .
   -- Fill VEC and TOR with values.
   . . .
   RESULT  := VEC + TOR;
   ANSWER := VEC * TOR;
end;
```

The overloading mechanism is general; it may also be used to combine objects of different types in an expression. For example, if we wish to allow division of a FLOAT by an INTEGER, returning a FLOAT value, we could define

```
function "/" (F : FLOAT; I : INTEGER) return FLOAT is
begin
   return F / FLOAT(I);
end;
```

And then

```
declare
   X, Y : FLOAT;
   M, N : INTEGER;
begin
   X := Y/N;       -- Legal. Uses newly defined "/"
   X := Y/X;       -- Legal. Uses STANDARD."/"
   X := N/Y;       -- Illegal. Wrong order
   M := Y/N;       -- Illegal. Can't assign FLOAT to INTEGER
end;
```

This capability might also be used to define an operation so that a scalar could be added to a vector object.

```
function "+" (SCALAR : INTEGER; V : VECTOR) return VECTOR is
  LOC_V : VECTOR;
begin
  for I in INDEX loop
    LOC_V(I) := SCALAR + V(I);
  end loop;
  return LOC_V;
end "+"; -- For INTEGER to VECTOR addition
```

We can also define a unary "+" operator to sum the elements of an array.

```
function "+" (V : VECTOR) return INTEGER is
  LOC_I : INTEGER := 0;
begin
  for I in INDEX loop
    LOC_I := LOC_I + V(I);
  end loop;
  return LOC_I;
end "+"; -- Sum the VECTOR
```

We can use these two new "+" operators as in the following block.

```
declare
  RESULT, VEC : VECTOR;
  M : INTEGER;
begin
  GET(VEC); GET(M);
  RESULT  := M + VEC;        -- Uses new "+"
  M       := +VEC;           -- Uses new unary "+"
  RESULT  := VEC + M;        -- Illegal. Wrong order
end;
```

14.3.2 New Operators

The operators ** and rem were briefly presented in chapter 6. They are discussed further in the following text, along with other additional Ada operations.

Exponentiation Operator

Ada provides the exponentiation operator as a standard language feature. Both INTEGER and FLOAT may be raised to INTEGER powers. For INTEGER numbers, the exponent must be nonnegative. Exponentiation is a highest-precedence-operator. Consider the examples:

```
INT__1   := INT__2 ** 3;
REAL__1 := REAL__2 ** −4;
INT__1   := INT__2 ** −2;      -- Illegal, negative exponent
REAL__1 := INT__1 ** 2;        -- Illegal, type mismatch
REAL__1 := REAL__2 ** 0.5;     -- Illegal, exponent must be INTEGER
```

Multiplying Operators

Ada adds the **rem** operator to the multiplying operators found in Pascal. The **rem** is the remainder after integer division. It always takes on the sign of the first operand. For example,

```
17 rem 3 = 2
−17 rem 3 = −2
11 rem 7 = 4
A = (A/B) * B + (A rem B)       -- For all integer A and B
```

There are differences between **rem** and **mod** when the operands are of different signs. These are explained in detail in the LRM.

Relational Operators

The domain of the relational operators extends beyond the comparison of scalar types to allow comparison of records and arrays and their derivatives.

The operations for equality and inequality, = and /=, are allowed for any type discussed this far. The equality of two records, or two arrays, or two arrays of records, and so on, is established by the equality of each of their matching components, as given by the predefined equality operator for each component. If any matching components of the two objects being compared are not equal, the two objects are not equal.

The ordering operators, <, <=, >, and >=, are defined for one-dimensional arrays whose components are integers or enumeration types. The operators return a result corresponding to the lexicographic order (collating sequence) based on the order relation of matching components. For example, for $<$, the matching components are compared from lowest index to highest index. The array that first has a component smaller than a matching component in the other array is the smaller of the two. For example,

```
"A" < "B"
"ACME" < "B"
"A" < "AAA"
" " < "A"
```

Logical Operators

Ada provides for short-circuit control forms of the logical operators **and** and **or**. The forms are **and then** and **or else**. In each case the short-circuit control form requires the compiler to cause the right-hand operand to be evaluated only if necessary to complete the evaluation of the expression. For example,

```
if NOT_EOF and then A > B then        . . . end if;
if B / = 0 and then A / B > 100 then        . . . end if;
```

In each case the right-hand expression (A $>$ B, A/B $>$ 100) is evaluated only if the left operator (NOT_EOF, B $/=$ 0) is true. If the left operator is false, the expression is false and the right-hand operator must not be evaluated. This approach differs from the evaluation of **and** and **or** without the short-circuit control form. In the latter case both operands must be evaluated, although the evaluation occurs in an undefined order.

The left operand is also evaluated first for the form **or else**. For example,

```
if A < 15 or else B ** A > INT_1 then        . . . end if;
if B = 0 or else A / B < = 100 then        . . . end if;
```

In the two examples, if the left operand is TRUE, the expression is true and the right operand is not evaluated. If the left operand is false, the right operand is evaluated and provides the value of the expression.

Ada adds a logical operator, **xor** (exclusive or), to those already discussed. It also extends the range of applicability of the logical operators **or** and **and** to include one-dimensional arrays of BOOLEAN as permissible operands.

Figure 14-1 shows the difference in operation between the inclusive **or** and the exclusive **or**. The only variation occurs when both operands are TRUE: **xor** returns a value of FALSE. Here are some examples of the use of the **xor** operator:

```
INT__1 := 6;
INT__2 := 1;
EOF := TRUE;
if INT__1 = 6   xor INT__2 = 6 . . .        -- TRUE
if INT__1 = 6   xor INT__2 = 1 . . .        -- FALSE
if EOF          xor INT__1 = 6 . . .        -- FALSE
```

The logical operators can be used to form the conjunction (**and**), inclusive disjunction (**or**), exclusive disjunction (**xor**), and logical negative (**not**) of one-dimensional arrays of BOOLEAN values. The arrays must have the same number of components, and the operations are performed on an individual component by component basis. Examples are provided in chapter 18.

X	Y	X or Y
T	T	T
T	F	T
F	T	T
F	F	F

a. Inclusive Disjunction (**or**)

X	Y	X xor H
T	T	F
T	F	T
F	T	T
F	F	F

b. Exclusive Disjunction (**xor**)

Figure 14-1   Truth Tables for Disjunction

Set Operators

In chapter 7 we introduced the notion of membership in a range. There is an even more general notion of membership in a set. We can introduce set operations into Ada through the use of overloaded operators. In the following example, APPLE__PIE and SPECIAL can be considered to be sets of GOOD-IES. The expression (GOODIES = > FALSE) sets all the BOOLEAN values in APPLE__PIE and SPECIAL to FALSE. It initializes the set to empty. The set is considered to contain only those values for which the corresponding BOOLEAN value is TRUE. For example, APPLE__PIE := (APPLES = >

TRUE, **others** => FALSE); puts APPLES into the set APPLE_PIE. The new overloaded operators "<=" (for subset) and "+" (for set union) will be defined in the following examples.

```
declare
    type GOODIES is (SUGAR, SYRUP, APPLES, PIE_CRUST, NUTS);
    type DESSERT is array (GOODIES) of BOOLEAN;
    APPLE_PIE, SPECIAL : DESSERT := (GOODIES => FALSE);
begin
    APPLE_PIE := (SUGAR => TRUE, APPLES => TRUE, PIE_CRUST
                    => TRUE, others => FALSE);

    .
    .
    .

    if SPECIAL = APPLE_PIE then          -- Legal. Use of Ada compari-
        ORDER_SPECIAL;                   -- son of equality for arrays
    end if;
    if SPECIAL <= APPLE_PIE then         -- The " <=" must be
                                         -- redefined,
                                         -- as a subset operator

    -- No syrup or nuts at this point since
    -- there are none in APPLE_PIE
    end if;
    SPECIAL := SPECIAL + APPLE_PIE;      -- The "+" must be
                                         -- redefined,
                                         -- as a set union operator
end;
```

The initialization of APPLE_PIE and SPECIAL and the assignment to AP-PLE_PIE is accomplished by the use of an array *aggregate*. The aggregate can be used to initialize arrays or to make assignment of values to arrays as in the assignment to APPLE_PIE. Positional assignment is allowed as well as the named notation, just used above. We could get the same effect by

```
APPLE_PIE := (TRUE, FALSE, TRUE, TRUE, FALSE);
```

Other features of named notation may be used, as in

```
APPLE_PIE := (SUGAR | APPLES | PIE_CRUST => TRUE, SYRUP |
                NUTS => FALSE);
```

The aggregate must be complete: partial assignments are not allowed. A discrete range is also allowed in named aggregates. Mixing positional and named aggregates is not allowed, except for the use of **others** at the end of a positional aggregate.

Where SPECIAL is equal to APPLE_PIE, we know that it contains SUGAR, APPLES, and PIE_CRUST. It does not contain anything else. Where SPECIAL is $<=$ APPLE_PIE, we know it does not contain SYRUP or NUTS (since APPLE_PIE does not contain them). It may or may not contain SUGAR, APPLES, or PIE_CRUST. Now we can provide the definition of overloaded Ada operators to accomplish set operations for objects of type DESSERT.

```
function " < =" (SUBSET, SET : DESSERT) return BOOLEAN is
    begin
      for THING in GOODIES loop
        if SUBSET(THING)  = TRUE and
          SET(THING)      = FALSE then
            return FALSE;  -- Something is in the SUBSET, but
                           -- not in the SET
        end if;
      end loop;
      return TRUE;
    end " < ="; -- Check for subset
```

This definition corresponds to the usual sense of subset in that the SUBSET (SPECIAL in this case) may contain (have a TRUE value for) fewer than, but not more than, the GOODIES contained in the SET (APPLE_PIE). The function loops to search and compare SET and SUBSET. If something is in the SUBSET but not in the SET, the function " $<=$ " is FALSE. If everything in the SUBSET is also in the SET, the loop terminates and the function returns TRUE. Of course since SUBSET(THING) and SET(THING) are BOOLEAN (since DESSERT is an array of BOOLEAN variables), an alternate style for writing the **if** statement is

```
if SUBSET(THING) and not SET(THING) then
    return FALSE;
end if;
```

We can also overload the "+" operator to add one set or array of GOODIES to another.

```
function "+" (ONE, ANOTHER : DESSERT) return DESSERT is
  SUM : DESSERT;
begin
  for THING in GOODIES loop
    SUM(THING) := ONE(THING) or ANOTHER(THING);
  end loop;
  return SUM;
end "+"; -- Set union
```

The THING takes on each of the values of the type GOODIES -- SUGAR, SYRUP, and so forth. If either ONE(THING) or ANOTHER(THING) is true, the corresponding item of GOODIES is placed in the set returned by the "+" operator.

The newly defined operators must now be grouped with their use. In skeleton form, we have

```
declare
  type GOODIES is . . .
  type DESSERT is . . .
  APPLE__PIE, SPECIAL . . .
  function "<=" . . .
  function "+" . . .
begin
  -- Use the new "<=" and "+"
end;
```

After leaving the block, the overloaded definitions of "<=" and "+" are no longer available.

The combination of additional operators in Ada and the ability to provide new definitions for old operators is a powerful mechanism for the expression of relationships between objects and for the manipulation of data.

14.4 PROGRAM STRUCTURE AND SCOPE

Pascal and related languages present difficulties for the construction of large programs because of their lack of control over the scope of names. This section discusses some of the problems and presents the **package**, the Ada mechanism for overcoming these difficulties.

The classic block structure of languages creates a problem with nested procedures and functions in that there is an *invasion* of names into the most deeply nested subprograms. That is, all of the names declared at higher levels of the program structure are visible at lower levels. For example,

```
procedure MAIN is
  M : INTEGER;
  procedure OUTER is
    OUTR : INTEGER;
    procedure INNER is
      INN : INTEGER;
      procedure NESTED is
        NEST : INTEGER;
      begin
        -- Visible names are NEST, INN, OUTR, and
        -- M, as well as MAIN, OUTER, and INNER.
      end NESTED;
    . . .
    . . .
  . . .
end MAIN;
```

A related problem involving lack of control over visibility is that if a data structure is available to several subprograms, it is also available to programs that use the subprograms.

We will discuss these issues by elaborating on the banking problem first presented in chapter 4. Suppose we wish to implement a mechanism for deposits and withdrawals from a bank account and for keeping track of the number of transactions.

```
procedure BANK is
  BALANCE : FLOAT range −1000.00 .. 10_000_000.00 := 0.0;
  NUMBER_OF_DEPOSITS : NATURAL := 0;
  NUMBER_OF_WITHDRAWALS : NATURAL := 0;

  procedure DEPOSIT (AMOUNT : in FLOAT) is
  begin
    BALANCE := BALANCE + AMOUNT;
    NUMBER_OF_DEPOSITS :=
      NUMBER_OF_DEPOSITS + 1;
  end DEPOSIT;
```

```
procedure WITHDRAW (AMOUNT : in FLOAT) is
begin
   BALANCE := BALANCE – AMOUNT;
   NUMBER_OF_WITHDRAWALS :=
     NUMBER_OF_WITHDRAWALS + 1;
end WITHDRAW;
begin -- BANK
   DEPOSIT (100.00);                         -- Legal use of DEPOSIT
   WITHDRAW (17.26);                         -- Legal use of WITH-
                                             -- DRAW

   PUT(NUMBER_OF_DEPOSITS);                  -- Legal output of infor-
                                             -- mation
   PUT(NUMBER_OF_WITHDRAWALS);               -- from main program
   BALANCE := BALANCE + 1_000_000.00;        -- Legal, but inappropri-
                                             -- ate. Should use
                                             -- procedure DEPOSIT

   NUMBER_OF_DEPOSITS := 100;                -- Legal, but
                                             -- inappropriate

   NUMBER_OF_WITHDRAWALS :=
     NUMBER_OF_WITHDRAWALS – 1;              -- Legal, but
                                             -- inappropriate

end BANK;
```

The bank policy is to limit accounts to $10 million. This account has a loan limit of $1000.00. The NUMBER_OF_DEPOSITS and NUMBER _OF_WITHDRAWALS are of type NATURAL and initialized to zero. NATURAL is a predefined type of Ada with range 0 .. INTEGER'LAST. Note that, when using nested procedures, in order to allow DEPOSIT and WITH-DRAW to have access to the shared variable BALANCE, it is necessary to also make it available to the main procedure that calls DEPOSIT and WITH-DRAW.* Further, if the main program is to output the variables that represent the number of transactions, it usually will have access to these values directly. The problem with this mechanism is shown in the example: the main program may tamper with the values that should be manipulated only by the subordinate procedures DEPOSIT and WITHDRAW. We can think of this as though a customer of a bank were able to increase his or her bank balance without actually making a deposit. Although in actual programming situations the

---

*FORTRAN is able to avoid this problem. Although it has other difficulties that have been solved by block-structured languages, it can provide an effective mechanism for several routines to share a private data structure inaccessible to either the calling routine or subordinate routines.

tampering may not be malicious, it can be accidental and lead to bugs difficult to detect in a large program.

The general problem is that shared or global data structures provide more information than necessary. The main or calling program has unnecessary information about the structure of the data and has the ability to modify the data in incorrect ways. This unnecessary visibility is inconsistent with modern notions of system design.

The mechanism for overcoming these difficulties must involve some means of *encapsulating* data along with the processes that operate on the data. Ada provides the **package** as a mechanism for building a wall around data and related procedures, yet allowing the necessary visibility through the wall so that external processes may access procedures within the **package.**

The package is a central concept in Ada. It may be the language's single most important feature. Chapter 21 will cover the package concept in detail. Here we will only provide a brief introduction and show how it solves the preceding problem. Packages will be used from time to time in the examples remaining in part 3.

Figure 14-2 repeats figure 3-3 to again illustrate features of the package. First there is a specification, which contains the part that is visible and available to the outside world. It can be considered a *contract* in that it is a specification of capabilities or resources to be provided. Then there is the package body, the implementation of the specification, which may include hidden data structures. The following example rewrites the bank problem and illustrates how the main routine no longer has access to unnecessary, potentially dangerous information.

```
procedure BETTER_BANK is

   package TRANSACTIONS
     procedure DEPOSIT (AMOUNT : in FLOAT);
     procedure WITHDRAW(AMOUNT : in FLOAT);
     procedure PRINT_NUMBER_OF_TRANSACTIONS;
   end;
   package body TRANSACTIONS is
     BALANCE : FLOAT range −1000.00 .. 10_000_000.00 := 0.0;
     NUMBER_OF_DEPOSITS : NATURAL := 0;
     NUMBER_OF_WITHDRAWALS : NATURAL := 0;

     procedure DEPOSIT (AMOUNT : in FLOAT) is
```

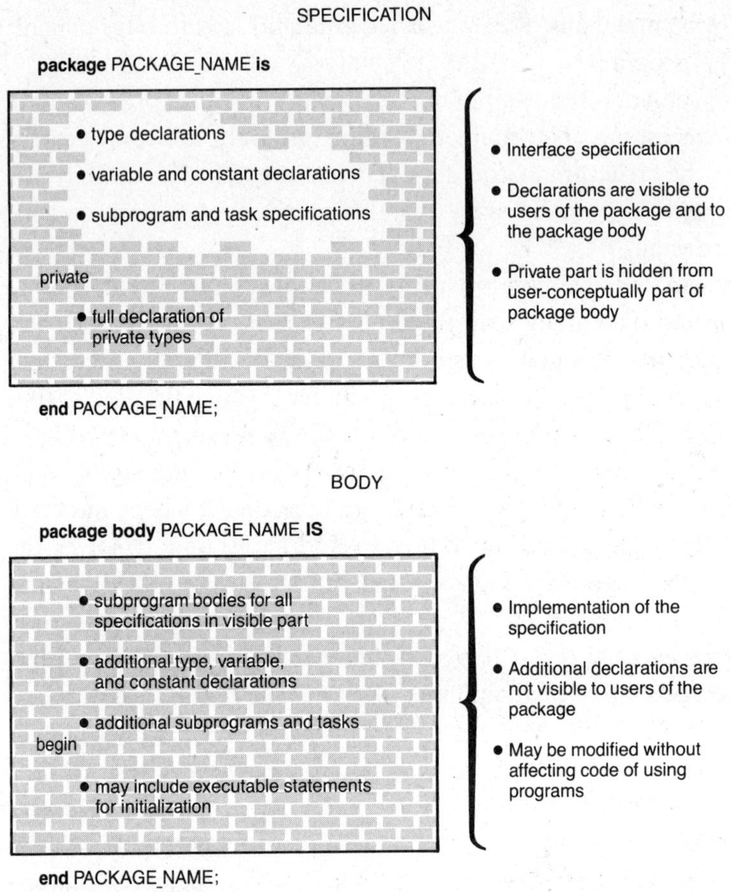

SPECIFICATION

package PACKAGE_NAME **is**

- • type declarations
- • variable and constant declarations
- • subprogram and task specifications

private

- • full declaration of
  private types

end PACKAGE_NAME;

- • Interface specification
- • Declarations are visible to users of the package and to the package body
- • Private part is hidden from user-conceptually part of package body

BODY

package body PACKAGE_NAME **IS**

- • subprogram bodies for all specifications in visible part
- • additional type, variable, and constant declarations
- • additional subprograms and tasks

begin

- • may include executable statements for initialization

end PACKAGE_NAME;

- • Implementation of the specification
- • Additional declarations are not visible to users of the package
- • May be modified without affecting code of using programs

Figure 14-2   Package Structure

```
  begin
    BALANCE := BALANCE + AMOUNT;
    NUMBER_OF_DEPOSITS :=
      NUMBER_OF_DEPOSITS + 1;
  end DEPOSIT;

  procedure WITHDRAW (AMOUNT : in FLOAT) is
  begin
    BALANCE := BALANCE − AMOUNT;
    NUMBER_OF_WITHDRAWALS :=
      NUMBER_OF_WITHDRAWALS + 1;
  end WITHDRAW;

  procedure PRINT_NUMBER_OF_TRANSACTIONS is
  begin
    PUT(NUMBER_OF_DEPOSITS);
    PUT(NUMBER_OF_WITHDRAWALS);
  end PRINT_NUMBER_OF_TRANSACTIONS;
 end TRANSACTIONS;

  use TRANSACTIONS;
begin -- BETTER_BANK
  DEPOSIT(100.00);
  WITHDRAW(17.26);
  BALANCE := BALANCE + 1_000_000.00;      -- Illegal. BALANCE
                                          -- not visible here

  PRINT_NUMBER_OF_TRANSACTIONS;
  NUMBER_OF_DEPOSITS := 100;              -- Illegal. Not visible
  NUMBER_OF_WITHDRAWALS :=
    NUMBER_OF_WITHDRAWALS − 1;            -- Illegal. Not visible
end BETTER_BANK;
```

The clause "**use TRANSACTIONS;**" just before the executable part of the BANK makes the procedures declared in the package specification immediately visible. Without the **use** clause, the procedures would have to be accessed using a fully qualified name as

```
TRANSACTIONS.DEPOSIT(100.00);
TRANSACTIONS.WITHDRAW(17.26);
```

The implementation just shown is safer in the sense that the main body of the procedure BANK can no longer directly access the BALANCE or other information in the package. The names BALANCE, NUMBER_OF_

DEPOSITS, and NUMBER_OF_WITHDRAWALS are not visible in the body of the procedure and therefore can not be modified. TRANSACTIONS encapsulates the data along with the processes that act on it. The package specification makes DEPOSIT and WITHDRAW (along with their specifications) visible and available to the main procedure and provides the only access to the data. Each deposit or withdrawal is now properly recorded, and the number of transactions is incremented. Further, the main procedure cannot tamper with the number of transactions. The NUMBER_OF_DEPOSITS and NUMBER_OF_WITHDRAWALS are monotonically increasing variables; they cannot be decremented.

Exercise_14

Modify PROGRAM_6 so that OBJECT is shared by the two procedures but is not available to the main program. You will need a package to do this.

Program_14

```
with TEXT_IO; use TEXT_IO;
procedure PROGRAM_14 is

  package HIDE_OBJECT is
    procedure ADD_N(N : in INTEGER);
    procedure SUB_N(N : in INTEGER);
  end;

  package body HIDE_OBJECT is
    OBJECT : INTEGER := 0;

    procedure ADD_N(N : in INTEGER) is
    begin
      OBJECT := OBJECT + N;
    end ADD_N;

    procedure SUB_N(N : in INTEGER) is
    begin
      OBJECT := OBJECT - N;
    end SUB_N;
  end HIDE_OBJECT;

  package IO is new INTEGER_IO(INTEGER); use IO;

  use HIDE_OBJECT;
```

```
begin -- PROGRAM__14
  ADD__N(10);
  SUB__N(5);
  OBJECT := OBJECT + 3; -- Now illegal
  <--------->
*** Semantic Error: Undeclared identifier OBJECT (RRM 3.1)
  <--------->
*** Semantic Error: incompatible types for +
  PUT(OBJECT);
  <--------->
*** Semantic Error: Ambiguous call to one of IO.PUT TEXT__IO.PUT TEXT
__IO.PUT (RRM 6.6, 8.3)
end PROGRAM__14;
3 translation errors detected
```

Discussion__14

We have used a package to encapsulate the OBJECT and the procedures that operate on it. The OBJECT can be shared between the two procedures but cannot be accessed by users of the package. Immediate visibility of the procedures ADD__N and SUB__N is gained by the clause

use HIDE__OBJECT;

Without the clause, we would use HIDE__OBJECT.ADD__N and HIDE __OBJECT.SUB__N to invoke the procedures. References to OBJECT during execution of the main program give rise to errors at compile time since neither OBJECT nor its type are known outside the package. This is a secure encapsulation of the OBJECT. This use of a package to control visibility is an important advance of Ada over other languages.

KEYS TO UNDERSTANDING

▶ A programmer is allowed to define new meanings for the predefined operators. Since they also retain their old meaning, the operators are said to be overloaded.

▶ The classic block structure of languages creates a problem with the invasion of names into inner scopes. It also requires that too much information be made globally available.

▶ The Ada package provides a superior mechanism for encapsulating data and for controlling the scope of names.

15

Type Definitions and Strong Typing

Objective: to discuss attributes of types, to present the Ada mechanism for defining new derived types, and to summarize the types in Ada

Ada provides a number of features to allow stronger differentiation among types than does Pascal, and it provides features to make types easier to use.

15.1 ATTRIBUTES

Attributes can provide information about the characteristics of a type. For types, an attribute is written as

    type__name ' attribute__identifier

The attribute identifier is always prefixed by an apostrophe. The type__name could also be a subtype name. Here are some examples:

```
COLOR ' FIRST        -- Value of the first component
                     -- of the enumeration type COLOR
INTEGER ' LAST       -- Value of the largest INTEGER
```

```
VECTOR'FIRST        -- The lower index bound of the
                    -- array type VECTOR
VECTOR'LAST         -- The upper index bound of VECTOR
VECTOR'RANGE        -- VECTOR'FIRST .. VECTOR'LAST
```

A complete list of attributes is provided in appendix E. Use of attributes can lead to the creation of general-purpose and portable subprograms.

In chapter 14 we wrote a function to add the elements of arrays of type VECTOR. We used subtype INDEX as the range. A more general implementation would use the attribute of the VECTOR type.

```
function "+" (V : VECTOR) return INTEGER is
   LOC_I : INTEGER := 0;
begin
  for I in VECTOR'RANGE loop
    LOC_I := LOC_I + V(I);
  end loop;
  return LOC_I;
end "+";
```

The 'RANGE attribute is also associated with *objects* of an array type. So we could have controlled the loop iteration with

```
for I in V'RANGE loop . . .
```

This can be important in writing general-purpose subprograms. As we will see in chapter 18, this method can allow an array to have different index ranges. We can operate in an appropriate range, dynamically defined at run time, by using the 'RANGE attribute of a formal array parameter.

15.2 *QUALIFIERS*

Sometimes the type of an object is ambiguous from its context. We can use a type qualifier to resolve the ambiguity. It is written as

```
type_name'(object_name)
```

For example, enumeration types may include overloaded names:

```
declare
   type COLOR is (WHITE, RED, YELLOW, GREEN, BLUE);
   type LIGHT is (RED, AMBER, GREEN);
   . . .
begin
   for BULB in RED .. GREEN loop -- Illegal. Ambiguous
   . . .
   end loop;
   for BULB in LIGHT ' (RED) .. GREEN loop -- OK
   . . .
   end loop;
end;
```

The first situation is ambiguous since RED and GREEN could be of type COLOR or of type LIGHT, and BULB is implicitly declared to be the same type as RED .. GREEN. The use of the qualifier in the second situation clears up the ambiguity. Note that

```
LIGHT ' (RED) .. LIGHT ' (GREEN)
```

is also appropriate, but unnecessary.

15.3 UNIVERSAL TYPES

Although Ada is very strict regarding the mixing of types, there are "universal" types that can be used with greater freedom. Literal values such as

```
6  , 256  , 1__000__000  -- Universal INTEGER
6.0 , 256.0 , 3.14159     -- Universal REAL
```

and numbers declared as

```
TABLE__SIZE   : constant := 1000;
PI            : constant := 3.14159;
```

are universal types. Note that literal real values must have a digit both before and after the decimal point. Universal integers can be used in expressions involving any of the integer types, and universal reals can be used in expressions with any of the real types. In addition, universal real and integer numbers may be mixed in expressions. Specifically,

```
256 * PI        -- integer times real
PI * 256        -- real times integer
PI / 256        -- real divided by integer
PI ** 2         -- real to integer power
```

are allowed and provide a result of universal real.

15.4 DERIVED TYPES

We have seen how it is possible to define subtypes of a base type in order to provide for types that have a restricted range of allowable values. We have also seen the situation in which two types, say arrays, have the same structure but are incompatible since each type declaration introduces a new and distinct type. It is often useful to be able to introduce new types for any type at all. The new types will have the same structure as the old types but will be incompatible and therefore cannot be inadvertently mixed. The format is

```
type MY__INT is range 1..1000;
type NEW__A is new MY__INT;
type NEW__B is new MY__INT;
```

Then we say that NEW__A and NEW__B are derived types with a parent type of MY__INT. A derived type inherits the properties of its parent, including the values that it may be assigned and the set of allowable operations. For user-defined parent types, the derived type also inherits certain applicable subprograms of the parent type. For a parent type and applicable subprograms defined in a package specification, derived types declared after the end of the specification will inherit the subprograms. Although NEW__A and NEW__B each have the same parent and the same structure, they are incompatible, both with each other and with the parent type. For example,

```
declare
  A_1, A_2 : NEW_A;
  B_1, B_2 : NEW_B;
  MY_1     : MY_INT := 10;
begin
  A_1 := 100;
  A_2 := A_1;
  A_2 := A_1 * A_2 + 5;
  B_1 := MY_1;                    -- Illegal
  B_2 := A_1;                     -- Illegal
  A_1 := A_2 * B_1;               -- Illegal
end;
```

Recall that in chapter 7 we had an example that distinguished between two books of different length:

```
declare
  subtype PAGES        is INTEGER range 1 .. 1000;
  subtype BOOK_PAGES   is PAGES range 1 .. 400;
  subtype SMALL_BOOK   is BOOK_PAGES range 1 .. 100;
  BOOK              : PAGES;
  ADA_BOOK          : BOOK_PAGES;
  FORTRAN_BOOK      : SMALL_BOOK;
begin
  FORTRAN_BOOK := 50;
  ADA_BOOK := FORTRAN_BOOK;              -- Always OK
  FORTRAN_BOOK := ADA_BOOK;              -- OK, but must have
                                         -- check at run time
  BOOK := ADA_BOOK + FORTRAN_BOOK;       -- Always OK
  BOOK := 425;
  ADA_BOOK := BOOK - FORTRAN_BOOK;       -- Needs run-time
                                         -- check
end;
```

Suppose, however, that we wished to ensure that operations on the two types of books were not mixed. We could replace the subtype declarations by

```
type PAGES        is range 1 .. 1000;
type BOOK_PAGES   is new PAGES range 1 .. 400;
type SMALL_BOOK   is new BOOK_PAGES range 1 .. 100;
```

The declaration of BOOK—PAGES is equivalent to

```
type HIDDEN        is new PAGES;
subtype BOOK—PAGES  is HIDDEN range 1 .. 400;
```

Then we would have

```
declare
   BOOK          : PAGES;
   ADA—BOOK      : BOOK—PAGES;
   FORTRAN—BOOK : SMALL—BOOK;
begin
   FORTRAN—BOOK := 50;                    -- OK
   ADA—BOOK := FORTRAN—BOOK;              -- Illegal.  Different
                                          -- types

   BOOK := ADA—BOOK + FORTRAN—BOOK;       -- Illegal.  Different
                                          -- types

   ADA—BOOK :=                            -- Legal. Use of type
      BOOK—PAGES(FORTRAN—BOOK);           -- name
                                          -- to change type

   FORTRAN—BOOK :=                        -- OK. Still needs
      SMALL—BOOK(ADA—BOOK);               -- run-time
                                          -- check

   BOOK := PAGES(ADA—BOOK);               -- Needs  the  type
                                          -- conversion
                                          -- to PAGES

end;
```

The use of derived types in the preceding example is consistent with the Ada philosophy of defining different types for different kinds of abstract objects. Such an approach helps the compiler detect instances of inadvertent mixing of objects and operations that ought to be incompatible. When it is necessary to mix objects or types, such as BOOK—PAGES and SMALL—BOOK, the explicit type conversion makes the programmer's intention visible to the compiler.

In chapter 11 we had a STUDENT—RECORD example using subranges of INTEGER and FLOAT. The example could be completely reworked with user-defined types as

```
declare
  TOP__GRADE : constant : = 4.0;
  COMPLETE : constant : = 50;
  type COURSE__RANGE is range 0 .. COMPLETE;
  type GRADE__RANGE   is range 0.0 .. TOP__GRADE;
  type POINT__RANGE   is range 0.0 .. TOP__GRADE * COMPLETE;
  type GRADE__ARRAY   is array (1 .. COMPLETE) of
                              GRADE__RANGE;
  type STUDENT__RECORD is
    record
      NAME                      : STRING(1 .. 25);
      NUMBER__OF__COURSES  : COURSE__RANGE;
      GRADE__POINTS            : GRADE__ARRAY;
    end record;
  GPA  : GRADE__RANGE;
  TGP  : POINT__RANGE;
  A    : STUDENT__RECORD;
begin
  GET(A.NAME);
  GET(A.NUMBER__OF__COURSES);
  for N in 1 .. A.NUMBER__OF__COURSES loop
    GET(A.GRADE__POINTS(N));
  end loop;
  If A.NUMBER__OF__COURSES > = 1 then
    TGP := 0.0;
    for N in 1 .. A.NUMBER__OF__COURSES loop
      TGP := TGP + POINT__RANGE(A.GRADE__POINTS(N));
    end loop;
    GPA := GRADE__RANGE( TGP /
      POINT__RANGE(A.NUMBER__OF__COURSES));
    PUT(A.NAME);
    PUT(GPA);
  end if;
end;
```

Of course, if our programming problem really only consisted of the simple task just illustrated, we would not go through as much type definition. The importance of taking such care to ensure that different types are not mixed in expressions only becomes evident in the construction of large programs. Ada gives the capability of using simple methods for simple programs, but also provides the more powerful and safe methods for the construction of large programming systems.

The use of derived types is more complex than expressed in these examples. There are a number of rules for the exact applicability of the use of type conversion, which are covered at length in the LRM. There is also a strong interaction between derived types, private types, and the advanced use of packages. These topics will be discussed in part 4.

15.5 *SUMMARY OF TYPES*

The types in Ada can be classified as

Private types can be defined as scalar, composite, or access types in the private part of a package. Private types are used to control the allowable set of operations on objects of the type. There is also a **task** type, discussed in chapter 25.

Exercise__15

Modify PROGRAM__7 so that the subtypes are now separate types. Indicate which of the previously legal assignments are now illegal.

Program__15

```
procedure PROGRAM__15 is
   type US__COLOR is (RED, WHITE, BLUE);
   type SKY is new US__COLOR range WHITE .. BLUE;
   type SHORT__INT is new INTEGER range −10 .. 10;
   US__FLAG          : US__COLOR;
   PARTLY__CLOUDY    : SKY;
   TENS              : SHORT__INT;
   ANY__SIZE         : INTEGER;
```

```
begin -- PROGRAM__15
  US__FLAG := BLUE;
  US__FLAG := "BLUE";                            -- Illegal
      <- - - - - - - - ->
    *** Semantic Error: incompatible types for :=
PARTLY__CLOUDY := WHITE;
PARTLY__CLOUDY := RED;                           -- Out of range error
                                                 -- at run time

      <- - - - - - - - ->
    *** Warning: Evaluation of expression will raise CONSTRAINT__ER-
    ROR
PARTLY__CLOUDY := US__FLAG;                       -- No longer legal
      <- - - - - - - - ->
    *** Semantic Error: incompatible types for :=
US__FLAG := PARTLY__CLOUDY;                       -- No longer legal
      <- - - - - - - - ->
    *** Semantic Error: incompatible types for :=
TENS := -2;
ANY__SIZE := 11;
TENS := ANY__SIZE;                               -- No longer legal
<- - - - - - - - ->
    *** Semantic Error: incompatible types for :=
ANY__SIZE := 1;
TENS := ANY__SIZE;                               -- No longer legal
      <- - - - - - - - ->
    *** Semantic Error: incompatible types for :=
ANY__SIZE := TENS;                               -- No longer legal
      <- - - - - - - - ->
    *** Semantic Error: incompatible types for :=
ANY__SIZE := 1.0;                                -- No mixing of
                                                 -- integer and real

      <- - - - - - - - ->
    *** Semantic Error: incompatible types for :=
ANY__SIZE := 'a';                                -- No mixing of
                                                 -- integer and
                                                 -- character

      <- - - - - - - - ->
    *** Semantic Error: incompatible types for :=
end PROGRAM__15;
8 translation errors detected
```

Discussion__15

We have now made SKY and SHORT__INT derived types. They have the same structure as the parent types from which they are derived, but they are no longer compatible (as the subtypes were with their base types). A number of the assignments legal in PROGRAM__7 are no longer legal.

Keys to Understanding

► Attributes provide information about the characteristics of a type, such as the range of indices for an array type.

► Ada provides for **new** types, called derived types, that have the same underlying structure as other types. The device allows for greater abstraction and differentiation between different types of objects.

16

Control Structures

Objective: to present additional Ada control structures

Ada provides a complete set of control structures to implement modern programming methods.

16.1 *SELECTION*

Ada has improved the selection mechanism of Pascal, without adding any complexity, through the use of features already described. We will summarize them here.

The **elsif**, rather than a series of **else if . . . else if ..** aids readability. It immediately draws attention to the fact that one alternative will be selected from a list, rather than allowing a nesting of conditions.

For the **case** statement Ada requires that all possible alternatives of the expression evaluated to make the choice (that is, the case selector) be present in the list of alternatives. That is, the choices preceding the alternative sequences of statements must include all possible values of the type of the expression to be evaluated. This requirement clarifies an ambiguity in Pascal as to what happens if the case selector evaluates to a value not included in the list of choices. This situation can not occur in Ada at run time since the possibility would be detected at compile time and the program would be illegal.

Ada allows **others** as a choice in a case statement to explicitly provide a sequence of statements to be executed when the expression does not evaluate to a choice otherwise listed. The **others** can, in certain circumstances, ease the programmer's task in making the list of choices include all possible values of the type of the expression. The use of **others** is required when all values of the type of the case selector have not been listed as previous choices.

Note that Ada's improvements to the **case** statement do not add any increased capability. The same result may be achieved in Pascal by careful use of enumeration types, use of subranges for integers, and use of an enclosing if__then__else around the case statement. What Ada does, and it is important, is enforce safe programming practice. If the programmer has erred (written unsafe code) the Ada compiler will discover the error at compile time rather than permit code that could create problems/erroneous execution during test or system operation.

16.2 *ITERATION*

We have seen how Ada directly implements the constructs DO__WHILE and FOR (including reverse counting). The REPEAT__UNTIL construct is implemented with the use of **exit when** < condition >. Ada generalizes the exit clause and allows loops to be labeled in order to provide greater flexibility in controlled iteration.

As shown in chapter 8, the **exit when** < condition > clause need not be at the end of the loop.

```
loop
    -- Statements
exit when  < condition > ;
    -- More statements
end loop;
```

The **exit** clause can be used in a general way to allow checking of conditions in the middle of a loop. A loop can have a name, and the exit can refer to the loop name. For example,

```
FOUND := FALSE;
MAIN__LOOP:
loop
  -- Statements
  while <condition> loop
    -- Statements
    -- Eventually sets FOUND to TRUE
    exit MAIN__LOOP when FOUND;
    -- More statements
  end loop;
  -- more statements
end loop MAIN__LOOP;
```

When FOUND becomes true, the outer loop is terminated. The repeat of the loop name at the end of the loop is required.

Exercise__16

Write a program with nested loops. From the inner loop, exit only the inner loop and also exit both loops by using an exit from a named loop.

Program__16

```
with TEXT__IO; use TEXT__IO;
procedure PROGRAM__16 is
begin
  LOOP__LABEL:
  for I in 1 .. 5 loop
    for J in 1 .. 5 loop
      PUT__LINE("In inner loop");
      exit when I = 2 and J = 2;
      exit LOOP__LABEL when I * J > 8;
    end loop;
    PUT__LINE("After inner loop"); NEW__LINE;
  end loop LOOP__LABEL;
end PROGRAM__16;
```

```
    No translation errors detected
    Begin Ada execution

    In inner loop
    In inner loop
```

In inner loop
In inner loop
In inner loop
After inner loop

In inner loop
In inner loop
After inner loop

In inner loop
In inner loop
In inner loop

Execution complete

Discussion—16

You can follow the execution sequence by looking at the printed values. The simple **exit** clause causes exit from the immediately enclosing loop. The named **loop exit** causes exit from the outer loop.

Keys to Understanding

▶ Ada's ability to exit from a loop is very general. Loops may be named, and an exit may be located anywhere in the loop, including within nested loops.

17

Subprograms

Objective: to present additional Ada features for using subprograms

The major ways in which Ada provides enhanced handling of subprograms—overloading, especially of operators, and improved specification of the modes (**in, out, in out**) of parameters—have already been discussed. The following sections address default parameters, overloading of procedure names, and the ability of a function to return a composite object.

17.1 *DEFAULT PARAMETERS*

Parameters of mode **in** may have default values specified as expressions given in the formal parameter list. If no value is provided in the actual parameter list, the corresponding parameter takes on the default value. For example, several options are usually available when ordering a chicken dinner.

```
type SIZE   is (INDIVIDUAL, FAMILY_PACK, FEAST);
type MEAT   is (WHITE, DARK, MIXED);
type STYLE  is (OLD_FASHIONED, EXTRA_CRISPY, BARBEQUE);
```

A procedure specification might be

```
procedure CHICKEN_DINNER (ORDER   : in SIZE   := INDIVIDUAL;
                          CHICKEN : in MEAT  := MIXED;
                          COATING : in STYLE :=
                                         OLD_FASHIONED);
```

This means that if no actual parameter is provided in the procedure call for one of the formal parameters (ORDER, CHICKEN, and COATING), the formal parameter takes on the default value given: INDIVIDUAL, MIXED, or OLD-FASHIONED respectively. The default values are read as "For SIZE use INDIVIDUAL, for MEAT use MIXED, and for STYLE use OLD_FASHIONED." Orders for chicken dinner could be

```
CHICKEN_DINNER(FEAST, MIXED,
               BARBEQUE);
CHICKEN_DINNER;                         -- Takes all default val-
                                        -- ues
CHICKEN_DINNER(FEAST, WHITE);           -- The default COATING
                                        -- is OLD_FASHIONED
CHICKEN_DINNER(FEAST, COATING = >
               BARBEQUE);               -- The default CHICKEN
                                        -- is MIXED
```

The last example illustrates named notation and is read "for COATING use BARBEQUE." Named notation may be used for any parameter of any mode in Ada subprograms, not just for parameters with defaults. Named notation can be an effective documentation device. Note that positional and named notation may be mixed as in the last example, and that the default value is taken for CHICKEN. Once the left-to-right order of positional notation is abandoned, named notation must be used. In this case the parameters may be provided in any order, with missing parameters taking default values. For instance,

```
CHICKEN_DINNER(COATING = > BARBEQUE, ORDER = > FEAST);
```

Default values can be effectively used in any circumstance that would otherwise call for long parameter lists containing mostly standard values. Named notation is an easy, flexible mechanism for selecting parameters that have other than default values.

17.2 *NAME OVERLOADING*

It is possible for subprogram names to be overloaded, that is, for the same name to refer to different subprograms:

```
procedure PROCESS(X : INTEGER);
procedure PROCESS(X : FLOAT);
```

The compiler is able to distinguish calls to the subprograms by parameter or (for functions) result type, parameter mode or name, number of parameters, and other criteria. For example,

```
declare
   INT : INTEGER;
   FLO : FLOAT;
begin
   PROCESS(INT);
   PROCESS(FLO);
end;
```

Overloading adds to clarity since we need not bother with separate names for operations that are essentially identical. We don't need REAL_PROC and INT_PROC, or STRING_PUT, FLOAT_PUT, and INT_PUT. This is of particular importance in Ada, since new types will be frequently defined, and the language carefully distinguishes and isolates one type from another. However, when carelessly used, overloading can create programs that are ambiguous and difficult to read. Overloading is a complex topic, and both the reader and the compiler may find it difficult to resolve subtle ambiguities in overloaded names. Nonetheless, when carefully used, subprogram overloading is a useful feature and aids readability.

17.3 *OPERATOR OVERLOADING*

Operator overloading was discussed in chapter 14. Operators and functions are closely related. An operator is actually just a function that accepts a limited number of actual parameters (one or two) and returns a single value. Whether the process is specified as a function or an operator is a matter of form. We needn't discuss operator overloading further, except to emphasize that, as with name overloading, operator overloading is both valuable and potentially dangerous. However, when carefully used, it is a useful, powerful feature for language extensibility.

17.4 FUNCTION RETURN VALUES

A function may return a value of reference or composite types. If a function returns a composite value (a record or an array), a component may be directly selected or indexed—for example, if we have a function that sums two VECTOR objects (one-dimensional arrays of INTEGER):

```
function SUM (V, T : VECTOR) return VECTOR is
  LOC_VEC : VECTOR;
begin
  for I in VECTOR ' RANGE loop
    LOC_VEC(I) := V(I) + T(I);
  end loop;
  return LOC_VEC;
end SUM;
```

Then for

```
HIS_VEC, HER_VEC : VECTOR;
A_NUMBER : INTEGER;
```

the assignment

```
A_NUMBER := SUM(HIS_VEC, HER_VEC)(5);
```

assigns the sum of the fifth components of HIS_VEC and HER_VEC to A_NUMBER.

Exercise_17

Write a program that overloads the "/" operator in the following way: it provides for division with truncation of a FLOAT value by an INTEGER value. That is, float__value / integer__value, with result of type INTEGER. Although operator overloading was discussed in chapter 14, it is also relevant to this chapter.

Program__17

```
with TEXT__IO; use TEXT__IO;
procedure PROGRAM__17 is
   F : FLOAT;
   I : INTEGER;

   function "/" (N : FLOAT; D : INTEGER) return INTEGER is
      return INTEGER (N / FLOAT(D) − 0.5);
   end "/"; -- For FLOAT / INTEGER division with truncation

   package IO is new INTEGER__IO(INTEGER); use IO;
begin -- PROGRAM__17
   F := 10.1;
   I := 4;
   PUT(F/I); NEW__LINE;
   I := 6;
   PUT(F/I); NEW__LINE;
   I := 12;
   PUT(F/I);
end PROGRAM__17;

Begin Ada execution

2
1
0
```

Discussion__17

Normally, a FLOAT variable cannot be divided by an INTEGER variable. The compiler would discover the type incompatibility and generate an error. However, here we explicitly state what we intend to accomplish by creating a function to define "/" for the division. The functioning of the new "/" is straightforward. The effect is similar to that for usual INTEGER division— the result is INTEGER with truncation. This capability to overload operators is somewhat controversial. However, it can aid readability of programs for functions such as matrix arithmetic. Experience will tell if its advantages outweigh the potential for misleading definition of operators.

Keys to Understanding

▶ Ada allows the specification of default parameters. Default values are taken for parameters not specified in the subprogram call.
▶ Named parameter association may be used to relate actual parameters to formal parameters.
▶ Subprogram names may be overloaded.

18

Arrays

Objective: to present additional Ada array manipulation capabilities

Ada provides a number of enhanced capabilities for dealing with arrays. This chapter discusses unconstrained arrays, aggregates, and special operations applicable to one-dimensional arrays.

18.1 *UNCONSTRAINED ARRAYS*

A serious limitation of arrays in Pascal is that arrays, once declared, are fixed in size. This limitation creates two problems. First, it does not allow us to create a type that includes a variety of arrays which are conceptually or abstractly similar but have different length. Second, it does not allow us to create general-purpose subprograms for the manipulation of arrays with similar characteristics but differing sizes.

18.1.1 *Array Declarations*

The usual definition of a fixed-length or constrained array type is

type VECTOR **is array** (1 .. 10) **of** INTEGER;

However, it is possible to also define an unconstrained array type: one in which the range constraint for the index is not provided. For example,

type VECTOR **is array** (POSITIVE **range** $<>$) **of** INTEGER;

The index is read as "POSITIVE range *box.*" Remember POSITIVE is a predefined type with range 1 .. INTEGER'LAST. Then we can declare

```
HIS_VEC      : VECTOR(1 .. 3);
HER_VEC      : VECTOR(28 .. 30);
THEIR_VEC : VECTOR(1 .. 6);
```

HIS_VEC and HER_VEC each have three components, while THEIR_VEC has six components. They are all of the same type. The attributes are

```
HIS_VEC'FIRST    = 1        HIS_VEC'LAST    = 3
HER_VEC'FIRST    = 28       HER_VEC'LAST    = 30
THEIR_VEC'FIRST = 1         THEIR_VEC'LAST = 6
```

Of course, there are alternate ways of specifying the discrete range:

```
type INDEX is range 1 .. 10;
THIS_VEC : VECTOR(INDEX);
THEIR_VEC : VECTOR(HIS_VEC'FIRST ..
   HIS_VEC'LAST + HER_VEC'LENGTH);
     -- Same as THEIR_VEC : VECTOR(1 .. 6);
```

Various objects of type VECTOR of the same length are compatible for assignment. In general, the discrete range can also include negative bounds (but not for VECTOR). For example, $(-10 .. 10)$ or $(-100 .. -10)$ are legal bounds for an INTEGER index.

18.1.2 *Arrays in Subprograms*

In chapter 14 we wrote a function to sum two vectors. The function was limited in its generality since it could only operate on objects with range given by INDEX. Using the unconstrained array VECTOR defined in this chapter, along with a range specification given by the attributes of the parameters to the function, we can write a general-purpose VECTOR addition routine:

```
function "+" (V, T : VECTOR) return VECTOR is
  LOC_VEC : VECTOR(V'RANGE);
begin
  for I in V'RANGE loop
    LOC_VEC(I) := V(I) + T(I);
  end loop;
  return LOC_VEC;
end "+"; -- For general VECTOR addition
```

The range of the formal parameters is the same as those on the corresponding actual parameters. The function contains an implicit assumption that V'RANGE $<=$ T'RANGE. The range of the result is taken from the expression returned, LOC_VEC.

We can use this function to add two vectors, such as

```
HIS_VEC := HIS_VEC + HER_VEC;
```

It will also allow, even if we didn't wish for this ability,

```
HIS_VEC := HIS_VEC + THEIR_VEC;
```

(using only the first three components of THEIR_VEC); but will fail on

```
HIS_VEC := THEIR_VEC + HIS_VEC;
```

since V'RANGE is 1 .. 6 and the constraints on the size of HIS_VEC will be violated on the fourth iteration of the loop in function "+". In order to prevent an uncontrolled failure, we could modify "+" to add the code

```
if V'LENGTH /= T'LENGTH then
  -- Raise an exception as discussed
  -- in chapter 24
end if;
```

as a guard for the loop.

18.2 *AGGREGATES*

An array aggregate is a list of values in parentheses, which provides a value for each component of an array.

    HIS_VEC:= (6, 8, 0);

Aggregates are frequently used to initialize arrays:

    HIS_VEC : VECTOR(1 .. 3) := (1, 2, 3);

It is possible to establish a named association between the index values and the value assigned:

    HER_VEC : VECTOR(28 .. 30) := (28 => 1, 29 => 5, 30 => 6);

The aggregate is read as "For 28 use 1, for 29 use 5, for 30 use 6." It is also possible to indicate ranges and combinations, similar to the choices in a case statement:

    THEIR_VEC : VECTOR(1 .. 6) :=
        (1 | 3 => 1, 4 .. 6 => 2, 2 => 3);

All components must have values assigned. The clause **others** has the expected effect:

    THEIR_VEC : VECTOR(1 .. 6) := (2 => 3, 5 => 1, **others** => 0);

The **others** must be the last assignment. Mixed positional and named notion is not permitted, except for the use of **others.**

    THEIR_VEC : VECTOR(1 .. 6) := (1 => 2, **others** => 0);

The use of aggregate assignment can also be used to establish the index constraints for an unconstrained array type.

```
CONST_VEC  : constant VECTOR  := (17, 3, 22);
THIS_VEC   : VECTOR            := (8 => 4, 9 => 16,
                                  10 => 256);
```

For CONST_VEC the lower bound is CONST_VEC'FIRST = POSITIVE'-FIRST = 1, and CONST_VEC'LAST = 3. However, THIS_VEC'FIRST = 8 and THIS_VEC'LAST = 10. Note that

```
THIS_VEC := CONST_VEC; -- Legal
```

The use of named aggregates combined with descriptive names can be a useful documentation device for initializing tables of values. The following declarations initialize the location and available weapons and aircraft at some airbases.

```
type COORD         is range −10_000 .. 10_000;
type ORDNANCE      is (BOMBS, ROCKETS, GUN_PACKS,
                       CRUISE_MIS);
type AIRCRAFT      is (A_1, A_2, A_3);
type BASES         is (A_BASE, B_BASE);
type STOCKPILE     is array(ORDNANCE) of INTEGER range 0 ..
                       10_000;
type SQUADRON      is array(AIRCRAFT) of INTEGER range 0 .. 100;
type BASE_RECORD   is
  record
    X, Y        : COORD;
    WEAPONS  : STOCKPILE;
    AC_LEFT  : SQUADRON;
  end record;
type BASE_STATUS is array (BASES) of BASE_RECORD;

BASE_IS : BASE_STATUS :=
(A_BASE => (X => 100, Y => 1000, WEAPONS =>(
    BOMBS => 1000,
    ROCKETS => 900,
    GUN_PACKS => 200,
    CRUISE_MIS => 400), AC_LEFT =>(
      A_1 => 10,
      A_2 => 30,
      A_3 => 2))),
B_BASE => (200, 400, (5000, 2000, 1000, 1000), (20, 90, 30)));
```

This is a complex initialization that is worthy of study. It reads "(For A__ BASE use (for X use 100, for Y use 1000, for WEAPONS use (for BOMBS use 1000, for . . .), for AC__LEFT use (for A__1 use 10, for . . .))), for *B* __BASE use (. . . (. . .), (. . .)))." So at A__BASE, the ROCKETS index of the WEAPONS array of the BASE__RECORD accesses the value 900. The equivalent value for the B__BASE index of BASE__IS is 2000. After the format has been established by use of named aggregates for A__BASE, positional notation is more concise and easier to read for B__BASE.

18.3 *ONE-DIMENSIONAL ARRAYS*

Ada provides a number of special operations on one-dimensional arrays in order to make them simple to use and to provide for more readable programs.

18.3.1 *Slices*

Assigning part of one array to part of another can be accomplished through iteration.

```
for I in 2 .. 3 loop
   HIS__VEC(I) := THEIR__VEC(I);
end loop;
```

Of course, the desired parts of the array to be assigned don't always fit so well.

```
for I in 1 .. 3 loop
   THEIR__VEC(I)   := HER__VEC(I + 27);
   HIS__VEC(I)     := THEIR__VEC(I + 3);
end loop;
```

Ada provides for the assignment of array slices to more easily accommodate such instances. The slices must be of the same length.

```
HIS__VEC(2 .. 3)     := THEIR__VEC(2 .. 3);
THEIR__VEC(1 .. 3)   := HER__VEC(28 .. 30);
HIS__VEC(1 .. 3)     := THEIR__VEC(4 .. 6);
```

The bounds of the array slices can be dynamic, as in

```
HIS_VEC(K .. L) := THEIR_VEC(M .. N);    -- Slices still must be same
                                         -- length
```

In fact, the bounds can be any expression. Of course, run-time checks will be performed to ensure all constraints are satisfied.

Array slices are applicable only to one-dimensional arrays. Of course, operations are permitted on the one-dimensional arrays which are components of other structures.

```
type VEC_LIST is array (1 .. 10) of VECTOR(1 .. 100);
VL_1, VL_2 : VEC_LIST;
```

Then we may have

```
for I in VEC_LIST ' RANGE loop
  VL_1(I) (2 .. 4) := VL_2(I) (8 .. 10);
end loop;
```

since VL_1(I) and VL_2(I) are each of type VECTOR.

18.3.2 *Catenation*

The catenation operator introduced in chapter 10 for strings is actually generally applicable to one-dimensional arrays.

```
THEIR_VEC := HIS_VEC & HER_VEC;
```

18.3.3 *Ordering*

The operators to test for ordering, $<$, $<=$, $>$, and $>=$, are applicable to one-dimensional arrays of discrete types. They were previously discussed for strings. If we define

```
type INT_VEC is array(1 .. 4) of INTEGER;
IV_1, IV_2 : INT_VEC;
```

and assign values as

```
IV__1 := (1, 2, 6, 0);
IV__2 := (1, 2, 5, 10);
```

the comparison

```
IV__2 < IV__1
```

produces a result of TRUE. The comparison proceeds element by element until there is a difference. In this case 5 is less than 6, so IV__2 is less than IV__1.

18.3.4 *Logical Operators*

The logical operators, **and, or, xor,** and **not**, can be applied to Boolean arrays, component by component, with the expected results. The following declarations provide some array objects to illustrate the functioning of logical operators and also show the declaration for a **constant** array. Such an array, like **constant** single elements, cannot be modified.

```
declare
   type LOGICAL__ARRAY is array (1 .. 3) of BOOLEAN;
   ALWAYS     : constant LOGICAL __ARRAY := (TRUE, TRUE, TRUE);
   NEVER      : constant LOGICAL __ARRAY := (FALSE, FALSE,
                                                       FALSE);
   MAYBE      : LOGICAL __ARRAY := (TRUE, FALSE, TRUE);
   COULDBE  : LOGICAL __ARRAY := (TRUE, TRUE, FALSE);
   RESULT     : LOGICAL __ARRAY;
begin
   RESULT := not ALWAYS;                -- FALSE, FALSE, FALSE
   if RESULT = NEVER . . . end if;      -- TRUE
   RESULT := MAYBE or NEVER;            -- TRUE, FALSE, TRUE
   RESULT := MAYBE and COULDBE;         -- TRUE, FALSE, FALSE
   RESULT := MAYBE xor COULDBE;         -- FALSE, TRUE, TRUE
end;
```

For **and, or,** and **xor** the two arrays must both be of the same type and have the same number of components.

Exercise__18

Modify PROGRAM__10 so that the procedure is not limited to arrays of size 10. It should be able to handle an array of any INTEGER size.

Program__18

```
with TEXT__IO; use TEXT__IO;
procedure PROGRAM__18 is
  type FLEX__ARRAY is array(INTEGER range < >) of FLOAT;
  A : FLEX__ARRAY(-6 .. 6);
  package IO is new FLOAT__IO (FLOAT); use IO;

  procedure READ__FLEX__ARRAY(P : out FLEX__ARRAY) is
    LOCAL__P : FLEX__ARRAY;
    SUM : FLOAT := 0.0;
    AVERAGE : FLOAT;
    NUMBER__OF__ELEMENTS : INTEGER;
  begin
    for I in P'RANGE loop
      GET(LOCAL__P(I));
      P(I) := LOCAL__P(I);
      SUM := SUM + LOCAL__P(I);
    end loop;
    NUMBER__OF__ELEMENTS := P'LENGTH;
    AVERAGE := SUM / FLOAT(NUMBER__OF__ELEMENTS);
    PUT(AVERAGE);
    for J in P'RANGE loop
      P(J) := LOCAL__P(J) + AVERAGE;
    end loop;
  end READ__FLEX__ARRAY;
begin -- PROGRAM__18
  READ__FLEX__ARRAY(A);
  for K in A'FIRST .. A'LAST loop
    PUT(A(K)); NEW__LINE;
  end loop;
end PROGRAM__18;
```

Discussion__18

Two major things must be done to make the program more flexible. The first is to establish a type declaration with an unconstrained array definition. That is the purpose of the FLEX_ARRAY declaration. The declaration of the object "A" then uses the unconstrained array definition with index constraints.

The other major consideration is to use the array attributes to define the operations on the array. The procedure READ_FLEX_ARRAY uses the 'RANGE and 'LENGTH attributes to establish the number of iterations of the **for loop** and to determine the NUMBER_OF_ELEMENTS. Since the attributes are those of the array object "P" (the formal parameter), the procedure is quite general. Any array of type FLEX_ARRAY may be used as an actual parameter (with any INTEGER index constraints), and the formal parameter P will have the appropriate index bounds and the appropriate attributes.

The main program uses an alternate form of stating the range of the index of the aray. Of course "P" is not visible here and it uses the attributes of the array object "A".

KEYS TO UNDERSTANDING

▶ Unconstrained array types allow for general-purpose subprograms with variable length arrays. Use of attributes is valuable.

▶ Array aggregates and slices are useful.

▶ Special capabilities, including logical operations, are provided for one-dimensional arrays.

19

Records

Objective: to present additional Ada features related to records

Ada provides extended use of the discriminant part of the record and for initialization of components including the discriminant. It also allows aggregate assignment to records and forbids unsafe or type-incompatible operations.

The primary extension of the use of records in Ada is to increase the uses of the discriminant. Earlier we saw the discriminant used, as in Pascal, to create a variant record. A discriminant can also be used in other ways to make a record more adaptable. Before examining discriminants, we will look at some additional factors related to the declaration of records.

19.1 *RECORD DECLARATIONS*

The definition of a record type is permitted to contain default values for components. For example,

```
type COMPLEX is
  record
    RE : FLOAT := 0.0;
    IM : FLOAT := 0.0;
  end record;
-- Both components of every complex record are initialized to 0
```

A record type with a default value is the only way in which objects of a type are allowed to have default initialization values. Consider another example,

```ada
type GARMENT is (SUIT, SPORT, JACKET);
type SLACKS is (SUIT, CASUAL);      -- Note SUIT is overloaded
type ATTIRE is
  record
    COAT         : GARMENT := SPORT;
    TROUSERS     : SLACKS   := CASUAL;
  end record;
CLOTHING : ATTIRE;                       -- The initial set of clothes
                                         -- is informal
```

The value of the components may be changed by an explicit initialization when an object is declared. For example,

```ada
ROOT : COMPLEX := (1.0, 1.0);
```

A record may not contain a constant declaration, as shown here,

```ada
type X is
  record
    COAT : constant GARMENT := SUIT; -- Illegal
    . . .
  end record;
```

but a data object of a record type can be a constant:

```ada
DRESS_UP : constant ATTIRE := (SUIT, SUIT);
```

Or, using named notation for clarity:

```ada
DRESS_UP : constant ATTIRE := (COAT => SUIT,
                               TROUSERS => SUIT);
```

19.2 *DISCRIMINANTS*

Recall in chapter 11 that we defined records with discriminants as variant records. For example, we had

```
type ITEM is (BOOK, TAPE);
type FILE__CARD (NEW__BUY : ITEM := BOOK) is
  record
    COST : FLOAT;
    case NEW__BUY is
      when BOOK =>
        AUTHOR            : STRING (1 .. 15);
      when TAPE =>
        TIME__TO__PLAY   : INTEGER range 1 .. 60;
    end case;
  end record;
```

This allowed us to mix records of books and tapes in a single file. It might also be desirable to use the discriminant to modify other parts of the record.

The discriminant may be used to specify a characteristic, such as the length of an array, of other components of the record. For example,

```
MAX : constant INTEGER := 1000;
subtype BUF__SIZE is INTEGER range 0 .. MAX;
type BUFFER (SIZE : BUF__SIZE := 100) is
-- The default value for SIZE is 100. Maximum is 1000
  record
    POS       : BUF__SIZE := 0;
    VALUE    : STRING (1 .. SIZE);
  end record;
MY__BUF  : BUFFER (20);              -- SIZE = 20
HIS__BUF  : BUFFER;                   -- SIZE = default of 100
HER__BUF : BUFFER (SIZE => 200);   -- SIZE = 200
```

The CONSTRAINED attribute applies to objects of types with discriminants. It is BOOLEAN, with its value dependent on whether a constraint was applied to the object when declared.

```
MY__BUF'CONSTRAINED  = TRUE
HIS__BUF'CONSTRAINED  = FALSE
```

If the object is 'CONSTRAINED, the discriminant value cannot be changed.

```
MY__BUF := (SIZE    => 7; -- Illegal size change
            POS     => 1;
            VALUE   => "Illegal");
```

If 'CONSTRAINED is FALSE, the discriminant and hence the SIZE of the object can be changed.

```
HIS__BUF := (SIZE    => 5;
             POS     => 1;
             VALUE   => "Legal");
```

Only one discriminant is permitted, but it may be used more than once in the record. For example,

```
type MATRIX is array (POSITIVE range <>, POSITIVE range <>) of
                   FLOAT;
type AREA(SIDE : INTEGER) is
  record
    SQUARE : MATRIX(1 .. SIDE, 1 .. SIDE);
  end record;
FARM : AREA(100); -- 100 by 100 units
```

The fact that SIDE did not have an initial value implies that objects of type AREA must be constrained. Thus,

```
NO__FARM : AREA; -- Illegal
```

19.3 AGGREGATE ASSIGNMENT

We have used the aggregate assignment to provide values for all components of a record, as in

```
CLOTHING := (JACKET, CASUAL);
```

We can use aggregate assignment to change the value of the discriminant. Assigning a complete record value is the only way to change a discriminant, and of course the assignment of the components of the record must be consistent with the discriminant. Recall that type FILE__CARD has a discriminant NEW__BUY with a default value of BOOK. For the declaration

```
    LIBRARY__REC : FILE__CARD;
```

we can have the assignments

```
    LIBRARY__REC.COST        := 15.98;
    LIBRARY__REC.AUTHOR      := "BLAISE PASCAL      ";
```

but not

```
    LIBRARY__REC.TIME__TO__PLAY := 45; -- Illegal
```

If we wish to make LIBRARY__REC a record of a tape, we can do so by

```
    LIBRARY__REC := (TAPE, 6.95, 45);
```

The net result of the Ada approach to assignment of values to components of discriminated records is that we are guaranteed that the record types and values are consistent.

Exercise__19

Write a program to define discriminated records, both constrained and unconstrained, in which the discriminant specifies the length of a component of type STRING. Use the unconstrained record to allow for assignment of strings of various lengths to the component. This is similar to the text example with type BUFFER and object MY__BUF.

Program__19

```
with TEXT__IO; use TEXT__IO;
procedure PROGRAM__19 is
   subtype STRING__LENGTH is INTEGER range 0 .. 100;
   type VARIABLE__STRING(LENGTH : STRING__LENGTH := 10) is
     record
        LETTERS : STRING(1 .. LENGTH);
     end record;
   RIGID      : VARIABLE__STRING(20);
   FLEXIBLE  : VARIABLE__STRING;
begin -- PROGRAM__19
   RIGID.LETTERS := "String of 20 chars      ";
   PUT__LINE(RIGID.LETTERS);
   FLEXIBLE := (8, "HI THERE");
   PUT__LINE(FLEXIBLE.LETTERS);
   FLEXIBLE.LETTERS := "CHANGEIT";
   PUT__LINE(FLEXIBLE.LETTERS);
   FLEXIBLE := (22, "QUITE FLEXIBLE INDEED!");
   PUT__LINE(FLEXIBLE.LETTERS);
end PROGRAM__19;
```

```
String of 20 chars
HI THERE
CHANGEIT
QUITE FLEXIBLE INDEED!
```

Discussion__19

VARIABLE__STRING is a discriminated record type with a discriminant
LENGTH. The type of LENGTH is STRING__LENGTH, a subtype of
INTEGER, and its default value is 10. The declaration of a record object, such
as RIGID, that specifies a value for the discriminant is then constrained: its
LENGTH cannot be changed dynamically. If no value for the discriminant is
given in the record object declaration, as in FLEXIBLE, the initial value is the
default value of 10. The record is unconstrained, however, and the LENGTH
may be changed. If no default value is provided for the discriminant, the object
declaration must be constrained.

   For an unconstrained record, the only way to change the value of the
discriminant is with an aggregate assignment that also provides legal values for
the other components of the record.

Keys to Understanding

▶ The definition of a record type may contain default values for components.

▶ Discriminants may be used in several ways to allow flexible record definitions.

▶ Protection for consistency of types is provided by changing a discriminant only when the entire record value is changed by use of an aggregate assignment.

20

Pointers

Objective: to provide further discussion of pointers in Ada

To understand how pointers work in Ada, little need be added to the material in chapter 12. Ada handles pointers in a precise way, allowing storage to be reclaimed and avoiding problems with dangling references. Access types may be private or limited private in order to control their use. Access objects can point to objects of any type in Ada, including tasks. Access objects may be returned by a function and be passed as subprogram parameters. Allocation may raise the STORAGE_ERROR exception, and the programmer can reserve storage using the 'STORAGE_SIZE attribute. Pointers can be used effectively with the other structured types to create complex data structures appropriate to the application being programmed.

Key to Understanding

▶ Ada pointer handling is similar to other languages but is also well integrated into Ada features.

PART 4

ADVANCED FEATURES

Parts 2 and 3 presented algorithmic Ada. The features presented will not solve the problems that prompted the development of Ada. As presented thus far, Ada has considerable similarity to Pascal. However, as previously pointed out, Ada is not Pascal; Ada is Ada. Programming style in Ada is likely to be quite different from programming style in Pascal. Design style will certainly be very different. Ada is a design language. Pascal is a language for writing small programs, while Ada is a language for designing and creating large software systems—for programming in the large. However, there is as yet no consensus as to how to teach the use of Ada for programming large systems. The methods of using Ada for design, as a program or system design language, are still under development. Parts 2 and 3 presented Ada as a modern, block-structured language suitable for general-purpose programming. The introduction to the algorithmic aspects of Ada has established the foundation for those features that will allow Ada to be used for the design and creation of large software systems.

The advanced features are those that *will* solve the problems for which Ada was designed. Some of the concepts are easy; some will be quite difficult for those who have not been previously exposed to them. Part 4 discusses the advanced features but does not provide an exposition of new design ideas. The intent is to introduce the Ada features, indicate how they might be effectively used, alert the reader to the fact that new design approaches are likely to develop, and demonstrate that Ada will support these new approaches.

21

Packages

Objective: to describe the capabilities of the Ada package and to introduce the notion of the abstract data type

This chapter amplifies the discussion of chapters 3, 4 and 14 and provides additional discussion of the package. It introduces the notion of the abstract data type and presents a new feature, the **limited private** type, which provides complete control over the operations allowed on data.

21.1 *THE USE OF PACKAGES*

The usual notion of a package is exemplified by a mathematical, statistical, or graphics package. Ada fully supports this notion of a package in whch related subprograms, usually sharing local data and providing a common service, are grouped together. The careful separation of specification from implementation in packages makes Ada particularly valuable in supporting a software components industry. By incorporating reusable software components specified as packages, it should be possible to construct major parts of large software systems out of standard parts, much as we now construct electronic hardware out of well-specified hardware components. The Ada generic capability, discussed in chapter 23, holds particular promise for the creation of reusable software components because it allows components to be fine tuned or parameterized to meet user requirements.

A second way to use packages is to group together declarations of related variables, constants, and types. To be suitably packaged, such declarations would be closely related to each other and accessed by subprograms needing to share the information. This use of packages in Ada is similar to the use of named common in FORTRAN. In fact, if we use the FORTRAN 77 PARAMETER statement for constants, BLOCK DATA for initialization, and (in most FORTRAN implementations) INCLUDE to ensure a single specification, we can use named common in a manner very similar in concept to this use of the package. Ada, however, allows greater control of data visibility (through the use of nested packages) and easier access to a name space (through the **use** clause and selected component notation).

The third and most innovative way to use packages is to create encapsulated or abstract data types: types for which the name and applicable operations are declared, but for which all details of structure, representation, and implementation are hidden. In this case the user of the package neither knows nor cares how the operations are implemented.

The importance of each of the three general forms of packages—grouping of subprograms, grouping of declarations, and encapsulation of data types—is that they are valuable for programming in the large, that is, for the design and implementation of large software systems. The package can be thought of as a wall around the information it contains, with some of the declarations exposed through a window. The window for the grouping of related variables, similar to FORTRAN's named common, is very large: all the declarations can be accessed. On the other hand the window for encapsulated data types is quite small: only names and operations are available. The ability to control the degree of information hiding, and to control the visibility of both processes and data structures, is likely to lead to a radical restructuring of the way in which large systems are designed. Recently developed design methods based on the principle of hiding design decisions, especially those related to data structures, will probably influence future Ada design methods. A real understanding of how to effectively use packages for design of large systems and how the package will influence design methodologies will come about only by actually implementing several real-time systems in Ada.

21.2 *PRIVATE TYPES*

We have defined a type as a set of values and the operations allowed on those values. The predefined and derived types have a large number of defined or inherited values and operations. Frequently the characteristics of the system being designed can limit the allowable range of values. Ada accommodates this situation by the use of subtypes with constraints. Furthermore, certain operations are frequently unnecessary, illogical, or even dangerous for certain types of objects. Ada accommodates this situation by the use of **private** types.

In chapter 3 we discovered that **package** BLOCKS allowed some illogical operations, such as division of a length by a width. To prevent such operations we defined package PRIVATE_BLOCKS, shown again in the following example.

```
package PRIVATE_BLOCKS is
    type LENGTH        is private;
    type WIDTH         is private;
    type AREA          is private;
    type PERIMETER     is private;
    function "*"(L : LENGTH; W : WIDTH)        return AREA;
    function BOUNDARY(L : LENGTH; W : WIDTH)   return PERIMETER;
    procedure GET(L : out LENGTH);
    procedure GET(W : out WIDTH);
private
    -- Types described as private must be defined here
    -- These type definitions are unavailable to users of the package
    type MEASURE      is range 0 .. INTEGER'LAST;
    type LENGTH       is new MEASURE;
    type WIDTH        is new MEASURE;
    type AREA         is new MEASURE;
    type PERIMETER    is new MEASURE;
end PRIVATE_BLOCKS;

package body PRIVATE_BLOCKS is
-- Implements functions and procedures defined in the package specification
end PRIVATE_BLOCKS;
```

By declaring the types LENGTH, WIDTH, AREA, and PERIMETER as **private**, we restrict the allowable operations to assignment and comparison for equality/inequality. The user of the package knows nothing about the internal structure or representation of these types; the declarations following the **private** clause are conceptually part of the package body and are therefore hidden from the user. Even the range of allowable values is restricted and unknown to the user of the package. An assignment such as

```
LEN__1 := 2; -- Illegal. LEN__1 is private, not an integer type
```

is illegal since, within SAFE__GEOM (see below), LEN__1 has lost all relationship to INTEGER. It could be FLOAT or CHARACTER, or an array or a record. Indeed, as far as SAFE__GEOM knows, LENGTH could be an array of records, while WIDTH could be a CHARACTER. The "*" operator is defined to operate on WIDTH and LENGTH and return an AREA, which also could have any internal structure. It is critical to remember that the **private** part *is not visible to the user of the package.* Procedure SAFE__GEOM has no knowledge of the underlying representation of LENGTH, WIDTH, AREA, and PERIMETER. They are not an integer type, they are a **private** type.

```
with PRIVATE__BLOCKS; use PRIVATE__BLOCKS;
procedure SAFE__GEOM is
     LEN__1, LEN__2   : LENGTH;
     WID              : WIDTH;
     AR               : AREA;
     PER              : PERIMETER;
begin
     . . .
     GET(LEN__1); GET(WID);
     LEN__2  := LEN__1;
     AR      := LEN__2 * WID;
     PER     := BOUNDARY(LEN, WID);
     LEN__2  := LENGTH(WID);            -- Illegal. No conversion for
                                        -- private types
     LEN__1  := 2;                      -- Illegal. Different types
     LEN__1  := LEN__1 * LEN__2;        -- Illegal. No "*" for type
                                        -- LENGTH
     LEN__1  := 2 * LEN__2;             -- Illegal. Different types
     LEN__1  := LEN__1 - LEN__2;        -- Illegal. No "-" for type
                                        -- LENGTH

     . . .
end SAFE__GEOM;
```

The package PRIVATE—BLOCKS is providing *types* that can be used to declare objects. The package provides the means to operate on objects of the given types. It can be viewed as a type manager. An alternate use of a package could be to provide an *object* that may be modified by using procedures. Such a package could be viewed as an object manager. The example in Chapter 23 (23.4) illustrates an object manager.

    Here is another example of a type manager. Rational numbers are ratios of integers: 3/4 , 9/10 , 4/17 , and so on. Operations on rational numbers should produce rational numbers. Numbers such as 3/4 , 9/12 , and 21/28 are equal since when the denominators are made the same, the numerators also will be the same. An early version of the LRM defined the following package for rational numbers:

```
package RATIONAL —NUMBERS is
  type RATIONAL is
    record
      NUMERATOR    : INTEGER;
      DENOMINATOR  : INTEGER range 1 .. INTEGER ' LAST;
    end record;
  function EQUAL (X, Y : RATIONAL) return BOOLEAN;
  function "+" (X, Y : RATIONAL) return RATIONAL;
  function "*" (X, Y : RATIONAL) return RATIONAL;
end;

package body RATIONAL—NUMBERS is

  procedure SAME—DENOMINATOR (X, Y : in out RATIONAL) is
  begin
    -- Reduces X and Y to the same denominator
  end;

  function EQUAL(X, Y : RATIONAL) return BOOLEAN is
    U, V : RATIONAL;
  begin
    U := X;
    V := Y;
    SAME—DENOMINATOR (U, V);
    return U.NUMERATOR = V.NUMERATOR;
  end EQUAL;

  function "+" (X, Y : RATIONAL) return RATIONAL is . . . end "+";

  function "*" (X, Y : RATIONAL) return RATIONAL is . . . end "*";
end RATIONAL —NUMBERS;
```

The preceding package defines the new type **RATIONAL** but leaves its structure available to the user of the package. A procedure using the package might be

```
use RATIONAL __NUMBERS;
procedure USE __RN is
  A, B : RATIONAL
begin
  A.NUMERATOR    := 3;
  A.DENOMINATOR := 7;
  B.NUMERATOR    := 5;
  B.DENOMINATOR := A.DENOMINATOR;
  A := (9, 10);      -- Using aggregate assignment
  A := A + B;
  A := A * B;
  B := A;
end USE__RN;
```

The individual operations on the individual components of the records A and B are necessary to create the rational numbers. They are not very natural, however, and allow undesirable user visibility into the structure of what could be a more abstract data type. A stronger encapsulation of **RATIONAL** is

```
package RATIONAL__NUMBERS is
  type RATIONAL is private;
  function EQUAL (X, Y : RATIONAL) return BOOLEAN;
  function "+" (X, Y : RATIONAL) return RATIONAL;
  function "*" (X, Y : RATIONAL) return RATIONAL;
  function "/" (N : INTEGER; D : POSITIVE) return RATIONAL;
private
  type RATIONAL is
    record
      NUMERATOR    : INTEGER;
      DENOMINATOR : POSITIVE;
    end record;
end;
```

In this case the package body would contain

```
function "/" (N : INTEGER; D : POSITIVE) return RATIONAL is
   R : RATIONAL;
begin
   R.NUMERATOR := N;
   R.DENOMINATOR := D;
   return R;
end "/"; -- To create rational numbers
```

With these definitions a better way to create and use a rational number is

```
A :=  3/7 ;
B :=  5/7 ;
B := 5/A.DENOMINATOR; -- Illegal. DENOMINATOR is not visible
A := B;
```

A.DENOMINATOR is illegal, since the components of the record are no longer available to the using procedure.

Notice that assignment, as in **A := B**, is still a permitted operation, as is comparison for equality. The explicit definition of an equality function (EQUAL) was necessary only to account for the fact that the characteristics of rational numbers are different from records in general.

Sometimes we would like to forbid the usual "=" operator for records and declare

```
function "=" (X, Y : RATIONAL) return BOOLEAN;
```

rather than declaring the function name of EQUAL. Then, for type RATIONAL all comparisons for equality would use the process we defined.

Such security and control over "=" can be achieved by using **limited private** types. The control over "=" is a by-product of the improved control over all operations.

21.3 *LIMITED PRIVATE TYPES*

The limited private type not only hides the structure of the type and forbids most operations, it forbids all operations except those explicitly provided for in the visible part of the encapsulating package. Therefore, even "=", "/=", and, most important, ":=" are not allowed. The fact that assignment is a forbidden operation makes limited private types ideal for the issuing of *keys* that are not allowed to be copied.

Suppose that a small company wishes to issue badges to its employees to allow access to the company facilities by using a badge reader to unlock the door. It would be desirable to not allow the copying of badges after they have been encoded or issued. However, usual methods do allow copying (assignment), as in

```
type PUBLIC_BADGE is range 0 .. 100;
MY_BADGE, COPY_BADGE, YOUR_BADGE : PUBLIC_BADGE;
. . .

. . .
ISSUE(MY_BADGE);                        -- Issue a valid badge
COPY_BADGE := MY_BADGE;                 -- Undesirable
YOUR_BADGE := COPY_BADGE;               -- Undesirable
```

If the type BADGE is declared as private, its internal structure will be hidden, but it still may be copied. The result is that multiple copies of a badge are allowed to exist, and the company has lost control over who has access to its offices. The **limited private** type gives greater control over the process of issuing and using badges. It forbids assignment or comparison outside the defining package. For example,

```
package BADGE_CONTROL is
  type WORK_SPACE is . . . -- Something appropriate
  type BADGE is limited private;
  procedure ISSUE (B : in out BADGE);
  procedure WORK (B : in BADGE; OFFICE: out WORK_SPACE);
private
  type LEGAL_NUMBER is range 0 .. INTEGER'LAST;
  type BADGE is
    record
      NUMBER : LEGAL_NUMBER := 0;
    end record;
end;

package body BADGE_CONTROL is
  LAST_NUMBER : LEGAL_NUMBER := 0;

  procedure ISSUE (B : in out BADGE) is
```

```
  begin
    if B.NUMBER = 0 then      -- Issue the next number
      LAST_NUMBER := LAST_NUMBER + 1;
      B.NUMBER := LAST_NUMBER;
    end if;
  end ISSUE;

  procedure WORK(B : in BADGE; OFFICE : out WORK_SPACE) is
  begin
    if B.NUMBER = 0 then
      -- Log invalid access attempt
      -- Deny office space
    else
      -- Log the valid entry
      -- Provide office space
    end if;
  end WORK;
end BADGE_CONTROL;
```

The package BADGE_CONTROL has a number of interesting features. Since BADGE is limited private, its complete type definition must be provided in the **private** part of the package specification. Remember that this private part is conceptually part of the package body and is not available to the user of the package. Since it is limited private, the assignment operation is not available outside the defining package. Some implications of this for procedures using the package are

- Declarations cannot include initialization:
  MY_BADGE : BADGE := . . .   -- Illegal
- Parameters cannot have default values:
  procedure B_PROC(B:BADGE := . . .   -- Illegal
- Constants of the limited private type cannot be declared:
  type C_BADGE **is constant** BADGE := . . .   -- Illegal

The restrictions against assignment also forbid **out** or **in out** mode for limited private types in subprograms external to the package that defines the limited private type. Subprograms having parameters of any mode are allowed within the defining package.

All objects declared to be of type BADGE will have a value of zero for the NUMBER component. The zero value represents an invalid badge, one for which no number has yet been issued. This default initial value for the type is possible only by the use of record components.

Procedures ISSUE and WORK take advantage of the easy way to recognize whether a badge needs to be encoded (in ISSUE) or is valid (in WORK). These two procedures represent the only allowable operations on objects of type BADGE.

A procedure to use the capabilities provided by BADGE__CONTROL might look like this:

```
use BADGE__CONTROL;
procedure GO__TO__WORK is
  MY__BADGE, COPY__BADGE, YOUR__BADGE : BADGE;
  DESK : WORK__SPACE;
begin
  ISSUE(MY__BADGE);
  ISSUE(YOUR__BADGE);
  ISSUE(MY__BADGE);                       -- Will not receive a new
                                          -- number
  COPY__BADGE := YOUR__BADGE;             -- Illegal
  if MY__BADGE = YOUR__BADGE then         -- Illegal
    . . .
  WORK(MY__BADGE, DESK);                  -- OK. Gets a desk
  WORK(COPY__BADGE, DESK);                -- Invalid. Does not get a
                                          -- desk
end GO__TO__WORK;
```

By using the limited private type we can create very secure programs with control over replication of keys or passwords. BADGE is an abstract data type. The definition of the package provides complete control over the allowable values and the allowable operations on objects of the type. Although we will not demonstrate the method here, it is possible to define an "=" (equality) operator for limited private types. This might have been desirable for the package RATIONAL__NUMBERS, previously discussed.

Exercise__21

Create a package to implement the abstract data type BED. Objects of type BED are to have two (externally visible) states: messy or not messy. The internal representation is not necessarily limited to two states. There are three (only three) operations allowed on objects of type BED. INITIALIZE establishes an initial value for the bed. MAKE cleans up a bed. SLEEP provides rest, when the bed is not messy. SLEEP has the property that if the bed is not messy, it sets an object of type CONDITION (with possible values of RESTED, TIRED) to RESTED. If the bed is messy, SLEEP does nothing. SLEEP may make the bed messy, depending on criteria specified within the package but hidden from the user. The BOOLEAN function MESSY can be used to determine the state of the BED. That is, MESSY is provided to the user of the package and is specified and implemented by the package. It is in addition to the three operations that may change the state of BED. Write a program to use the package.

Program__21

```
package SLEEP__TIGHT is
  type BED is limited private;
  type CONDITION is (RESTED, TIRED);
  procedure INITIALIZE(B : out BED);
  procedure SLEEP(B : in out BED; C : in out CONDITION);
  procedure MAKE (B : out BED);
  function MESSY(B : BED) return BOOLEAN;
private
  type BED is range 0 .. 6;
end;

with TEXT__IO; use TEXT__IO;
package body SLEEP__TIGHT is

  procedure INITIALIZE(B : out BED) is
  begin
    PUT__LINE("In INITIALIZE");
    B := 0;
  end INITIALIZE;

  procedure SLEEP(B : in out BED; C : in out CONDITION) is
  begin
    PUT__LINE("In SLEEP");
    if B < BED'LAST then
      C := RESTED;
      B := B + 1;
    end if;
  end SLEEP;

  procedure MAKE(B : out BED) is
```

```
    begin
      PUT_LINE("In MAKE");
      B := 0;
    end MAKE;

    function MESSY(B : BED) return BOOLEAN is
    begin
      PUT_LINE("In MESSY");
      if B = BED'LAST then
        return TRUE;
      else
        return FALSE;
      end if;
    end MESSY;
  end SLEEP_TIGHT;


  with SLEEP_TIGHT, TEXT_IO; use SLEEP_TIGHT, TEXT_IO;
  procedure PROGRAM_21 is
    FIRM_BED : BED;
    CAPABILITY : CONDITION := RESTED;
  begin
    INITIALIZE(FIRM_BED);
    for I in 1 .. 13 loop
      PUT_LINE("In loop in PROGRAM_21");
      CAPABILITY := TIRED;
      if MESSY(FIRM_BED) then
        MAKE(FIRM_BED);
      end if;
      SLEEP(FIRM_BED, CAPABILITY);
      if CAPABILITY = RESTED then
        PUT_LINE("Now rested");
      end if;
    end loop;
  end PROGRAM_21;


  Begin Ada execution

  In INITIALIZE
  In loop in PROGRAM_21
  In MESSY
  In SLEEP
  Now rested
```

In loop in PROGRAM__21
In MESSY
In SLEEP
Now rested
In loop in PROGRAM__21
In MESSY
In SLEEP
Now rested
In loop in PROGRAM__21
In MESSY
In SLEEP
Now rested
In loop in PROGRAM__21
In MESSY
In SLEEP
Now rested
In loop in PROGRAM__21
In MESSY
In SLEEP
Now rested
In loop in PROGRAM__21
In MESSY
⟶ in MAKE
In SLEEP
Now rested
In loop in PROGRAM__21
In MESSY
In SLEEP
Now rested
In loop in PROGRAM__21
In MESSY
In SLEEP
Now rested
In loop in PROGRAM__21
In MESSY
In SLEEP
Now rested
In loop in PROGRAM__21
In MESSY
In SLEEP
Now rested

```
In loop in PROGRAM__21
In MESSY
In SLEEP
Now rested
In loop in PROGRAM__21
In MESSY
In MAKE
In SLEEP
Now rested
```

Discussion__21

The visible part of the package defines the type BED, a type CONDITION (that will be used to observe the effect of SLEEP), and the required subprograms. The private part of the package is not visible to the user of the package, and it is illegal to attempt to take advantage of the fact that the representation of BED is an integer type. Internal to the package, objects of type BED have seven states. The external view is that of only two states: messy and not messy.

The package body implements the required subprograms. INITIALIZE sets its parameter, of type BED, to zero. (We could also have used the attribute BED'FIRST for ease of later changes.) The actual type of BED is known in the package body. INITIALIZE and MAKE are the same in this package, but of course they need not be, and we may later wish for the flexibility to initialize to something other than zero. SLEEP "uses" the bed if it is not already at a value of 6, using the 'LAST attribute for flexibility for possible later changes. Using the bed involves changing the condition to RESTED. If the bed is messy, SLEEP silently does nothing. Of course, other decisions may have been made, but here SLEEP assumes that the user of the bed has checked to ensure that it is not messy (or doesn't care). MESSY simply returns TRUE or FALSE depending on whether or not the bed is messy. Since the condition check has a BOOLEAN value, an alternate form for the body of MESSY is

return B = BED'LAST;

B = BED'LAST is a *condition,* with value TRUE or FALSE, which will be returned.

The body of procedure PROGRAM__21 simply uses the capabilities of the package, looping enough times to show the various calls. Inspection of the output shows that MAKE is called when it is needed.

By abstracting the type BED and concealing knowledge of its actual implementation, we are free to implement the type in any way. Since there is no change in the package specification, using programs need not be changed —not even recompiled—as a result of change of implementation.

For example, if we wished to ensure that all variables of the type were initialized, we could implement BED as a record.

```
type BED_USE is range 0 .. 6;
type BED is
  record
    USED : BED_USE := 0;
  end record;
```

A component of a record type such as BED may have a default initialization value. A declaration of an object of type BED automatically causes the component USED to be initialized to zero. Then the bodies of the procedures would become

```
SLEEP becomes
  if B.USED < BED'LAST then
    C        := RESTED;
    B.USED   := B.USED + 1;
  end if;

MAKE becomes
  B.USED := 0;

MESSY becomes
  return B.USED = BED'LAST;
```

We can also change the type of BED to completely diverge from the idea of a numeric type. For example, we might declare in the private part

```
type BED is new BOOLEAN;
```

The procedure bodies would then be

```
INITIALIZE and MAKE become
  B := TRUE;


SLEEP becomes
  if B then
    C := RESTED;
    B := FALSE;
  end if;


MESSY becomes
  return not B;
```

We would not have to change or recompile procedures using the package.

We made a decision in the procedure SLEEP that it would be silent about not providing any REST (of course, the status of the condition might be checked). An alternate approach might be to return an error indicator if an attempt was made to sleep in a messy bed.

```
procedure SLEEP(B       : in out BED;
                C       : in out CONDITION;
                FILTH   :    out BOOLEAN);
```

then the body would include

```
if B < BED'LAST then
  C     := RESTED;
  B     := B + 1;
  FILTH := FALSE;
else
  FILTH := TRUE;
end if;
```

Each call to SLEEP then might be followed by the check

```
if FILTH then
  -- Do something, likely including a call to MAKE
end if;
```

Exercise 24 in chapter 24 illustrates an alternate method of indicating errors.

Keys to Understanding

▶ The **package** is the Ada mechanism for structuring programs. It allows the specification of groups of logically related items.

▶ Packages may be used to group collections of type and data declarations, to group logically related subprograms, or to encapsulate data types.

▶ A data abstraction is an object (or set of objects) and a set of operations that characterize the the state and the behavior of the objects. The user of an encapsulated data type (a definition for an abstract object) is not aware of the underlying representation of the type.

▶ Since the package allows the definition of types, the declaration of objects of that type, and the specification and definition of operations (procedures and functions) on objects of the type, it is a natural mechanism for the specification of abstract data types.

▶ The **private** and **limited private** types are important to the creation of secure data abstractions.

22

Separate Compilation

Objective:	to describe Ada capabilities for separate compilation

The capability to separately compile different parts of a program and have the parts work together is essential for a language used by teams of programmers to create large software systems. The separately compiled parts of a program belong to a *program library*. It is vital that complete type checking be accomplished across the boundaries of compilation units in order to maintain the protection of strong typing. Ada provides these capabilities by supporting the package concepts discussed in the previous chapter. Ada supports both top-down and bottom-up development approaches. The following sections introduce ideas about compilation, outline a standard program, and show top-down and bottom-up approaches for implementing the program.

22.1 *GENERAL IDEAS*

An Ada program is made up of one or more compilation units. A compilation unit can be either a library unit or a secondary unit.

- •Library Unit
  - Subprogram declaration or body
  - Package declaration
  - Generic declaration or instantiation (generics are discussed in chapter 24)

- •Secondary Unit
  - Subprogram body
  - Package body
  - Subunit

All compilation units (library units and secondary units) of a program are contained in a program library. While declarations may be compiled separately from bodies, they must be compiled before or at the same time as the body. Library units must have unique names. Subunits are implementations of specifications that have been declared within other compilation units (parent units). The combination of the subunit name and the parent unit name must be unique.

There is a package, STANDARD, described in appendix C, which is part of the predefined language environment for all library units. Among other capabilities, STANDARD provides for input and output.

Access to packages within STANDARD, or to other library units, is gained by use of the **with** clause. To gain direct visibility into the package named in the **with** clause, the **use** clause is invoked. The **use** clause also provides direct visibility into a package compiled at the same time as the using subprogram.

The following example, from the LRM, illustrates **with** and **use** in the context of the predefined package STANDARD. The program consists of a single compilation unit, a procedure that prints the real roots of a quadratic equation. The predefined package TEXT__IO and a user-defined package REAL__OPERATIONS (containing the definition of the type REAL and of the packages REAL__IO and REAL__FUNCTIONS) are assumed to be already present in the program library.

```
with TEXT__IO, REAL __OPERATIONS; use REAL__OPERATIONS;
procedure QUADRATIC__EQUATION is
   A,B,C,D : REAL;
   use REAL__IO,            -- Defines GET and PUT for REAL
       TEXT__IO,            -- Defines PUT for strings and NEW__LINE
       REAL__FUNCTIONS;     -- Defines SQRT
```

```
begin
  GET(A); GET(B); GET(C);
  D := B**2 − 4.0*A*C;
  if D < 0.0 then
    PUT("Imaginary Roots.");
  else
    PUT("Real Roots : X1 = ");
    PUT((−B − SQRT(D))/(2.0*A)); PUT(" X2 = ");
    PUT((−B + SQRT(D))/(2.0*A));
  end if;
  NEW__LINE;
end QUADRATIC__EQUATION;
```

The language does not define how a subprogram is identified as a *main* program. Note that to accomplish input or output, it is necessary to invoke appropriate I/O routines from within **STANDARD.** Heretofore we have usually not done so for the sake of simplicity of exposition and illustration.

The capability to defer creation of a stub for the body of a subprogram, package, or task declared in a compilation unit is provided by the use of the **separate** clause. The body of a program unit may be declared, within a (parent) compilation unit, as **separate.** When the body is later compiled, it refers back to its parent unit, again using the separate clause, and compilation occurs in the context of the parent. For example,

```
procedure PARENT__UNIT is
  procedure SUB__UNIT is separate;
  . . .
begin
  . . .
  SUB__UNIT;
end PARENT__UNIT;
```

For a later compilation,

```
separate (PARENT__UNIT)
procedure SUB__UNIT is
. . .
begin
  . . .
end SUB__UNIT;
```

The use of **with** and **separate** clauses have implications for the order in which programs are compiled and for necessary recompilation. For one thing package specifications for all packages named in a **with** clause must be compiled prior to the unit that names them. For another, parent units must be compiled before subunits. Rules for recompilation can be quite complex; they are discussed in detail in the LRM.

22.2 *A STANDARD PROGRAM*

Let's look at a standard program that might be submitted as a single compilation unit, then see how top-down and bottom-up development of the program might differ. The program structure is shown in figure 22-1; a skeleton of the code is shown in figure 22-2. STUFF__IO is assumed to be a standard library package. The program is shown in the form of a block structured language as a single compilation unit.

The program is a general form of a typical application; it takes some information, processes it, and delivers it elsewhere. For other than trivial programs, a development strategy is required.

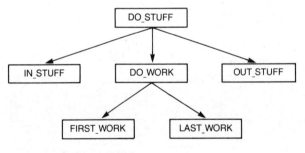

Figure 22-1   DO__STUFF Structure

22.3 *TOP-DOWN DEVELOPMENT*

Top-down development requires the ability to compile the top levels of a program before the subordinate units have been developed. It is convenient to be able to compile the top levels without having to explicitly create stubs of the subordinate levels. Figure 22-3 demonstrates how Ada supports top-down development for the example program. The subprogram specifications are declared as **separate.** The example shows only a simple declaration: the name of

```
with STUFF__IO; use STUFF__IO;
procedure DO__STUFF is
    -- Type declarations and
    -- other global information
    . . .
    procedure IN__STUFF is

    . . .
    end IN__STUFF;

    procedure DO__WORK is

        procedure FIRST__WORK is
        . . .
        end FIRST__WORK

        procedure LAST__WORK is
        . . .
        end LAST__WORK;
    . . .
    end DO__WORK;

    procedure OUT__STUFF is

    . . .
    end OUT__STUFF;
begin -- DO__STUFF
    IN__STUFF;
    DO__WORK;
    OUT__STUFF;
    . . .
end DO__STUFF;
```

Figure 22-2   Standard Program Skeleton

the procedure. In actual practice the specification would include the parameter list for subprograms and more information for packages and tasks.

```
procedure DO__STUFF is
    -- Type declarations and
    -- other global information
    . . .
    procedure IN__STUFF    is separate;
    procedure DO__WORK    is separate;
    procedure OUT__STUFF is separate;
begin -- DO__STUFF
    IN__STUFF;
    DO__WORK;
    OUT__STUFF;
    . . .
end DO__STUFF;
```

Figure 22-3   Top-Down Structure

```
with STUFF_IO; use STUFF_IO; -- Note that subunits may access library units
                             -- via with and use
separate (DO_STUFF)
procedure IN_STUFF is

. . .

end IN_STUFF;
```
                                    (a) IN_STUFF

```
separate (DO_STUFF)
procedure DO_WORK is

  procedure FIRST_WORK is

  . . .

  end FIRST_WORK;

  procedure LAST_WORK is

  . . .

  end LAST_WORK;
. . .
end DO_WORK;
```
                                    (b) DO_WORK

```
with STUFF_IO; use STUFF_IO;
separate (DO_WORK)
procedure OUT_STUFF is
. . .
end OUT_STUFF;
```
                                    (c) OUT_STUFF

Figure 22-4   Separate Subunits

Figure 22-4 shows how the subunits are tied back to the parent units. The dashed lines indicate the individual compilation units. The **separate** clause names the parent unit and indicates that the subunit is to be compiled in the context of the parent unit. The subunit compilation occurs exactly as if it were in the same physical place in the program text as its declaration. All type definitions, constraints, names of library units, and so forth, are visible to the subunit, just as though the subunit were compiled at the place of the declaration. Furthermore, the declaration of the subunit (which is an interface specification) is repeated in the separate compilation. For subprograms the specification is repeated; for packages and tasks each specification is validated and restrictions enforced during compilation of the body. The subunit declaration may mention additional library units in **with** and **use** clauses. Note that STUFF_IO was not mentioned in the declaration of DO_STUFF but instead is mentioned by IN_STUFF and OUT_STUFF.

In top-down development it is necessary to provide for additional levels of decomposition and separate compilation. This is illustrated for procedure DO_STUFF in figure 22-5. Note that the identification of the parent unit must be complete, as in DO_STUFF.DO_WORK. This is necessary because DO_WORK is not required to be a distinct name in a library. It is also desirable since it provides a complete path back to the top level of the program. Of course, FIRST_WORK could have subordinate procedures to be separately compiled, and so on. All previous rules apply to further compilations. For example, in figure 22-5 the

```
-- Type declarations and
-- other global information
```

in the top level of DO_STUFF are visible throughout all compilation units.

22.4 BOTTOM-UP DEVELOPMENT

Bottom-up development is generally based on library units written for general support that will be brought together for a specific function. We will illustrate bottom-up development with a modification of our example program (figure 22-2). The original program structure is probably not suitable for bottom-up

```
separate (DO_STUFF)
procedure DO_WORK is
  procedure FIRST_WORK is separate;
  procedure LAST_WORK  is separate;
begin
  . . .
end DO_WORK;
```
                           (a) DO_WORK

```
separate (DO_STUFF.DO_WORK)
procedure FIRST_WORK is

. . .
end FIRST_WORK;
```
                           (b) FIRST_WORK

```
separate (DO_STUFF.DO_WORK)
procedure LAST_WORK is

. . .
end LAST_WORK;
```
                           (c) LAST_WORK

Figure 22-5   Additional Subunits

development since it is likely that the "type declarations and other global information" are necessary for the context of IN—STUFF, DO—WORK, and OUT—STUFF. However, using packages, it is possible to uncouple the physical location of the subprogram declarations (which are physically within the procedure DO—STUFF) from the requirements for access to the information in the global area. To further illustrate this uncoupling, we will assume that some of the global information is universally required, but that some is required only by IN—STUFF and DO—WORK, not by OUT—STUFF. Figure 22-6 presents the new structure as a single compilation unit; this is more typical of Ada style than is the original program structure. Note that we are now protected from the inadvertent use by OUT—STUFF of information that should be private to IN—STUFF and DO—WORK. For OUT—STUFF to access such information, it must use the dot notation, as IN—DO—SHARE.INFORMATION. If the packages GLOBAL and IN—DO—SHARE included abstract data types with specified operations, package bodies would also be required.

22.4.1 *Packages as Resources*

The first approach to bottom-up development might be to provide the separately compiled packages GLOBAL and IN—DO—SHARE as resources for the support of the rest of the program development. Figure 22-7 shows this approach. The dashed lines indicate the compilation units. It would be particularly appropriate if the packages contained general services such as SQRT, LOG, and so on, or specific functions to support STUFF processing. The packages GLOBAL and IN—DO—SHARE, at least the package specifications, would be developed and compiled and then would be available to be **with,** and provide a context for, the procedure DO—STUFF.

The next step is to encapsulate the procedures IN—STUFF, DO—WORK, and OUT—STUFF into packages to allow their development before the creation of DO—STUFF. One way would be to create a package containing all the procedures. This is shown in figure 22-8. Note that the **with** clauses are shown with the package body. If the procedure specifications required information from the packages, the **with** and **use** clauses would have to precede the package specification. The **with** and **use** clauses then could (but need not) be repeated prior to the package body. The compilation unit of DO—STUFF then mentions STUFF—PROCEDURES in a **with** clause to indicate the dependency.

```
with STUFF_IO; use STUFF_IO;
procedure DO_STUFF is

   package GLOBAL is
   -- Type declarations and
   -- other global information
   -- required by all subprograms
   end GLOBAL;

   package IN_DO_SHARE is
   -- The information for
   -- IN_STUFF and DO_WORK
   end IN_DO_SHARE;

   use GLOBAL;  -- To allow
                -- direct visibility to the
                -- contents of GLOBAL

   procedure IN_STUFF is
     use IN_DO_SHARE;
   . . .
   end IN_STUFF;

   procedure DO_WORK is
     use IN_DO_SHARE;
     procedure FIRST_WORK is
     . . .
     end FIRST_WORK;

     procedure LAST_WORK is
     . . .
     end LAST_WORK;
   . . .
   end DO_WORK;

   procedure OUT_STUFF is
   . . .
   end OUT_STUFF;
begin -- DO_STUFF
   IN_STUFF;
   DO_WORK;
   OUT_STUFF;
. . .
end DO_STUFF;
```

Figure 22-6   Packages in Single Compilation Unit

```
package GLOBAL is
   -- Type declarations and
   -- other global information
   -- required by all subprograms
end GLOBAL;
```
                              (a) Package Global

```
package IN_DO_SHARE is
   -- The information for
   -- IN_STUFF and DO_WORK
end IN_DO_SHARE;
```
                              (b) Package IN_DO_SHARE

```
with STUFF_IO, GLOBAL, IN_DO_SHARE; use STUFF_IO;
procedure DO_STUFF is
   use GLOBAL; -- To allow
               -- direct visibility to the
               -- contents of GLOBAL

   procedure IN_STUFF is
     use IN_DO_SHARE;
     . . .
   end IN_STUFF;
   procedure DO_WORK is

     use IN_DO_SHARE;
     procedure FIRST_WORK is
       . . .
     end FIRST_WORK;

     procedure LAST_WORK is
       . . .
     end LAST_WORK;
     . . .
   end DO_WORK;
   procedure OUT_STUFF is
     . . .
   end OUT_STUFF;
begin -- DO_STUFF
   IN_STUFF;
   DO_WORK;
   OUT_STUFF;

   . . .
end DO_STUFF;
```
                              (c) Main Program DO_STUFF

Figure 22-7   GLOBAL and In_DO_SHARE as Resources

```
package STUFF_PROCEDURES is
  procedure IN_STUFF;
  procedure DO_WORK;
  procedure OUT_STUFF;
end;


with GLOBAL, IN_DO_SHARE, STUFF_IO; use STUFF_IO;
package body STUFF_PROCEDURES is

  use GLOBAL;
  procedure IN_STUFF is
    use IN_DO_SHARE;

  . . .
  end IN_STUFF;

  procedure DO_WORK is
    use IN_DO_SHARE;

    procedure FIRST_WORK is

    . . .
    end FIRST_WORK;

    procedure LAST_WORK is

    . . .
    end LAST_WORK;

  . . .
  end DO_WORK;

  procedure OUT_STUFF is

  . . .
  end OUT_STUFF;
end STUFF_PROCEDURES;
```
                    (a) Package STUFF_PROCEDURES

```
with STUFF_PROCEDURES;
procedure DO_STUFF is
  use STUFF_PROCEDURES;
begin -- DO_STUFF
  IN_STUFF;
  DO_WORK;
  OUT_STUFF;

. . .
end DO_STUFF;
```
                    (b) Main Program DO_STUFF

Figure 22-8   Package STUFF_PROCEDURES

The package specification of STUFF_PROCEDURES must be compiled prior to compilation of DO_STUFF, but the package body need not be compiled. In fact, the package body of STUFF_PROCEDURES can be compiled and recompiled without causing a requirement for recompilation of DO_STUFF. The algorithms or internal data representations of a package body can change freely without requiring recompilation of program units using the package. If the package specification changes and is recompiled, the using program units must also be recompiled.

Note that a combination of top-down and bottom-up development is possible. We have been discussing bottom-up development for STUFF_PROCEDURES, but its development could also proceed in a top-down fashion, using **separate** clauses for the procedures.

22.4.2 *Increasing Independence*

An alternate approach to the packaging of the procedures is to treat IN_STUFF, DO_WORK, and OUT_STUFF independently. As shown in figure 22-9, it is possible to completely uncouple the physical position of the text from the individual subprogram's required visibility. Package DO_PROCESS has no need for STUFF_IO and is not burdened with visibility to the name. We have not only protected OUT_STUFF from inadvertent access to components of IN_DO_SHARE (as we had done previously), but we have also completely uncoupled the two units. OUT_STUFF is out of the scope of IN_DO_SHARE. The name is not visible, and access such as IN_DO_SHARE.INFORMATION is impossible. This formulation is more secure than combining the procedures into a STUFF_PROCEDURES package as we did in figure 22-8.

To use the capabilities of the given packages, the main procedure DO_STUFF is compiled as

```
with IN_PROCESS, DO_PROCESS, OUT_PROCESS;
procedure DO_STUFF is
-- Perhaps some local declarations
begin
   IN_PROCESS.IN_STUFF;
   DO_PROCESS.DO_WORK;
   OUT_PROCESS.OUT_STUFF;

   . . .
end DO_STUFF;
```

```
package IN_PROCESS is
  procedure IN_STUFF;
end;

with GLOBAL, IN_DO_SHARE, STUFF_IO; use STUFF_IO;
package body IN_PROCESS is

  procedure IN_STUFF is
    use GLOBAL, IN_DO_SHARE;
  . . .
  end IN_STUFF;
end IN_PROCESS;
```

```
package DO_PROCESS is
  procedure DO_WORK;
end;

with GLOBAL, IN_DO_SHARE;
package body DO_PROCESS is

  procedure DO_WORK is
    use GLOBAL, IN_DO_SHARE;

    procedure FIRST_WORK is
    . . .
    end FIRST_WORK;

    procedure LAST_WORK is
    . . .
    end LAST_WORK;
  . . .
  end DO_WORK;
end DO_PROCESS;
```

```
package OUT_PROCESS is
  procedure OUT_STUFF;
end;

with GLOBAL, STUFF_IO; use STUFF_IO;
package body OUT_PROCESS is

  procedure OUT_STUFF is
    use GLOBAL;
  . . .
  end OUT_STUFF;
end OUT_PROCESS;
```

Figure 22-9   Independent Packages

Note that DO__STUFF mentions in the **with** clause only those packages for which the names must be directly visible. It does not mention packages such as STUFF__IO or IN__DO__SHARE, which are necessary for IN__PROCESS, and so forth. If GLOBAL were necessary to other processing of DO__ STUFF, it could be added to the **with** clause.

An allowable order of compilation for this last example (figure 22-9) is

- First: specifications for GLOBAL and IN__DO__SHARE, in any order.
- Second: specifications for IN__PROCESS, DO__PROCESS, and OUT__ PROCESS.
- Third: procedure DO__STUFF.
- Other: The package bodies may be compiled anytime after their corresponding specification; they may be recompiled without affecting units depending on the specification.

The basic recompilation rule is that *a unit must be recompiled following a recompilation of any unit upon which it depends.* Note that a unit is never dependent on a package body but only on the specification. A body may be changed and recompiled without causing recompilation of a unit that depends on the package. This is so even if there is a major change to the package body, say changing the implementation of a stack from use of an array to use of a linked list. As long as the package specification remains unchanged, the unit dependent on the package need not be recompiled. The fact that a package body can be changed without affecting units dependent on the specification will ease both development and maintenance of large systems.

The last example is most typical of an Ada structure and use of packages. The likely order of development using a generally top-down philosophy is

- Write procedure DO__STUFF and the package specifications for IN__PROCESS, DO__PROCESS, and OUT__PROCESS. These can be compiled together to validate the consistency of interface specifications. Note that none of the package specifications is dependent on other packages.
- Complete GLOBAL and IN__DO__SHARE to provide necessary type definitions and data structures.
- Incrementally develop, compile, and test the package bodies for IN__PROCESS, DO__PROCESS, and OUT__PROCESS. The development of DO__ PROCESS may use the capabilities of **separate** development for FIRST __WORK and LAST__WORK.

Such a development process is particularly important on a large system of many thousands of lines of code. It combines separation of development responsibilities, validation of interfaces, ease of testing, and good control over visibility of data.

Exercise__22

Modify PROGRAM__21 so that the bodies of the subprograms in the package body are implemented as separate subunits.

Program__22

```
package SLEEP_TIGHT is
  type BED is limited private;
  type CONDITION is (RESTED, TIRED);
  procedure INITIALIZE(B : out BED);
  procedure SLEEP(B : in out BED; C : in out CONDITION);
  procedure MAKE (B : out BED);
  function MESSY (B : BED) return BOOLEAN;
private
  type BED is range 0 .. 6;
end;

with TEXT_IO; use TEXT_IO;
package body SLEEP_TIGHT is
  procedure INITIALIZE(B : out BED) is separate;
  procedure SLEEP(B : in  out BED; C : in  out CONDITION) is  separate;
  procedure MAKE(B : out BED) is separate;
  function MESSY(B : BED) return BOOLEAN is separate;
end SLEEP_TIGHT;

  separate (SLEEP_TIGHT)
  procedure INITIALIZE(B : out BED) is
  begin
    PUT_LINE ("In INITIALIZE");
    B := 0;
  end INITIALIZE;

  separate(SLEEP_TIGHT)
  procedure SLEEP(B : in out BED; C : in out CONDITION) is
```

```ada
begin
  PUT_LINE ("In SLEEP");
  if B < BED'LAST then
    C := RESTED;
    B := B + 1;
  end if;
end SLEEP;

separate(SLEEP_TIGHT)
procedure MAKE(B : out BED) is
begin
  PUT_LINE("In MAKE");
  B := 0;
end MAKE;

separate (SLEEP_TIGHT)
function MESSY(B : BED) return BOOLEAN is
begin
  PUT_LINE ("In MESSY");
  if B = BED'LAST then
    return TRUE;
  else
    return FALSE;
  end if;
end MESSY;


with SLEEP_TIGHT, TEXT_IO; use SLEEP_TIGHT, TEXT_IO;
procedure PROGRAM_22 is
  FIRM_BED : BED;
  CAPABILITY : CONDITION := RESTED;
begin
  INITIALIZE (FIRM_BED);
  for I in 1 .. 13 loop
    PUT_LINE("In loop in PROGRAM_22");
    CAPABILITY := TIRED;
    if MESSY(FIRM_BED) then
      MAKE(FIRM_BED);
    end if;
    SLEEP(FIRM_BED, CAPABILITY);
    if CAPABILITY = RESTED then
      PUT_LINE("Now rested");
    end if;
  end loop;
end PROGRAM_22;
```

Begin Ada execution
In INITIALIZE
In loop in PROGRAM__22
In MESSY
In SLEEP
Now rested
In loop in PROGRAM__22
In MESSY
In SLEEP
Now rested
In loop in PROGRAM__22
In MESSY
In SLEEP
Now rested
In loop in PROGRAM__22
In MESSY
In SLEEP
Now rested
In loop in PROGRAM__22
In MESSY
In SLEEP
Now rested
In loop in PROGRAM__22
In MESSY
In SLEEP
Now rested
In loop in PROGRAM__22
In MESSY
⟶ In MAKE
In SLEEP
Now rested
In loop in PROGRAM__22
In MESSY
In SLEEP
Now rested
In loop in PROGRAM__22
In MESSY
In SLEEP
Now rested
In loop in PROGRAM__22
In MESSY
In SLEEP
Now rested

```
        In loop in PROGRAM__22
        In MESSY
        In SLEEP
        Now rested
        In loop in PROGRAM__22
        In MESSY
        In SLEEP
        Now rested
        In loop in PROGRAM__22
        In MESSY
───▶    In MAKE
        In SLEEP
        Now rested
```

Discussion__22

The subprogram bodies are provided separately, but the execution is identical. There is somewhat more work for the compiler to do, so the compilation takes longer.

Keys to Understanding

▶ Complete type checking is maintained across compilation units.

▶ The **with** clause defines a partial ordering of compilation.

▶ Facilities are provided for both bottom-up and top-down methods of development.

23

Generics

Objective: to introduce the notion of generic
             routines and to describe the Ada ge-
             neric feature

Ada introduces a concept new to many programmers: that of generic program units. Generic subprograms and packages can be considered as templates to construct programs that differ only in some well-defined way. Figure 23-1 shows how a series of **SWAP** routines might be written for different types. The overloading of the procedure name is appropriate here since all the routines shown accomplish the same function. Figure 23-2 shows how the same effect is accomplished through the use of a generic procedure. The generic procedure is written once, then additional instances of the procedure are created (that is, *instantiated*) when they are required. Note that we must give separately both the procedure specification and body. Even this simple example illustrates several important points.

First, the use of the generic facility allows us to write, only once, code that will be used many times. In this sense a generic procedure is an extension of the concept of the subroutine or of a generalized macro facility.

Second, since the code is used only once, the same algorithm is used for each **SWAP** procedure. This leads to consistency across a large programming project and text that is smaller and easier to read. It also simplifies the examination of programs for correctness and makes programs easier to change and test. Using a generic approach, the programmer also uses fewer keystrokes and thus has less chance to make clerical errors. The greatest savings are likely to be in

```
procedure SWAP (X , Y : in out INTEGER) is
  TEMP : INTEGER := X;
begin
  X := Y; Y := TEMP;
end SWAP;

procedure SWAP (X , Y : in out APPLE) is
  TEMP : APPLE := X;
begin
  X := Y; Y := TEMP;
end SWAP;

procedure SWAP (X , Y : in out ORANGE) is
  TEMP : ORANGE := X;
begin
  X := Y; Y := TEMP;
end SWAP;

procedure SWAP (X , Y : in out DAY) is
  TEMP : DAY := X;
begin
  X := Y : Y := TEMP;
end SWAP;
```

Figure 23-1   Swap Procedures

program maintenance. A change may only need to be made in one place, rather than in many places.

Third, the instantiation of the generic does not lead to any run time overhead. It is instead completed at compile time, and the run-time execution

```
generic
  type SWAP_TYPE is private;
procedure EXCHANGE (X, Y : in out SWAP_TYPE);

procedure EXCHANGE (X, Y : in out SWAP_TYPE) is
  TEMP : SWAP_TYPE := X;
begin
  X := Y; Y := TEMP;
end EXCHANGE;

procedure SWAP is new EXCHANGE (INTEGER);

procedure SWAP is new EXCHANGE (APPLE);

procedure SWAP is new EXCHANGE (ORANGE);

procedure SWAP is new EXCHANGE (DAY);
```

Figure 23-2   A "SWAP" Generic Unit

is identical to that resulting from the separate creation of nongeneric procedures. In fact, the use of generics may lead to more compact code. The translator may be able to take advantage of the fact that the algorithms are identical and use the same code when appropriate.

Last, the example shows how a type is passed as a parameter to the generic procedure. The following sections amplify on types as parameters and illustrate how values and subprograms may also be used for parameterization.

23.1 *TYPES AS PARAMETERS*

Many functions or procedures specify algorithms that are identical except for the type of the objects being operated on. Ada provides for passing a type as a parameter to a generic unit. Of course, since a type defines a range of allowable values and a set of operations, the allowable operations in the generic unit are limited by the type to be passed as a parameter. For example, if the generic operates on discrete types (including enumeration types) the "+" operator is not allowed, since RED + GREEN is meaningless (even though 6 + 10 is appropriate). The legal types for generic units and the operations allowed with each type are shown in the following list. Note that the declaration following the generic clause specifies allowable operations.

Type	*Allowable Operations*
type T **is**	
limited private;	-- No operations
private;	-- Assignment and equality comparison
(< >);	-- Operations for discrete types
range < >;	-- Integer types
delta < >;	-- Fixed types
digits < >;	-- Floating types
access;	-- Access types
array (INDEX) **of** STUFF;	-- Array types

For the SWAP example of figure 23-2, we specified the SWAP_TYPE as **private** since we had need of the assignment operator. If we were creating a generic package that used a SUCC function, we could specify

```
type T is ( < >); -- Read "box"
```

Doing this, we would be able to perform more operations than if we had specified a **private** type declaration, but we would lose in generality. For example, the generic procedure would not be applicable to FLOAT types, since there is no SUCC function for floating-point types. Similarly for the other types, the type declaration influences the allowable operations and the generality of the procedure.

An example of a generic function using discrete types follows. It is a generic routine, for any enumeration type, that finds the second successor. If the value is last or next to last for the type, the function provides for wraparound to the first value.

```
generic
  type ENUM is (< >);
function AFTER_AFTER(E : ENUM) return ENUM;

function AFTER_AFTER (E : ENUM) return ENUM is
  G : ENUM := E;
begin
  for I in 1 .. 2 loop
    if G = ENUM'LAST then
      G := ENUM'FIRST;
    else
      G := ENUM'SUCC (G);
    end if;
  end loop;
  return G;
end AFTER_AFTER;
```

To instantiate the function for type **DAY**, we simply pass the type as a parameter:

```
function DOUBLE_SUCC is new AFTER_AFTER (DAY);
```

Then to use the function where X is of type **DAY** (the enumeration type previously specified), we invoke it like any other function:

```
X := DOUBLE_SUCC (MON) ; -- X = WED
X := DOUBLE_SUCC (SAT)  ; -- X = MON
```

23.2 *VALUES AS PARAMETERS*

Suppose we wish to modify AFTER__AFTER to be a more general-purpose generic function that finds the *n*th successor. We can do this by making the number of loops (the number of times we apply the SUCC function) a parameter passed to the function:

```
generic
  type ENUM is ( < > );
  N : INTEGER := 2;
function AFTER__N(E : ENUM) return ENUM;

function AFTER__N(E : ENUM) return ENUM is
  G : ENUM := E;
begin
  for I in 1 .. N loop
    if G = ENUM ' LAST then
      G := ENUM ' FIRST;
    else
      G := ENUM ' SUCC (G);
    end if;
  end loop;
  return G;
end AFTER__N;
```

The second generic parameter, N, controls the number of times through the loop. Now we can instantiate new functions:

```
function TRIPLE__SUCC  is new AFTER__N(DAY, 3);
function QUAD__SUCC    is new AFTER__N(DAY, 4);
```

or using named parameter association:

```
function PENT__SUCC is new AFTER__N(ENUM => DAY, N => 5);
```

with the expected effect of

```
X := TRIPLE__SUCC(SAT);    -- X = TUE
X := QUAD__SUCC(SAT);      -- X = WED
X := PENT__SUCC(SAT);      -- X = THU
```

Notice that there is a default value of N, similar to a subprogram parameter, so that

function DEFAULT__SUCC **is new** AFTER__N(DAY);

causes DEFAULT__SUCC to provide the second successor.

23.3 *SUBPROGRAMS AS PARAMETERS*

Ada allows us to pass a subprogram as a parameter to a generic unit. Let's first look at a simple generic procedure that is similar to the standard package for input and output of enumeration types. We will see how it works using 'IMAGE as a standard function, and then see how we can pass a different function as a parameter to the generic procedure.

Here is a generic procedure that provides for output of the value of an enumeration type as a string. The default value for the function ENUM__ STRING is the attribute 'IMAGE of enumeration types. The attribute 'IMAGE acts as a function to provide the string corresponding to the identifier of a value of an enumeration type.

```
generic
  type ENUM is (< >);
  with function ENUM__STRING(X : ENUM)
    return STRING is ENUM ' IMAGE;
procedure PUT__ENUM (IT : in ENUM);

procedure PUT__ENUM (IT : in ENUM) is
begin
  PUT(ENUM__STRING(IT)); -- PUT for strings
end PUT__ENUM; -- for ENUM
```

Then the instantiation for type DAY is

procedure PUT **is new** PUT__ENUM(DAY);

with the effect

```
DAY__THING := WED;
PUT(DAY__THING); -- Output the string "WED"
```

The generic subprogram parameter **ENUM__STRING** has a default value of **ENUM'IMAGE**. It returns the string corresponding to the value of the parameter. Since the generic parameter has a default, the instantiation need not provide a function. However, it is possible to define a new function and pass it as a parameter to the generic procedure.

Suppose we wish to output either "WORK" or "REST" depending on the day. We first define

```
function EFFORT (D : DAY) return STRING is
begin
  case D is
    when MON .. FRI => return "WORK";
    when SAT .. SUN => return "REST";
  end case;
end EFFORT;
```

Then we instantiate the generic procedure:

```
procedure WHAT__TO__DO is new PUT__ENUM(DAY, EFFORT);
```

The result is

```
DAY__THING := WED;
WHAT__TO__DO (DAY__THING);      -- Output "WORK"
WHAT__TO__DO (SAT);             -- Output "REST"
```

The function **EFFORT** is the actual parameter that replaces the formal parameter **ENUM__STRING**. The default of **ENUM'IMAGE** is not used. The net effect of the instantiation is to create a procedure such as the following one.

```
procedure WHAT__TO__DO (IT : in DAY) is
  function EFFORT . . .
    . . .
  end EFFORT;
begin -- WHAT__TO__DO
  PUT (EFFORT(IT));
end WHAT__TO__DO;
```

The passing of subprograms as parameters is usually used for mathematical applications in which processing depends on the function provided as an actual parameter.

23.4 *GENERIC PACKAGES*

The following examples, adapted from the LRM, show generic packages for implementing stacks of various types. In the first method the size of the stack and the type of the stack elements are provided as generic parameters.

```
generic
  SIZE : POSITIVE;
  type ITEM is private;
package STACK is
  procedure PUSH (E : in ITEM);
  procedure POP   (E : out ITEM);
end STACK;

package body STACK is
  type TABLE is array (POSITIVE range  < >) of ITEM;
  SPACE : TABLE (1 .. SIZE);
  INDEX : NATURAL := 0;

  procedure PUSH(E : in ITEM) is
  begin
    INDEX := INDEX + 1;
    SPACE(INDEX) := E;
  end PUSH;

  procedure POP(E : out ITEM) is
  begin
    E := SPACE(INDEX);
    INDEX := INDEX − 1;
  end POP;
end STACK;
```

The package has two generic formal parameters, SIZE and ITEM. SIZE is the capacity of the stack and ITEM is the type of object to be placed on the stack. The operations provided are PUSH and POP. Implementation of the stack is through use of an array. The declaration of the array makes use of the values of the generic parameters, as does the declaration of PUSH and POP. This example does not check for proper use of the stack, that is, check the values of INDEX. A natural way to do so would be by use of an *exception,* which will be explained in the next chapter. We can create instances of the package

```
package STACK_INT is new STACK(SIZE = > 200, ITEM = >
                              INTEGER);
package STACK_FLOAT is new STACK(100, FLOAT);
```

and can use the procedures

```
STACK_INT.PUSH (20);
STACK_FLOAT.PUSH (3.14);
STACK_FLOAT.POP (X);
```

The creation of an instance of a generic package, say STACK_INT, creates a package that can be used just as if it were individually created. STACK_INT is an encapulation of the stack. The package can be veiwed as an object manager, as discussed in chapter 21. The STACK_INT package provides a stack that can handle up to 200 objects of type INTEGER. If we had needed a larger stack, we might have used SIZE = > 1000 rather than SIZE = > 200. PUSH and POP are used just like any other procedures in a package. While we used STACK_INT.PUSH (20), in a program that contained

```
use STACK_INT;
```

we would just have PUSH(20), POP(INT_1), and so on. However,

```
use STACK;
```

is inappropriate since a generic package cannot be used, only instantiated.

Now it should be clear what we have been doing in the exercises when we were instantiating packages such as,

```
package IO is new INTEGER_IO (INTEGER);
use IO;
```

The generic package INTEGER_IO has procedures GET and PUT for integer types. So for declarations such as

```
type MY_INT is range 1 .. 10;
type TENS is range −10 .. 10;
```

or for INTEGER (the predefined type), we need to instantiate the generic package with the type as a parameter in order to be able to use GET and PUT.

It is interesting to see how various features in Ada interact. Here is a generic package specification that indicates an alternate method of implementing the stack package, using a discriminated record to provide the flexibility for stack size:

```
generic
  type ITEM is private;
package ON_STACKS is
  type STACK(SIZE : POSITIVE) is limited private;
  procedure PUSH(S : in out STACK; E : in ITEM);
  procedure POP (S : in out STACK; E : out ITEM);
private
  type TABLE is array (POSITIVE range < >) of ITEM;
  type STACK(SIZE : POSITIVE) is
    record
      SPACE : TABLE (1 .. SIZE);
      INDEX : NATURAL := 0;
    end record;
end;

package body ON_STACKS is
-- Not provided
end ON_STACKS;
```

The type of the elements of the stack is still passed as a generic parameter. STACK is declared **limited private** and is an abstract data type with allowable operations PUSH and POP. PUSH and POP operate on a stack passed as a parameter, pushing the **in** parameter of the appropriate type onto the stack or popping the top of the stack into the variable **out** parameter. Objects of type STACK, of a specified size, can be created after an instantiation of the generic package for a certain type of stack element. The instantiation is

package ANOTHER__STACK__INT **is new** ON__STACKS (INTEGER);

Package ANOTHER__STACK__INT is a *type* manager, as contrasted to the previous STACK__INT which is an *object* manager. The type manager allows multiple stacks to be created, while still controlling the implementation mechanism and the allowable operations. STACK objects can be created as

```
use ANOTHER__STACK__INT;
MY__STACK     : STACK(100);
YOUR__STACK : STACK(5000);
```

The declaration of MY__STACK creates an object that can contain 100 integers. The actual implementation is as a record with an array to hold the values pushed onto the stack. The array has an upper bound of SIZE $=>$ 100, and the current top of stack is indicated by the value of INDEX.
The procedures in ANOTHER__STACK__INT can be used as

```
PUSH(MY__STACK, 700);
PUSH(YOUR__STACK, 200);
POP(MY__STACK, INT__1);
```

The first statement above puts the value 700 on the top of the stack. As implemented, 700 will be assigned to the array SPACE at the location marked by INDEX, which is incremented.

23.5 *GENERICS AND TEXT SUBSTITUTION*

It may appear that generic instantiation is a mechanism for text substitution at the point of instantiation. In simple cases, the effect is the same, but actually the generic instantiation takes effect in the context of the location of the generic declaration. Differences arise in which nonlocal identifiers (not also used as actual generic parameters) are involved. Such identifiers take their meaning at the point of declaration, not at the point of instantiation. For example,

```
declare
  type FUNNY is new DAY; -- Funny is a derived type of DAY

  generic
  procedure USE_FUNNY;

  procedure USE_FUNNY is
    A : DAY := MON;
    B : FUNNY;
  begin
    B := FUNNY(A);
  end USE_FUNNY;

  procedure FUNNY_WORKS is new USE_FUNNY;
begin
  FUNNY_WORKS;
end;
```

Everything works fine in the example since the type transformation FUN-
NY(A) is appropriate. An object of type **DAY** may be converted to type
FUNNY. However, consider the following:

```
declare -- Outer block
  type FUNNY is new DAY; -- Funny is a derived type of DAY

  generic
  procedure USE_FUNNY;

  procedure USE_FUNNY is
    A : DAY := MON;
    B : FUNNY;
  begin
    B := FUNNY(A);
  end USE_FUNNY;
begin

  declare -- A new block
    type FUNNY is new FLOAT; -- Now a derived type of FLOAT
    procedure DOES_FUNNY_WORK is new USE_FUNNY;
  begin
    DOES_FUNNY_WORK; -- Yes
  end; -- Of new block

end; -- Of outer block
```

If generic instantiation implied simple text substitution, the instantiation would fail since type FUNNY would be a derived type of FLOAT and the transformation FUNNY(A) would be illegal. It would be an attempt to transform an object of type DAY to a numeric type—a forbidden operation. However, since identifiers take their meaning at the point of declaration, type FUNNY (in the generic procedure) is still a derived type of DAY, and DOES__FUNNY__ WORK does work.

23.6 *USE OF GENERICS*

Generics provide a powerful way to control complexity in large programming projects. In turn, however, they can be difficult to use, particularly when creating templates, the generic programs for later instantiation. This book avoids discussing the more complex issues of writing generic programs. On most projects, and for most applications, the great majority of programmers will not write or create generics; they will instantiate and use generics. Instantiation is fairly straightforward and should be an easily attainable skill. Only a small cadre of users will need to be familiar with the rules and precautions necessary to create generic packages and subprograms.

Exercise__23

Modify PROGRAM__21 so that it is a generic package with the type of BED as a generic parameter. The generic package should allow BED to be of any discrete type. Instantiate the package for three different types.

Program__23

```
generic
  type BED is (< >);

  package SLEEP__TIGHT is
    type CONDITION is (RESTED, TIRED);
    procedure INITIALIZE(B : out BED);
    procedure SLEEP(B : in out BED; C : in out CONDITION);
    procedure MAKE (B : out BED);
    function MESSY(B : BED) return BOOLEAN;
  end;
```

```
with TEXT_IO; use TEXT_IO;
package body SLEEP_TIGHT is

  procedure INITIALIZE(B : out BED) is
  begin
    PUT_LINE("In INITIALIZE");
    B := BED'FIRST;
  end INITIALIZE;

  procedure SLEEP(B : in out BED; C : in out CONDITION) is
  begin
    PUT_LINE("In SLEEP");
    if B < BED'LAST then
      C := RESTED;
      B := BED'SUCC(B);
    end if;
  end SLEEP;

  procedure MAKE(B : out BED) is
  begin
    PUT_LINE("In MAKE. The bed will be refreshed. *****");
    B := BED'FIRST;
  end MAKE;

  function MESSY(B : BED) return BOOLEAN is
  begin
    PUT_LINE("In MESSY");
    if B = BED'LAST then
      return TRUE;
    else
      return FALSE;
    end if;
  end MESSY;

end SLEEP_TIGHT;

with SLEEP_TIGHT, TEXT_IO; use TEXT_IO;
procedure MAIN_PROGRAM_23 is

  procedure PROGRAM_23 is
    type SACK is range 0 .. 6;
    package SACK_SLEEP_TIGHT is new SLEEP_TIGHT(SACK);
    use SACK_SLEEP_TIGHT;
    FIRM_BED : SACK;
    CAPABILITY : CONDITION := RESTED;
```

```
begin
  INITIALIZE(FIRM__BED);
  for I in 1 .. 13 loop
    PUT__LINE("In loop in PROGRAM__23");
    CAPABILITY := TIRED;
    if MESSY(FIRM__BED) then
      MAKE(FIRM__BED);
    end if;
    SLEEP(FIRM__BED, CAPABILITY);
    if CAPABILITY = RESTED then
      PUT__LINE("Now rested");
    end if;
  end loop;
end PROGRAM__23;


procedure PROGRAM__23__ENUM is
  type SACK is (CLEAN, USED, PRETTY__BAD, MESSY__DIRTY);
  package SACK__SLEEP__TIGHT is new SLEEP__TIGHT(SACK);
  use SACK__SLEEP__TIGHT;
  FIRM__BED : SACK;
  CAPABILITY : CONDITION := RESTED;
begin
  INITIALIZE(FIRM__BED);
  for I in 1 .. 13 loop
    PUT__LINE("In loop in PROGRAM__23__ENUM");
    CAPABILITY := TIRED;
    if MESSY(FIRM__BED) then
      MAKE(FIRM__BED);
    end if;
    SLEEP(FIRM__BED, CAPABILITY);
    if CAPABILITY = RESTED then
      PUT__LINE("Now rested");
    end if;
  end loop;
end PROGRAM__23__ENUM;


procedure PROGRAM__23__BOOL is
  subtype SACK is BOOLEAN;
  package SACK__SLEEP__TIGHT is new SLEEP__TIGHT(SACK);
  use SACK__SLEEP__TIGHT;
  FIRM__BED : SACK;
  CAPABILITY : CONDITION := RESTED;
```

```
      begin
        INITIALIZE(FIRM_BED);
        for I in 1 .. 13 loop
          PUT_LINE("In loop in PROGRAM_23_BOOL");
          CAPABILITY := TIRED;
          if MESSY(FIRM_BED) then
            MAKE(FIRM_BED);
          end if;
          SLEEP(FIRM_BED, CAPABILITY);
          if CAPABILITY = RESTED then
            PUT_LINE("Now rested");
          end if;
        end loop;
      end PROGRAM_23_BOOL;


    begin -- MAIN_PROGRAM_23
      PUT_LINE("MAIN_PROGRAM_23 ----------"); NEW_LINE;
      NEW_LINE;
      PROGRAM_23;
      PUT_LINE("MAIN_PROGRAM_23 ----------"); NEW_LINE;
      NEW_LINE;
      PROGRAM_23_ENUM;
      PUT_LINE("MAIN_PROGRAM_23 ----------"); NEW_LINE;
      NEW_LINE;
      PROGRAM_23_BOOL;
    end MAIN_PROGRAM_23;


    MAIN_PROGRAM_23 ----------

    In INITIALIZE
    In loop in PROGRAM_23
    In MESSY
    In SLEEP
    Now rested
    In loop in PROGRAM_23
    In MESSY
    In SLEEP
    Now rested
    In loop in PROGRAM_23
    In MESSY
    In SLEEP
    Now rested
```

In loop in PROGRAM__23
In MESSY
In SLEEP
Now rested
In loop in PROGRAM__23
In MESSY
In SLEEP
Now rested
In loop in PROGRAM__23
In MESSY
In SLEEP
Now rested
In loop in PROGRAM__23
In MESSY
In MAKE. The bed will be refreshed. *****
In SLEEP
Now rested
In loop in PROGRAM__23
In MESSY
In SLEEP
Now rested
In loop in PROGRAM__23
In MESSY
In SLEEP
Now rested
In loop in PROGRAM__23
In MESSY
In SLEEP
Now rested
In loop in PROGRAM__23
In MESSY
In SLEEP
Now rested
In loop in PROGRAM__23
In MESSY
In SLEEP
Now rested
In loop in PROGRAM__23
In MESSY
In MAKE. The bed will be refreshed. *****
In SLEEP
Now rested

MAIN PROGRAM__23 ----------

In INITIALIZE
In loop in PROGRAM__23__ENUM
In MESSY
In SLEEP
Now rested
In loop in PROGRAM__23__ENUM
In MESSY
In SLEEP
Now rested
In loop in PROGRAM__23__ENUM
In MESSY
In SLEEP
Now rested
In loop in PROGRAM__23__ENUM
In MESSY
In MAKE. The bed will be refreshed. *****
In SLEEP
Now rested
In loop in PROGRAM__23__ENUM
In MESSY
In SLEEP
Now rested
In loop in PROGRAM__23__ENUM
In MESSY
In SLEEP
Now rested
In loop in PROGRAM__23__ENUM
In MESSY
In MAKE. The bed will be refreshed. *****
In SLEEP
Now rested
In loop in PROGRAM__23__ENUM
In MESSY
In SLEEP
Now rested
In loop in PROGRAM__23__ENUM
In MESSY
In SLEEP
Now rested

In loop in PROGRAM__23__ENUM
In MESSY
In MAKE. The bed will be refreshed. *****
In SLEEP
Now rested
In loop in PROGRAM__23__ENUM
In MESSY
In SLEEP
Now rested
In loop in PROGRAM__23__ENUM
In MESSY
In SLEEP
Now rested
In loop in PROGRAM__23__ENUM
In MESSY
In MAKE. The bed will be refreshed. *****
In SLEEP
Now rested

MAIN__PROGRAM__23 ----------

In INITIALIZE
In loop in PROGRAM__23__BOOL
In MESSY
In SLEEP
Now rested
In loop in PROGRAM__23__BOOL
In MESSY
In MAKE. The bed will be refreshed. *****
In SLEEP
Now rested
In loop in PROGRAM__23__BOOL
In MESSY
In MAKE. The bed will be refreshed. *****
In SLEEP
Now rested
In loop in PROGRAM__23__BOOL
In MESSY
In MAKE. The bed will be refreshed. *****
In SLEEP
Now rested

In loop in PROGRAM__23__BOOL
In MESSY
In MAKE. The bed will be refreshed. *****
In SLEEP
Now rested
In loop in PROGRAM__23__BOOL
In MESSY
In MAKE. The bed will be refreshed. *****
In SLEEP
Now rested
In loop in PROGRAM__23__BOOL
In MESSY
In MAKE. The bed will be refreshed. *****
In SLEEP
Now rested
In loop in PROGRAM__23__BOOL
In MESSY
In MAKE. The bed will be refreshed. *****
In SLEEP
Now rested

Discussion__23

PROGRAM__MAIN__23 encloses the generic package and three nested procedures that instantiate the package for different types.

The important difference in the generic specification is that the type BED is now a generic parameter. It may be of any discrete type. Considerable care must be taken in the generic package body to use operations that are valid for any discrete type, not just numeric types. For example, in SLEEP, the value of B becomes the successor ('SUCC) of B, not B + 1. For numeric types the effect is the same.

PROGRAM__23 instantiates the package for a type as in PRO-GRAM__21. Since the frequency of calls to MAKE is going to be dependent on the type, we emphasize (in the output) these calls. The effect of the program is the same as in the original PROGRAM__21.

PROGRAM__23__ENUM instantiates the package for an enumeration type. Now it becomes clear why the generic package had to take care to use 'SUCC rather than addition! The selection of names for the enumerated values can be used to indicate the current status of the bed in a more meaningful way than integer values.

PROGRAM__23__BOOL instantiates the package for a BOOLEAN type. Similar considerations apply for BOOLEAN as for enumeration types. Of course, the bed can be slept in only one time before being messy.

MAIN__PROGRAM__23 executes the three embedded procedures. The generic package had to be written only once and was then useful for three different purposes. Perhaps even more important, since it is so common in the maintenance phase of the life cycle, is that if the functioning of the package were to change, the program modification would only have to be made in one place. The instantiations remain the same, but the programs are all updated—and in the same way. Of course, the three procedures PROGRAM__23, PROGRAM__23__ENUM, and PROGRAM__23__BOOL are so similar that they could also be created as generic procedures. Nesting of generics is allowed.

Keys to Understanding

► Generic subprograms and packages are templates for processes that differ only in some well-defined way.
► Generic methods allow us to write, only once, code that will be used many times. It ensures that the same algorithm is used and simplifies code reading and testing.
► The parameters to **generic** routines are: types, values for data items, and subprograms. They are the differences between one generic process and another.
► Generic methods are of particular importance for the maintenance period of the software life cycle.

24

Exceptions

Objective: to explain what an exception is and to present the Ada facilities for dealing with exceptions

Exceptions are errors or other abnormal (exceptional) situations that arise during program execution. (Strictly speaking, an **exception** is a *name* for an error that may occur.) Since embedded computer systems are typically real-time, continuously operating systems that must not fail, a mechanism must be provided to handle unusual occurrences and still allow the program to continue running and the system to operate. Exception handling is an important feature of Ada, but one that is difficult to use effectively. It is not always clear what ought to be done when certain sorts of errors occur; the proper action must depend on the state of the system and on how control has reached the point of execution. Ada provides mechanisms that cater to this requirement for determining dynamically how an exception ought to be handled, by allowing the designer/programmer to create exception handlers.

Certain terms have special meanings when discussing exceptions. They are:

> *Exceptions:* events that cause suspension of normal program execution. Declaring the exception involves introducing a name for it.
> *Raising* the exception: draws attention to the event during program execution. Raising the exception transfers control to the exception handler.

Handling the exception: executes actions in response to the occurrence of the event.

In Ada, once the exception event occurs, the handler carries out the remaining execution of the unit, after which the unit exits.

For example, we may wish to handle an overflow situation in a subprogram:

```
function CUBE ( V : FLOAT ) return FLOAT is
   CUBE_VALUE : FLOAT;
begin
   CUBE_VALUE := V * V * V;
   return CUBE_VALUE;
exception
   when NUMERIC_ERROR =>
      PUT ("ERROR IN FUNCTION CUBE");
      return FLOAT'LARGE;
end CUBE;
```

If the product operation (V * V * V) yields a value larger than the implementation can support, the numeric error is handled by the code following the *exception* clause. This code replaces execution of the code in the function CUBE following the occurrence of the exception.

Exceptions are one of the few features of Ada that can be omitted from use without adversely affecting other features of the language. Even when coding embedded computer systems, a programmer could effectively employ some simple characteristics of exceptions without understanding everything about their use. A simple use of exceptions might be to check for and trap unusual data items, handling the exception immediately in an enclosing block. A more advanced use of exceptions would be to return an error indication to a calling program. This use is similar to the *alternate* return provided for in some languages to allow different processing for error returns. Of course, this violates the notion of a subprogram as a single-exit box. Exceptions can also replace what would otherwise be a *goto* fatal_error_label out of the current process. The following sections provide an overview of the declaration, occurrence, and handling of exceptions.

24.1 *DECLARING EXCEPTIONS*

A user-defined exception is declared by placing the identifier in a list followed by the reserved word **exception.** For instance,

    CRITICAL_TEMP, MISSILE_FAILURE, DANGER, HAZARD: **exception;**

These identifiers can then be used within their scope to indicate the exceptional circumstances and to specify the actions to be taken when the exception occurs. Five exceptions are predeclared in Ada. They are

CONSTRAINT_ERROR	Occurs in a large number of circumstances, including violating a range constraint of a type or subtype.
NUMERIC_ERROR	Occurs when the result of a numeric operation does not lie within the range of the numeric type. Division by zero is a typical example.
PROGRAM_ERROR	Occurs in a variety of circumstances, often related to program inconsistencies, not covered by other exceptions.
STORAGE_ERROR	Occurs when the dynamic storage allocated to a task is exceeded, or when allocators (pointers) use up available space.
TASKING_ERROR	Occurs during problems with the invocation of concurrent processes (tasks) or intertask communication.

24.2 *RAISING EXCEPTIONS*

An exception can be explicitly **raised** by a program:

```
if TEMP > MAX_TEMP then
    raise CRITICAL_TEMP;          -- A user-defined exception
end if;
raise NUMERIC_ERROR;              -- Raising a predefined exception
```

Raising the exception causes control to be transferred to a handler for the exception.

Certain conditions will cause exceptions to be raised automatically, as the following example shows:

```
declare
  A, B, C : INTEGER;
  SHORT : INTEGER range 0 .. 10;
begin
  A := 0;
  B := 20;
  C := B/A;          -- Raises NUMERIC_ERROR when executed
  SHORT := B;        -- Would raise CONSTRAINT_ERROR
end;
```

A user can raise predefined exceptions. A user-defined exception can never be raised automatically. Raising the exception causes the current thread of execution to be abandoned and control to be transferred to an exception handler.

24.3 HANDLING THE EXCEPTION

An exception handler may appear at the end of any block or at the end of a subprogram, package, or task body. It has a form similar to a case statement. It uses the vertical bar to indicate alternatives for a choice and uses others as a final choice.

```
begin
-- Sequence of statements
exception
  when CRITICAL_TEMP => 
  -- This is a handler
  when MISSILE_FAILURE => 
  -- This is another handler
  when DANGER | HAZARD => 
  -- This is a handler for two exceptions
  when others => 
  -- This is the handler for other exceptions
    raise; -- Raise without an identifier
end;
```

The **raise** statement without an identifier is allowed only within a handler. It has the effect of reraising the exception that caused control to transfer to the handler. Reraising the exception causes it to be propagated out of the enclosing block to the next enclosing exception handler.

Once control is passed to the handler, it may not return back to the point

```
procedure EXCEPTION_HANDLER (TEMPERATURE : in out CENTIGRADE;
                             PEOPLE : in BOOLEAN) is
  TEMP_RATIO : CENTIGRADE; -- Range is -276 .. 5_000;
  MAX_TEMP   : constant CENTIGRADE := 500;
  CRITICAL_TEMP, DANGER : exception;
begin
  if TEMPERATURE > MAX_TEMP then          ----------------------- (1)
    raise CRITICAL_TEMP;

  begin -- Inner block
    TEMP_RATIO := MAX_TEMP / TEMPERATURE;   ------------- (2)
    TEMPERATURE := TEMPERATURE + 300;       -------------------- (3)
    if TEMPERATURE > MAX_TEMP then
      raise CRITICAL_TEMP;                --------------------------------------- (4)
    end if;

  exception -- Handler for inner block
    when CRITICAL_TEMP = >
      if PEOPLE then
        raise DANGER;
      end if;          ---------------------------------------------------------------- (5)
    when NUMERIC_ERROR = >
      TEMP_RATIO := CENTIGRADE ' LAST;
  end; -- Inner block
    .
    .
    .
  -- other code          ---------------------------------------------------------- (6)
    .
    .
    .
exception
  when CRITICAL_TEMP = >
    PUT ("REDUCE TEMPERATURE IMMEDIATELY");
    ADD_COOLING_MATERIAL;
    TEMPERATURE := MAX_TEMP;
  when CONSTRAINT_ERROR = >
    PUT ("TEMPERATURE OVER 4700");
  when DANGER = >
    PUT ("CLEAR THE AREA");
end EXCEPTION_HANDLER;
```

Figure 24-1   Exception Example

at which the exception was raised. Specifically, the handler may not *goto* back into the unit containing the exception. Once the handler completes execution, the block, or subprogram, package, or task body is abandoned. The only way to return to the point at which the exception occurred is through a normal entry "through the top" of the unit.

Figure 24-1 shows the interaction between raise statements and handlers in a block nested within a procedure. The code is somewhat contrived, but it sufficiently "raises" a number of interesting points. We will investigate the effect of each statement and discuss each with reference to the statement numbers in the figure.

(1) Raising the exception causes control to transfer to the exception handler for the procedure. The warning "REDUCE TEMPERATURE IMMEDIATELY" is output, and the procedure ADD_COOLING _MATERIAL is called.

(2) If TEMPERATURE is 0, NUMERIC_ERROR will be raised. The exception will be handled by the handler local to the block containing this statement; the TEMP_RATIO will be set to 5000. Execution will continue with the first statement following the block. The exception replaces execution of the remainder of the block. Control is not returned to the point at which the exception was raised.

(3) If TEMPERATURE has a value greater than 4700, this statement will raise CONSTRAINT_ERROR. Since there is no handler in the block, the exception will be passed (or propagated) to the procedure. Since there is a handler for CONSTRAINT_ERROR in the procedure, it will be handled there before control returns to the program unit that invoked the procedure EXCEPTION_HANDLER.

(4) The raising of CRITICAL_TEMP at this point will cause transfer of control to the exception handler local to the block. Note that the handler to which an exception causes transfer depends on the point at which the exception occurs.

(5) The action of this differs from that of the handler used for the exception occurring in statement (1). Note that it makes use of the visibility

available to it as part of the procedure EXCEPTION__HANDLER. Also note that it raises an exception, to be handled elsewhere.

(6) If NUMERIC__ERROR is raised here, there is no handler available, as opposed to the situation at statement (2). The exception will be propagated to the calling environment. This is essentially an abnormal termination.

We now return to the generic STACK example of chapter 23 to illustrate a mechanism for handling underflow and overflow. Here is the new version of the generic package.

```
generic
  SIZE : POSITIVE;
  type ITEM is private;
package STACK is
  procedure PUSH(E : in ITEM);
  procedure POP  (E : out ITEM);
  OVERFLOW, UNDERFLOW : exception;
end STACK;

package body STACK is
  type TABLE is array (POSITIVE range < >) of ITEM;
  SPACE : TABLE (1 .. SIZE);
  INDEX : NATURAL := 0;

  procedure PUSH(E : in ITEM) is
  begin
    if INDEX > = SIZE then
      raise OVERFLOW;
    end if;
    INDEX := INDEX + 1;
    SPACE(INDEX) := E;
  end PUSH;

  procedure POP(E : out ITEM) is
  begin
    If INDEX = 0 then
      raise UNDERFLOW;
    end if;
    E := SPACE(INDEX);
    INDEX := INDEX − 1;
  end POP;
end STACK;
```

We can then instantiate the package and use it as in

```
procedure USE_GENERIC_EXCEPTION(U_INT : in out INTEGER) is
    THIS_INT, THAT_INT : INTEGER := U_INT;
    package STACK_INT is new STACK(200, INTEGER);
    use STACK_INT;
begin
-- Code using the stack
. . .
    PUSH(THIS_INT);      -- Could raise OVERFLOW
    . . .                -- More PUSH and POP
    POP(THAT_INT);       -- Could raise UNDERFLOW
. . .
exception
    when OVERFLOW =>
        POP(THAT_INT);
        SAVE(THAT_INT);
        PUSH(THIS_INT);
    when UNDERFLOW =>
        U_INT : = 0;
end USE_GENERIC_EXCEPTION;
```

This procedure appears in some context in which it is called, and in which the generic package STACK is immediately visible. It has available to it a procedure (SAVE) that saves things for later use.

On an OVERFLOW, it POPs a value, saves it, then uses the extra space to PUSH the current value of THIS_INT. It returns to the calling program. On UNDERFLOW, it sets the formal parameter U_INT to zero, then returns.

The exception-handling mechanism is important for critical portions of real-time programs. It is also complex. The rules for propagating unhandled exceptions are more complex than these simple examples illustrate. Additional rules cover exceptions that occur during the elaboration of declarations, generics/exceptions, and tasks/exceptions. Exceptions should be embedded within the design of the entire program. In developing large systems it might be possible for a small group to establish general policy for use of exceptions and write all the major handlers. As with many other facets of Ada, how exceptions can be used most effectively will be determined only from experience—after a major system has been successfully developed.

Exercise__24

Modify PROGRAM__21 so that an exception is returned when there is an attempt made to sleep in a messy bed. Provide a handler in the using program.

Program__24

```
package SLEEP__TIGHT is
  type BED is limited private;
  type CONDITION is (RESTED, TIRED);
  procedure INITIALIZE(B : out BED);
  procedure SLEEP(B : in out BED; C : in out CONDITION);
  procedure MAKE (B : out BED);
  function MESSY(B : BED) return BOOLEAN;
  DIRTY : exception;     -- Raised when an attempt is made to sleep in a
                         -- messy bed
private
  type BED is range 0 .. 6;
end;

with TEXT__IO; use TEXT__IO;
package body SLEEP__TIGHT is

  procedure INITIALIZE(B : out BED) is
  begin
    PUT__LINE("In INITIALIZE");
    B := 0;
  end INITIALIZE;

  procedure SLEEP(B : in out BED; C : in out CONDITION) is
  begin
    PUT__LINE("In SLEEP");
    if B = BED'LAST then
      raise DIRTY;
    end if;
    C := RESTED;
    B := B + 1;
  end SLEEP;

  procedure MAKE(B : out BED) is
  begin
    PUT__LINE("In MAKE");
    B := 0;
  end MAKE;
```

```
        function MESSY(B : BED) return BOOLEAN is
        begin
          PUT_LINE("In MESSY");
          if B = BED'LAST then
            return TRUE;
          else
            return FALSE;
          end if;
        end MESSY;
      end SLEEP_TIGHT;

      with SLEEP_TIGHT, TEXT_IO; use SLEEP_TIGHT, TEXT_IO;
      procedure PROGRAM_24 is
        FIRM_BED : BED;
        CAPABILITY : CONDITION := RESTED;
      begin
        INITIALIZE(FIRM_BED);
        for I in 1 .. 13 loop
          PUT_LINE("In loop in PROGRAM_24");
          CAPABILITY := TIRED;

          begin            -- Block to handle exception in SLEEP
            SLEEP(FIRM_BED, CAPABILITY);
            PUT_LINE("If we get here, there was no exception and must be"
                    & "rested.");
          exception
            when DIRTY =>
              PUT_LINE("In the exception handler.");
              MAKE (FIRM_BED); -- Maybe should try to SLEEP again
            when others =>
              PUT_LINE("Other exception in SLEEP");
              raise;
          end;             -- Block to handle exception in SLEEP

          if CAPABILITY = RESTED then
            PUT_LINE("Now rested");
          end if;
        end loop;
      end PROGRAM_24;
```

```
In INITIALIZE
In loop in PROGRAM_24
In SLEEP
If we get here, there was no exception and must be rested.
Now rested
```

In loop in PROGRAM__24
In SLEEP
If we get here, there was no exception and must be rested.
Now rested
In loop in PROGRAM__24
In SLEEP
If we get here, there was no exception and must be rested.
Now rested
In loop in PROGRAM__24
In SLEEP
If we get here, there was no exception and must be rested.
Now rested
In loop in PROGRAM__24
In SLEEP
If we get here, there was no exception and must be rested.
Now rested
In loop in PROGRAM__24
In SLEEP
If we get here, there was no exception and must be rested.
Now rested
In loop in PROGRAM__24
In SLEEP
In the exception handler.
In MAKE
In loop in PROGRAM__24
In SLEEP
If we get here, there was no exception and must be rested.
Now rested
In loop in PROGRAM__24
In SLEEP
If we get here, there was no exception and must be rested.
Now rested
In loop in PROGRAM__24
In SLEEP
If we get here, there was no exception and must be rested.
Now rested
In loop in PROGRAM__24
In SLEEP
If we get here, there was no exception and must be rested.
Now rested
In loop in PROGRAM__24
In sleep
If we get here, there was no exception and must be rested.
Now rested

In loop in PROGRAM__24
In SLEEP
If we get here, there was no exception and must be rested.
Now rested

Discussion__24

This program illustrates an Ada approach toward the handling of error conditions. The user-defined exception **DIRTY** is declared in the package specification. It will be raised when an attempt is made to sleep in a messy bed. The function **MESSY** is still provided and can be used by the calling programs when appropriate. However, if the calling program does invoke SLEEP when the bed is messy, it should be prepared to cope with the exception being raised.

In procedure SLEEP, the code

```
if B = BED'LAST then
  raise DIRTY;
end if;
```

causes the exception to be raised when the bed is messy. Since there is no handler in SLEEP, the result is to propagate the exception to the calling program. Of course, it would also be possible to have a handler in SLEEP that might call MAKE and then (recursively) call SLEEP. Then SLEEP would be executed (successfully), control would return to the handler in the earlier instance of SLEEP, and then control could be returned to the calling program.

The calling program now has an exception handler for the exception DIRTY as well as others that might occur. There are alternate possible placements of the handler depending on the desired effect. Here we provide a block around the call to SLEEP. The handler fixes up the situation by calling MAKE and then the block exits. The message about being rested is not printed when the exception occurs. The execution of the block is abandoned after the handler executes.

Keys to Understanding

▶ An **exception** is an error or other exceptional situation that may arise during program execution. To prevent such errors from halting an operational system, Ada provides mechanisms for programmer-defined handlers for exceptions.

▶ Ada provides both predefined exceptions and the facility for programmer-defined exceptions.

▶ An exception causes execution of an exception handler and the abandonment of the block in which the exception occurred. Exceptions are propagated in a dynamic manner, depending on the run-time sequence of execution of subprograms and tasks.

25

Tasks

Objective:

to define a task and describe Ada's
tasking mechanism

Tasks are entities that operate in parallel. There is concurrent execution of two
or more threads of control. The concurrency may be actual, as in the case of
system configurations with multiple processors, or apparent, as in a multipro-
gramming environment with interleaved execution on a single processor. The
following sections introduce the general nature of parallel processes and describe Ada tasks.

25.1 PARALLEL ACTIONS

Suppose that the accounting office of a small firm is responsible for carrying
out these functions or tasks:

    Ordering supplies
    Paying bills
    Preparing invoices

With one accountant the process might be represented as

```
procedure ACCOUNTING is
begin
   ORDER_SUPPLIES;
   PAY_BILLS;
   INVOICE;
end ACCOUNTING;
```

With three accountants, however, the tasks could be performed in parallel. The Ada representation of such a situation is

```
procedure ACCOUNTING is

   task ORDER;
   task body ORDER is
   begin
      ORDER_SUPPLIES;
   end ORDER;

   task PAY;
   task body PAY is
   begin
      PAY_BILLS;
   end PAY;

begin
   INVOICE;
end ACCOUNTING;
```

Notice the similarity between a task and a package. There is a distinct and separate specification,

```
task ORDER;
```

followed by a body or implementation describing what the task does:

```
task body ORDER is
   . . .
end ORDER;
```

The task specification is used to describe the interface presented to other tasks. In this case the task presents no interface, so the declaration involves only the statement of the name.

The way we organized the tasks in procedure ACCOUNTING, which is the parent procedure of the tasks, has the effect of assigning the INVOICE function to the chief accountant, with ORDER and PAY being left to the assistants. Of course, the chief accountant first sets the assistants to work. Hence, in Ada, the tasks are declared in the declaration part of the parent procedure. Then, upon reaching the **begin** of the parent procedure, they are set active in parallel. The statements of the parent procedure (which accomplish the invoicing function) are then activated and execute in parallel with the other tasks. Note that it would have been also permitted to have declared all three processes as tasks. The net effect is that there are three separate threads of control. As the following example shows, the three processes all execute at the same time.

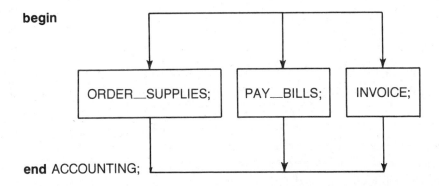

Each task terminates normally when it completes execution. However, a parent or master unit cannot terminate until all the dependent tasks have terminated. A parent unit, which can be a subprogram, block, task body, or library package, is a unit in which tasks have been declared. This termination rule is important since it implies that tasks are not autonomous agents but are completely nested within some other unit. The rule also ensures that the resources necessary to the task, likely to be declared in the parent unit, will be in scope during the lifetime of the task. For our example this means that if INVOICE is complete prior to completion of the tasks ORDER and PAY, procedure ACCOUNTING waits for termination of the subordinate tasks before it is complete.

25.2 *INTERPROCESS COMMUNICATION*

In the accounting example the tasks had no need to coordinate their actions in time and no need to pass information while they were executing—capabilities most parallel-processing applications require. We will illustrate these Ada capabilities, based on a mechanism known as a *rendezvous*, through an example of a message-processing system. We will refer to this example throughout the chapter.

The message-processing system has two components: a writer of messages and a sender of messages. The WRITER creates the message and provides it to the SENDER, who transmits it to some other location. The SENDER is clearly providing the service here and must have an **entry** into its process by which it can **accept** a MESSAGE. Here is an example of a task specification that shows the **entry** being offered as an interface:

```
task SENDER is
  entry SEND(M : in MESSAGE);
end SENDER;
```

The task specification, like a package specification, is a contract. It may not contain type definitions, but it may contain entry declarations to establish an interface to the services provided by the task body. The entry declaration is much like a procedure declaration. It has the same format and may have **in, out,** and **in out** parameters. The corresponding task body defines the processing done in the task, including an **accept** to fulfill the promise of the **entry** specification. The body of SENDER is

```
task body SENDER is
  OUT_GOING : MESSAGE;
  procedure TRANSMIT(ANY : in MESSAGE) is
  . . .
  end TRANSMIT;
begin
  loop
    accept SEND(M : in MESSAGE) do
      OUT_GOING := M;
    end SEND;
    TRANSMIT(OUT_GOING);
  end loop;
end SENDER;
```

The general form of the accept statement,

> **accept** SEND(. . .) **do**
>   . . .
> **end** SEND;

repeats the specification provided in the corresponding **entry**. The body of the accept statement consists of a sequence of statements with no declarative part. The structure and use of a task are summarized in figure 25-1. The entry is called by another task:

> SENDER.SEND(X);

in which the task__name.entry__name is used as in selected component notation. In WRITER it might appear as

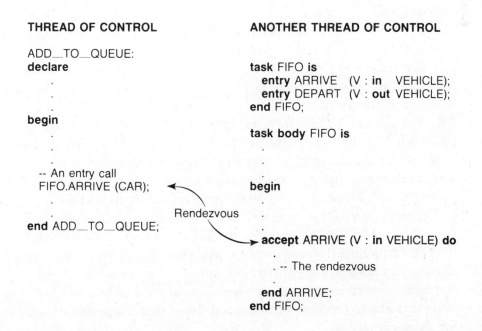

THREAD OF CONTROL

```
ADD__TO__QUEUE:
declare
    .
    .
    .
begin
    .
    .
    .
  -- An entry call
  FIFO.ARRIVE (CAR);
    .
    .
end ADD__TO__QUEUE;
```

ANOTHER THREAD OF CONTROL

```
task FIFO is
    entry ARRIVE  (V : in   VEHICLE);
    entry DEPART  (V : out  VEHICLE);
end FIFO;

task body FIFO is
    .
    .
    .
begin
    .
    .
    .
  accept ARRIVE (V : in VEHICLE) do
    .
    . -- The rendezvous
    .
  end ARRIVE;
end FIFO;
```

Rendezvous

Figure 25-1   Task Structure

```
task WRITER;
task body WRITER is
  STORY : MESSAGE;
  procedure WRITE(S : out MESSAGE) is
    . . .
  end WRITE;
begin
  loop
    WRITE(STORY);
    SENDER.SEND(STORY);
  end loop;
end WRITER;
```

The call SENDER.SEND(STORY) looks like a procedure call. However, remember that WRITER and SENDER are operating in parallel. This has two important consequences for the interaction of the rendezvous.

First, the rendezvous does not occur (the information is not passed from one task to another) until a task calls the entry and the task containing the entry reaches the accept statement. If the entry call occurs first, the calling task is suspended. It waits for the called task to reach the accept statement. If the task providing the entry reaches the accept statement first, it waits until the entry is called. When both conditions have been satisfied, the tasks are synchronized and the information in the parameter list is exchanged.

Second, the sequence of statements contained in the accept are considered to be executed on behalf of both tasks. They stay synchronized until the accept statement is complete.

The rendezvous joins together, into a single synchronized thread of control, what had been two separate threads of control. Information may be transmitted while the tasks are executing as a single thread of control. Hence the rendezvous is the Ada mechanism both for task coordination and for sharing of information. The joining of the threads of control is shown in figure 25-2. Initially, SENDER must wait for WRITER to complete the WRITE. Then they rendezvous, followed by parallel processing of TRANSMIT and WRITE. If multiple processors were available, TRANSMIT and WRITE could be actually executing at the same time. On a single processor the execution may be interleaved for an apparent concurrency. Whichever task completes its message processing first waits for the other. Then they rendezvous, and the cycle repeats.

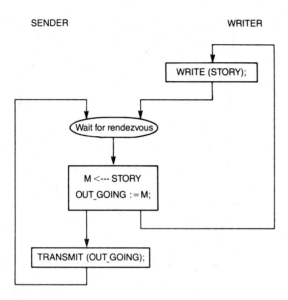

Figure 25-2   The Rendezvous

To improve the amount of parallel processing by decreasing the amount of time spent waiting for a rendezvous, we might use a separate task as a buffer. Here is a task that can buffer a single item:

```
task MESSAGE__BOX is
  entry PUT(IN__BOX : in MESSAGE);
  entry TAKE(FROM__BOX : out MESSAGE);
end MESSAGE__BOX;

task body MESSAGE__BOX is
  HOLD : MESSAGE;
begin
  loop
    accept PUT(IN__BOX : in MESSAGE) do
      HOLD := IN__BOX;
    end PUT;
    accept TAKE(FROM__BOX : out MESSAGE) do
      FROM__BOX := HOLD:
    end TAKE;
  end loop;
end MESSAGE__BOX;
```

In this case the WRITER task would no longer call an entry in SENDER but instead would use the call

```
MESSAGE_BOX.PUT(STORY);
```

and the SENDER task would no longer have an accept statement. Instead, whenever it was ready to send another message, it would also call an entry in MESSAGE_BOX:

```
MESSAGE_BOX.TAKE(OUT_GOING);
```

Notice that MESSAGE_BOX is designed to alternate between PUTs and TAKEs. It can buffer only one message, and after a PUT it will wait until a TAKE call has occurred before being prepared for another rendezvous with a call to PUT. Therefore, either SENDER or WRITER could still be waiting for a rendezvous.

So far we have considered only a single WRITER and single SENDER. Suppose, however, that there are several WRITER tasks, each of which issues calls to MESSAGE_BOX. The PUT entry may be called several times while MESSAGE_BOX is waiting to rendezvous with SENDER. In this case the calls are queued on a first-come-first-served basis. Of course, there could also be multiple SENDER tasks that could issue calls to be queued for the TAKE rendezvous. Within the body of the task providing the entries, there is an attribute to allow the determination of how many tasks are on the queue for an entry. The attributes PUT'COUNT and TAKE'COUNT are the number of tasks queued for each of the two entries. Knowledge of the queue length might be used to choose among alternate accepts. Ada also provides some built-in mechanisms for selecting among accepts and for controlling entry calls. These are discussed in the next section.

Before leaving the rendezvous concept, we should pause and point out the asymmetric nature of the rendezvous and differentiate between active and passive tasks.

The rendezvous is asymmetric in two ways:

• The calling task must know the name of the accepting task as well as the specification of the entry point. The accepting task does not know the name of the caller. The task providing the entries and accepts is essentially passive: it provides a service to any task that knows its name.

• A task calling an entry point may be on only one queue at a time. It may choose between calls to alternate tasks but is not allowed to wait for two entries so as to be served by the first one ready for rendezvous. On the other hand a task providing entries may have a number of tasks queued waiting for service, at a number of different entry points.

This asymmetry allows us to distinguish between active and passive tasks. Passive tasks are those that provide services through entries and accepts. Such tasks must be general in purpose, able to cope with the indeterminacy of when they are called, and able to administer the queues of tasks waiting for service. Active tasks use the services provided, by issuing entry calls. General-purpose passive tasks have some of the characteristics of operating systems and require the same skills to create. Active tasks are similar to application tasks that use the capabilities of a real-time operating system. The next section will introduce additional tools for writing both active and passive tasks.

25.3 CONTROL OVER THE RENDEZVOUS

Each of the two types of tasks we have been considering, the calling task and the called task, has a mechanism for controlling the rendezvous. For the called task it is the *selective wait,* and for the calling task it is *conditional* and *timed entry calls.* These mechanisms are described in the context of the message-processing system previously described.

25.3.1 Selective Wait

To improve the capabilities of the task MESSAGE—BOX, we will allow it to accept either a PUT or a TAKE, whichever is available. Of course, this implies that two or more PUT entry calls with a TAKE will cause overwriting of old messages, and multiple TAKE calls without an intervening PUT will receive the same information. For systems passing perishable information, such as aircraft location, this is a realistic situation. Task LOCATION—MESSAGE will **select** either a PUT **or** a TAKE.

```
task LOCATION_MESSAGE is
  entry PUT(IN_BOX : in MESSAGE);
  entry TAKE(FROM_BOX : out MESSAGE);
end LOCATION_MESSAGE;

task body LOCATION_MESSAGE is
  HOLD : MESSAGE;
```

```
begin
  accept PUT(IN__BOX : in MESSAGE) do
    HOLD := IN__BOX;
  end PUT;
  loop
    select
      accept PUT(IN__BOX : in MESSAGE) do
        HOLD := IN__BOX;
      end PUT;
    or
      accept TAKE(FROM__BOX : out MESSAGE) do
        FROM__BOX := HOLD;
      end TAKE;
    end select;
  end loop;
end LOCATION__MESSAGE;
```

LOCATION__MESSAGE does not accept only alternating PUT and
TAKE calls as did MESSAGE__BOX. It ensures that it first accepts a PUT
in order to provide a value for HOLD, but it then will accept multiple calls to
the same entry to prevent queuing of calling tasks awaiting a call to the other
entry. However, if LOCATION__MESSAGE entries are called at a faster rate
than they can be serviced, there may still be a queue for each of the two entries
in the **select** statement. The method of choosing among the alternatives depends
on the implementation. The language definition requires that the selection be
arbitrary. That is, the same alternative must not always be chosen.

Suppose we have a message-processing requirement in which the task
SENDER (or group of similar tasks) wishes only to send unique MESSAGES.
That is, if HOLD in LOCATION__MESSAGE has not received a new message, the SENDER task does not wish a rendezvous. However, the information
is still perishable, so PUT entries will always be accepted. This is exactly the
situation in aircraft tracking situations in which a number of sites share ("cross-
tell") information on tracks. We can accomplish this type of processing by using
the selective wait with a condition. Thus modified, LOCATION__MESSAGE
becomes UNIQUE__MESSAGE:

```
task UNIQUE__MESSAGE is
  -- Same entry declarations
    . . .
end UNIQUE__MESSAGE;
```

```
task body UNIQUE_MESSAGE is
  HOLD : MESSAGE;
  NEW_MESSAGE : BOOLEAN := FALSE;
begin
  loop
    select
      accept PUT . . .

        . . .

      end PUT;
      NEW_MESSAGE := TRUE;
    or
      when NEW_MESSAGE => 
        accept TAKE . . .

          . . .

        end TAKE;
        NEW_MESSAGE := FALSE;
    end select;
  end loop;
end UNIQUE_MESSAGE;
```

The **when** clause stipulates that the condition NEW_MESSAGE must be TRUE for the TAKE entry to be available for rendezvous. The operations on NEW_MESSAGE ensure the correct ordering of rendezvous. Note that the assignments to NEW_MESSAGE are not part of the rendezvous. The calling task does not have to wait for their completion. However, they do have to be completed before UNIQUE_MESSAGE is ready to loop and again execute the **select** statement. The task UNIQUE_MESSAGE meets the stated requirement and also, by initializing NEW_MESSAGE to FALSE, prevents the TAKEing of a message before one has been PUT.

25.3.2 *Conditional and Timed Entry Calls*

The calling task has two tools that allow it to control the conditions under which a rendezvous may occur. One control mechanism is to issue an entry call only if a rendezvous is immediately available. This is a conditional entry call. For example, in task body WRITER the entry call MESSAGE_BOX.PUT (STORY) could be replaced by

```
select
   MESSAGE_BOX.PUT(STORY);
   -- Optional sequence_of_statements
else
   -- Do alternative action
   -- Could be null;
end select;
```

The result is that the rendezvous will occur only if no other entry calls are queued (or being serviced) for **MESSAGE_BOX.PUT**. If the rendezvous cannot take place immediately, the alternative action is executed. The calling task cannot perform the alternative action while at the same time being on the queue for the entry.

The second control mechanism allows the calling task to enter the queue for an entry. If the rendezvous does not occur within a specified time, the calling task leaves the queue and continues execution. This is a timed entry call. For example,

```
select
   MESSAGE_BOX.PUT(STORY);
   -- Optional sequence_of_statements
else
   delay 5.0; -- Seconds
   -- Alternative optional sequence_of_statements
end select;
```

The task **WRITER** will be suspended waiting for the rendezvous for no more than 5.0 seconds. If the rendezvous occurs before 5.0 seconds has passed, **WRITER** will participate in the rendezvous, execute the optional sequence _of_statements, and then exit the select statement. If no rendezvous occurs within 5.0 seconds, the alternative optional sequence_of_statements will be executed.

25.4 *TASK TYPES AND FAMILIES*

Ada allows the definition of task types for declaring multiple tasks of similar nature, in much the same way as generics are allowed for subprograms and packages. Ada also allows tasks to have a family of entries where each entry of the family is to accomplish a similar function.

Suppose we required multiple copies of the task MESSAGE__BOX. The only change necessary to create MESSAGE__BOX as a task type is that the word **type** is included in the task specification:

```
task type MESSAGE__BOX is
  -- No other changes
  . . .
end MESSAGE__BOX;
```

We can create instances of the type by:

```
POST__OFFICE, MAIL__BOX : MESSAGE__BOX;
LETTER : MESSAGE;                        -- Create a LETTER object
```

and then use them.

```
POST__OFFICE.TAKE(LETTER);       -- Get a LETTER
MAIL__BOX.PUT(LETTER);           -- Mail the LETTER
```

The calling task gets a letter from the POST__OFFICE and delivers it to a MAIL__BOX.

If we require tasks of type MESSAGE__BOX to accept messages based on the precedence of the entry call, we could use a *family* of entries. First we define the precedence:

```
type PRECEDENCE is (ROUTINE, PRIORITY, IMMED, FLASH);
```

Then in the task type specification of MESSAGE__BOX we would have

```
entry PUT(PRECEDENCE)(IN__BOX: in MESSAGE);
```

to define a family of entries. There are really four entries of the family PUT: one each for ROUTINE, PRIORITY, IMMED, and FLASH. Each will accomplish the same processing. In the body of the task an accept statement for routine messages would be

```
accept PUT(ROUTINE)(IN__BOX: in MESSAGE) do
  . . .
end PUT;
```

Here is an example of accepting messages according to precedence, always taking FLASH before IMMED, IMMED before PRIORITY, and PRIORITY before ROUTINE:

```
loop
  for URGENCY in reverse PRECEDENCE loop
    select
      accept PUT(URGENCY)(IN__BOX : in MESSAGE) do
        . . .
      end PUT;
      exit;
    or
      null; -- Do nothing
    end select;
  end loop;
  . . .
end loop;
```

This method will empty the FLASH queue before accepting a rendezvous with a task on the IMMED queue, and so on.

For the declaration

```
MESSAGE__CENTER : MESSAGE__BOX;
```

the entry call for a letter that must be delivered quickly would be

```
MESSAGE__CENTER.PUT(FLASH)(LETTER);
```

Of course, since many other tasks would also use the facilities of MESSAGE__CENTER, its effective operation would depend on calling tasks being careful in their use of high precedence, especially FLASH.

As a final example, we will combine the concepts of task type and family to declare an Ada representation of AUTODIN, the U.S. Government's Automatic Digital Network. Using the previous declaration of families of entries for the task type MESSAGE__BOX, we can declare an array of tasks of that type:

```
AUTODIN : array (1 .. 100) of MESSAGE__BOX;
```

A call to an entry, of a family, of a specific task, of the given type is

AUTODIN(25).PUT(ROUTINE)(LETTER);

The LETTER (of type MESSAGE) will be processed by the ROUTINE entry of the PUT family of entries. It will be processed by the twenty-fifth element of the array of tasks AUTODIN. This is a very complex situation, and the Ada representation is correspondingly complex. It is not Ada that is complex: it is the situation. Ada provides the expressive power to state the complex situation in a very succinct way.

25.5 *MORE ON TASKS*

Tasks are complicated, as are the ways in which they are used. We have only briefly described the major features of tasks in this book. We have not mentioned other points:

- The **abort** statement controls stopping of task execution.
- Tasks can have static priorities.
- Tasks can be treated generally as objects, including being accessed by access objects (pointers).
- Tasks have additional attributes.
- The language specifies in great detail the rules for task control and interaction, including complex rules for the operation of a selective—wait.
- There is substantial and complex interaction between tasks and exceptions.

Despite their complexity, tasks are an important and necessary concept. The control of concurrent processes is necessary in most real-time systems. Having features in a high-level language to control concurrency allows programmers to avoid assembly language for this aspect of system development. The Ada tasking mechanism allows a high level of abstraction in the design of real-time systems and has the potential to increase reliability and lead to more maintainable software.

Exercise—25

Modify PROGRAM—21 so that SLEEP is provided as an entry to a task and is available to many (at least two) users. The using programs should be able to go about their business (whatever makes them TIRED) concurrently. In order to make it easier to use the bed for sleeping (and to make this exercise easier!), have the SLEEP entry guarantee the bed. If the bed is messy, SLEEP takes the responsibility for MAKEing it.

Exercise—25A

Write a program with a SENDER task and a WRITER task. The SENDER has an entry that accepts (mode **in**) an object of type MESSAGE (a private type). WRITER generates messages using a procedure WRITE and then calls the entry in SENDER. SENDER accepts the entry and then disposes of the message using the procedure TRANSMIT. The two tasks operate in parallel, with synchronization at the rendezvous. This exercise has the same components as the example in this chapter. The problem is to integrate them into a complete program.

Exercise—25B

Write a program containing three tasks. Two tasks generate values and the other task accepts the values and prints them out. The print task will accept a value from either of the generating tasks and print them as they become available.

Exercise—25C

Write a complete program implementing task buffering using a selective wait. Use LOCATION—MESSAGE (used as an example in this chapter) as a starting point.

Program—25

```
package SLEEP_TIGHT is
   type BED is limited private;
   type CONDITION is (RESTED, TIRED);
   procedure INITIALIZE(B : out BED);
   task HOTEL is
      entry SLEEP (B : in out BED; C : out CONDITION);
   end HOTEL;
private
   type BED is range 0 .. 6;
end;
```

```
with TEXT__IO; use TEXT__IO;
package body SLEEP__TIGHT is

    procedure INITIALIZE(B : out BED) is
    begin
      PUT__LINE("In INITIALIZE");
      B := 0;
    end INITIALIZE;

    procedure MAKE(B : out BED) is
    begin
      PUT__LINE("In MAKE");
      B := 0;
    end MAKE;

    function MESSY(B : BED) return BOOLEAN is
    begin
      PUT__LINE("In MESSY");
      if B = BED'LAST then
        return TRUE;
      else
        return FALSE;
      end if;
    end MESSY;

    task body HOTEL is
    begin
      for I in 1 .. 26 loop
        PUT__LINE("Waiting for an entry call to SLEEP");
        accept SLEEP(B : in out BED; C : out CONDITION) do
          PUT__LINE("In SLEEP");
          if MESSY(B) then
            MAKE(B);
          end if;
          C := RESTED;
          B := B + 1;
        end SLEEP;
      end loop;
    end HOTEL;
end SLEEP__TIGHT;


with SLEEP__TIGHT, TEXT__IO; use SLEEP__TIGHT, TEXT__IO;
procedure PROGRAM__25 is
    task FIRM__BED;
    task COUCH;
```

```
task body FIRM_BED is

  procedure FIRM_BED is
    FIRM_BED : BED;
    CAPABILITY : CONDITION := RESTED;
  begin -- Procedure FIRM_BED
    INITIALIZE(FIRM_BED);
    for I in 1 .. 13 loop
      PUT_LINE("In loop in FIRM_BED");
      CAPABILITY := TIRED;
      HOTEL.SLEEP(FIRM_BED, CAPABILITY);
      if CAPABILITY = RESTED then
        PUT_LINE("Now rested by FIRM_BED");
      end if;
    end loop;
  end FIRM_BED; -- Procedure
begin -- Task FIRM_BED
  FIRM_BED;
end FIRM_BED; -- Task

task body COUCH is

  procedure COUCH is
    COUCH : BED;
    CAPABILITY : CONDITION := RESTED;
  begin -- Procedure COUCH
    INITIALIZE(COUCH);
    for I in 1 .. 13 loop
    PUT_LINE("In loop in COUCH");
      CAPABILITY := TIRED;
      HOTEL.SLEEP(COUCH, CAPABILITY);
      if CAPABILITY = RESTED then
        PUT_LINE("Now rested by COUCH");
      end if;
    end loop;
  end COUCH; -- Procedure
  begin -- Task COUCH
    COUCH;
  end COUCH; -- Task
begin -- PROGRAM_25
  null;
end PROGRAM_25;
```

Waiting for an entry call to SLEEP
In INITIALIZE
In INITIALIZE
In loop in COUCH
In loop in FIRM__BED
In SLEEP
In MESSY
Now rested by COUCH
In loop in COUCH
Waiting for an entry call to SLEEP
In SLEEP
In MESSY
Now rested by FIRM__BED
In loop in FIRM__BED
Waiting for an entry call to SLEEP
In SLEEP
In MESSY
Now rested by COUCH
In loop in COUCH
Waiting for an entry call to SLEEP
In SLEEP
In MESSY
Waiting for an entry call to SLEEP
In SLEEP
Now rested by FIRM__BED
In loop in FIRM__BED
In MESSY
Waiting for an entry call to SLEEP
Now rested by COUCH
In SLEEP
In MESSY
In loop in COUCH
Waiting for an entry call to SLEEP
Now rested by FIRM__BED
In loop in FIRM__BED
In MESSY
Waiting for an entry call to SLEEP
Now rested by COUCH
In SLEEP
In MESSY
In loop in COUCH

Waiting for an entry call to SLEEP
In SLEEP
Now rested by FIRM__BED
In loop in FIRM__BED
In MESSY
Waiting for an entry call to SLEEP
In SLEEP
In MESSY
Now rested by COUCH
In loop in COUCH
Waiting for an entry call to SLEEP
Now rested by FIRM__BED
In loop in FIRM__BED
In SLEEP
In MESSY
Waiting for an entry call to SLEEP
Now rested by COUCH
In loop in COUCH
In SLEEP
In MESSY
Waiting for an entry call to SLEEP
Now rested by FIRM__BED
In loop in FIRM__BED
In SLEEP
In MESSY
In MAKE
Waiting for an entry call to SLEEP
In SLEEP
Now rested by COUCH
In loop in COUCH
In MESSY
In MAKE
Waiting for an entry call to SLEEP
Now rested by FIRM__BED
In loop in FIRM__BED
In SLEEP
In MESSY
Waiting for an entry call to SLEEP
Now rested by COUCH
In loop in COUCH
In SLEEP
In MESSY
Now rested by FIRM__BED
In loop in FIRM__BED

Waiting for an entry call to SLEEP
In SLEEP
In MESSY
Now rested by COUCH
In loop in COUCH
Waiting for an entry call to SLEEP
In SLEEP
In MESSY
Now rested by FIRM__BED
In loop in FIRM__BED
Waiting for an entry call to SLEEP
In SLEEP
In MESSY
Now rested by COUCH
In loop in COUCH
Waiting for an entry call to SLEEP
In SLEEP
In MESSY
Waiting for an entry call to SLEEP
In SLEEP
Now rested by FIRM__BED
In loop in FIRM__BED
In MESSY
Waiting for an entry call to SLEEP
Now rested by COUCH
In SLEEP
In MESSY
In loop in COUCH
Now rested by FIRM__BED
In loop in FIRM__BED
Waiting for an entry call to SLEEP
In SLEEP
In MESSY
Now rested by COUCH
In loop in COUCH
Waiting for an entry call to Sleep
In SLEEP
In MESSY
Now rested by FIRM__BED
In loop in FIRM__BED
Waiting for an entry call to SLEEP
In SLEEP
In MESSY
In MAKE

```
        Waiting for an entry call to SLEEP
        Now rested by COUCH
        In SLEEP
        In MESSY
        In MAKE
        Now rested by FIRM__BED
```

Program__25A

```
with TEXT__IO; use TEXT__IO;
procedure PROGRAM__25A is

    package SENDWRITE is
      type MESSAGE is private;
      task SENDER is
        entry SEND(M : in MESSAGE);
      end SENDER;
      task WRITER;
    private
      type MESSAGE is range 0 .. 100;
    end;

    package body SENDWRITE is

      task body SENDER is
        OUT__GOING: MESSAGE;

        procedure TRANSMIT(ANY : in MESSAGE) is
        begin
          PUT__LINE("IN TRANSMIT");
        end TRANSMIT;
      begin -- Task SENDER
        PUT__LINE("BEGINNING OF SENDER");
        for I in 1 .. 5 loop
          PUT__LINE("IN LOOP IN SENDER");
          accept SEND(M : in MESSAGE) do
            OUT__GOING := M;
          end SEND;
          TRANSMIT(OUT__GOING);
        end loop;
      end SENDER;

      task body WRITER is
        STORY : MESSAGE;
```

```
        procedure WRITE(S : out MESSAGE) is
        begin
          S := 1;
          PUT__LINE(" IN WRITE");
        end WRITE;
      begin -- Task WRITER
          PUT__LINE("BEGINNING OF WRITER");
          for I in 1 .. 5 loop
            PUT__LINE("IN LOOP IN WRITER");
            WRITE(STORY);
            SENDER.SEND(STORY);
            PUT__LINE("AFTER SENDER.SEND");
          end loop;
      end WRITER;
    begin
      PUT__LINE("PACKAGE BODY SENDWRITE INITIALIZATION");
    end SENDWRITE;
begin -- PROGRAM__25A
    PUT__LINE("BEGIN PROGRAM__25A");
end PROGRAM__25A;


BEGINNING OF WRITER
IN LOOP IN WRITER
PACKAGE BODY SENDWRITE INITIALIZATION
BEGIN PROGRAM__25A
BEGINNING OF SENDER
IN WRITE
IN LOOP IN SENDER
IN TRANSMIT
AFTER SENDER.SEND
IN LOOP IN WRITER
IN WRITE
IN LOOP IN SENDER
AFTER SENDER.SEND
IN LOOP IN WRITER
IN WRITE
IN TRANSMIT
IN LOOP IN SENDER
IN TRANSMIT
AFTER SENDER.SEND
IN LOOP IN WRITER
IN LOOP IN SENDER
IN WRITE
```

```
AFTER SENDER.SEND
IN LOOP IN WRITER
IN WRITE
IN TRANSMIT
IN LOOP IN SENDER
IN TRANSMIT
AFTER SENDER.SEND
```

Program__25B

```
with TEXT__IO; use TEXT__IO;
procedure PROGRAM__25B is
   type PASSIT is range 0 .. 110;
   package IO is new INTEGER__IO(PASSIT); use IO;
   THING : PASSIT := 0;

   task PRINT is
      entry OUTPUT(PARM : PASSIT);
   end PRINT;

   task body PRINT is
   begin
      for I in 1 .. 10 loop
         PUT__LINE("IN PRINT");
         accept OUTPUT(PARM : PASSIT) do
            PUT(PARM + 100); NEW__LINE;
         end OUTPUT;
      end loop;
   end PRINT;

   task ONE;
   task body ONE is
   begin
      for J in 1 .. 5 loop
         THING := PASSIT(J);
         PUT("IN TASK ONE. THING IS: "); PUT(THING); NEW__LINE;
         PRINT.OUTPUT(THING);
      end loop;
   end ONE;

   task TWO;
   task body TWO is
```

```
      begin
        for J in 6 .. 10 loop
          THING := PASSIT(J);
          PUT("IN TASK TWO. THING IS: "); PUT(THING); NEW_LINE;
          PRINT.OUTPUT(THING);
        end loop;
      end TWO;
    begin -- PROGRAM_25B
      PUT_LINE("MAIN BODY OF PROGRAM_25B");
    end PROGRAM_25B;
```

Program_25C

```
    with TEXT_IO; use TEXT_IO;
    procedure PROGRAM_25C is

      package LOCMSG is
        type MESSAGE is private;
        task LOCATION_MESSAGE is
          entry PUT (IN_BOX : in MESSAGE);
          entry TAKE(FROM_BOX : out MESSAGE);
        end LOCATION_MESSAGE;
        task SENDER;
        task WRITER;
      private
        type MESSAGE is range 0 .. 100;
      end;

      package body LOCMSG is

        task body LOCATION_MESSAGE is
          HOLD : MESSAGE := 0;
          begin
            for I in 1 .. 10 loop
              select
                accept PUT(IN_BOX : in MESSAGE) do
                  HOLD := IN_BOX;
                end PUT;
              or
                accept TAKE(FROM_BOX : out MESSAGE) do
                  FROM_BOX := HOLD;
                end TAKE;
              end select;
            end loop;
        end LOCATION_MESSAGE;
```

```
task body SENDER is
  OUT_GOING : MESSAGE;

  procedure TRANSMIT(ANY : in MESSAGE) is
  begin
    PUT_LINE("IN TRANSMIT");
  end TRANSMIT;
begin -- Task SENDER
  for I in 1 .. 5 loop
    LOCATION_MESSAGE.TAKE(OUT_GOING);
    TRANSMIT(OUT_GOING);
  end loop;
end SENDER;

task body WRITER is
  STORY : MESSAGE;

  procedure WRITE(S : out MESSAGE) is
  begin
    S := 1;
    PUT_LINE("IN WRITE");
  end WRITE;
begin -- Task WRITER
  for I in 1 .. 5 loop
    WRITE(STORY);
    LOCATION_MESSAGE.PUT(STORY);
  end loop;
end WRITER;
end LOCMSG;
begin -- PROGRAM_25C
  null; -- Tasks are activated
end PROGRAM_25C;
```

Discussion_25

The capabilities provided in the package specification are INITIALIZE and the
SLEEP entry in the task HOTEL. The package body contains the body of the
task HOTEL and also contains some support procedures not visible to users
of the package. These are the same procedures that were previously called by
users of the package. The entry accomplishes the same function that was
performed by the procedure SLEEP, but it guarantees the availability of a bed.
The task HOTEL can execute concurrently with other tasks.

PROGRAM__25 contains two nested tasks, FIRM__BED and COUCH. These tasks use the capability provided by HOTEL. The task declarations are simple since they do not provide any entries. Each task declares a procedure that will do the processing for the task. The executable part of each task is simply a call to the procedure.

The task COUCH, the procedure COUCH, and the object COUCH all have the same name. It is overloaded. There is no ambiguity since they are quite different sorts of constructs. The compiler can differentiate between them. Similarily for FIRM__BED.

Immediately prior to the execution of PROGRAM__25, the package SLEEP__TIGHT is elaborated. At this time task HOTEL begins to execute. It prints a message and then waits at its entry point. Then the two tasks in the procedure begin to execute. The three tasks then continue to execute in parallel, until their job is complete. The messages printed as a result of the program execution are somewhat repetitious, but are worthy of study since they show the task interactions and the indeterminacy of the task execution.

Discussion__25A

There are two tasks, which execute in parallel and also concurrent with the main body of the program. Task SENDER has an entry called SEND. When the other task calls the entry, the task execution is synchronized, the value is passed, and the code of the accept statement is executed.

The "task" of the body of the procedure completes its simple job (an output statement) before the other tasks, but control waits before the end statement until all tasks have completed. Then the procedure may terminate.

Execution of the tasks is indeterminate. One cannot tell from a static analysis of the code what the order of execution of statements is going to be. Different executions of PROGRAM__25A may produce different sequences of execution of statements, as though multiple processors were being used for varying sets of concurrent functions.

Discussion__25B

The situation is very similar to PROGRAM__25A, but here we have two tasks competing for attention of the PRINT task.

Discussion___25C

The situation is similar again to PROGRAM___25A, but here there is a buffer between the SENDER and WRITER. The buffer task LOCMSG has two entries, one for reading and one for writing. The mode of the formal parameters in the task specification makes the direction of information flow apparent. The buffer may select either a PUT or a TAKE, depending on which entry has been called. If there is a queue for each of the entries, it may select either, in an arbitrary way. The initialization of the object HOLD to zero is necessary since it is possible to have a call to TAKE prior to a call to PUT. Of course, the accepts could be ordered to ensure that a PUT occurred first. An easy way would be to have

```
          .
          .
          .
     accept PUT(IN__BOX : in MESSAGE) do
        HOLD := IN__BOX;
     end PUT;
     for I in 1 .. 9 do
     -- and now the select statement
```

This problem was discussed in the chapter.

Keys to Understanding

▶ Tasks are entities that operate in parallel, with real or apparent concurrency. Tasks typically interact and exchange information with each other.

▶ Ada's mechanism for controlling concurrent execution is the rendezvous. It provides both for task *synchronization* and for *transfer of information*. Ada provides extensive control over the rendezvous.

PART 5

ALL ABOUT ADA

An important part of Ada development is the environment surrounding the language itself: programming support, validation, design methodologies, and the Ada community. The first two of the following chapters discuss the Ada Programming Support Environment (APSE) and the Ada Compiler Validation Capability (ACVC). The next chapter summarizes the entire book; it does so by structuring Ada information into twelve categories that you can use to discuss the language development. The final chapter presents some notions on the relationship of design methods to Ada use and points out the changing nature of the Ada programming community.

26

The Ada Programming Support Environment

Objective: to discuss the Ada Programming Support Environment (APSE)

The Ada Programming Support Environment (APSE) is an important part of the development of Ada. It is the set of software tools that will be used to design, develop, and maintain Ada programs—the programmer's workbench. The programming support environment is a necessary adjunct to the language itself since the environment plays a critical role in effectively using the language and in influencing the cost and maintainability of the resulting programs. A sophisticated environment that allows easy programmer communication, effective integration, and control over alternate configurations is particularly important in creating the large embedded computer systems for which Ada is intended to be used.

The importance of the APSE was recognized early in the Ada program. The APSE definition underwent the same sort of careful development as did the Ada language itself, with the APSE concept being refined through Sandman, Pebbleman, and Stoneman phases. Early in 1978 the Sandman document was distributed to about fifty people in the DoD. Comments on Sandman resulted in Pebbleman, which was widely distributed, and in 1979 Pebbleman yielded to Stoneman. The *Department of Defense Requirements for Ada Programming Support Environments "Stoneman,"* published by DoD in February 1980, then became the requirements document for the APSE, as did the Steelman requirements document for Ada itself.

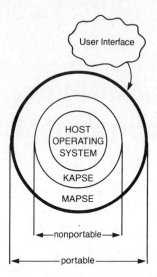

Figure 26-1   Stoneman Architecture

There was a difference, however, in the level of definition between Steelman and Stoneman. While the computing community by and large felt comfortable with specifying requirements for a language, there was a general sense that not enough was known about relative advantages of alternative features of a support environment. Stoneman, therefore, is less definitive for the APSE than Steelman is for Ada. Stoneman provides a general sort of guide to developers of a potential APSE and provides for an open-ended environment in which new tools can be added to a basic support environment.

Figure 26-1 shows the general architecture of the APSE; figure 26-2 elaborates the concept. At the heart is the *Kernel* APSE, or KAPSE. The KAPSE is the interface to the host operating system. Built on the KAPSE is a *Minimum,* or essential, set of tools, the MAPSE. The addition of more tools, including special-purpose tools for specific instances of an Ada environment, yields an APSE.

The KAPSE is machine—and operating system—dependent. It is intended to be the only machine-dependent part of the environment. It uses the facilities available at a primitive level, even residing on a bare machine, and provides a constant interface to MAPSE tools. It is required for transportability of an entire APSE or of individual tools from one machine environment to another. Rehosting the APSE (that is, making Ada and its environment available in a new host processor) should require only that the KAPSE be modified.

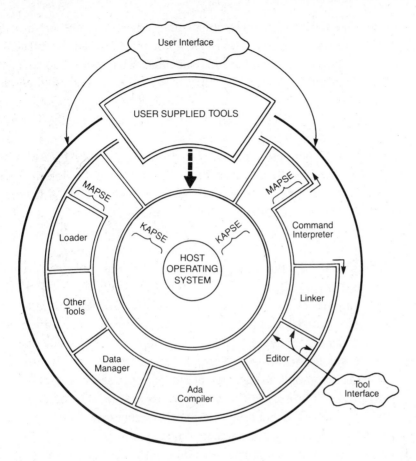

Figure 26-2   APSE Architecture

Relatively easy rehosting will help make Ada widely available, make it useful in a wide variety of circumstances, and make it the language of choice in real-time commercial environments as well as in DoD embedded computer systems.

The MAPSE uses the facilities provided by the KAPSE to provide a suitable set of tools for creating Ada programs. The MAPSE, provided with a standard interface to the KAPSE, should be transportable among host machines. To the extent to which it presents a standard interface to the programmer, the MAPSE will also facilitate the transportability of programmers from project to project. Unfortunately, neither of these two sorts of transportability currently exists. The KAPSE-MAPSE external interface has not been completely standardized, although government and industry teams are working toward such standardization. Nor has the MAPSE-programmer interface been specified as a standard. Stoneman left the issue open, since there is no consensus on what a specific interface ought to be. Nonetheless, the framework is available for standardization in the near future. As Ada use becomes common through the 1980s and into the 1990s, standards will evolve and yield the hoped-for benefits of a standard environment.

Even without a completely standard environment, the KAPSE-MAPSE-APSE notion is being used to create effective Ada software development environments. The MAPSE, of course, is available with the first DoD Ada compilers. There is no wide consensus as to what constitutes a MAPSE, but two key tools are the compiler itself and the programmer interface to the remaining tools.

Ada compilers are large, complex pieces of software. Not surprisingly, they can be (and for DoD, are) built in the Ada language itself. Various methods, including use of an Ada-to-Pascal translator, are being used to bootstrap initial versions of Ada compilers. In a typical compiler-generation effort the machine-independent front end is developed separately from the machine-dependent code generator. In Ada compiler development the intermediate language Diana is commonly used as a machine-independent representation of an Ada program, to link parts of the compiler. Separating the code generator eases the task of targeting the compiler to another processor. Retargeting is of particular importance, since development of large DoD programs in Ada will typically be carried out on a large host machine, with cross-compilers to generate code for a variety of different targets. Associated with retargeting is the creation of the run-time environment. Because of Ada's sophisticated features like tasking and error handling, creating an Ada run-time environment will be in many ways similar to developing a real-time executive. For each target it is important that the code produced be small in size and execute quickly.

The issue of the efficiency of generated object code is crucial to the success of Ada. In embedded computer system applications Ada often will not compete against other high-level languages; it will compete against assembly language. During studies leading to the initiation of the Ada program, DoD analysts discovered that even when DoD high-level languages (such as Jovial and CMS-2) were used for embedded computer systems, sometimes 50 percent or more of the lines of source code were in assembly language. The assembly-level code was used to implement features such as concurrency and to efficiently implement required functionality. Ada has features that allow all programming to be accomplished in Ada. But Ada must be efficient as well, if it is to meet with favor among system developers. To meet efficiency requirements, DoD Ada compilers will use sophisticated optimization techniques to produce compact and efficient code.

Optimizing compilers, however, are likely to take an extended amount of time to translate source code into executable form. Since compilation time is also important, and since Ada compilers have a great deal to accomplish, the compilers themselves must be efficient. The first generation of compilers are likely to be deficient in one respect or another, but if Ada is to succeed, the second-generation compilers of the late 1980s must both run quickly and generate efficient code.

The primary interface to the programmer using the MAPSE will be the command language that deals with the other tools in the environment. The command language will be modeled on Ada itself. It is probable that the command language interpreter will allow the programmer to program in the command language to some extent and to access a tree-structured set of directories and files. Such a user interface is likely to incorporate a number of features of the popular operating system UNIX.*

The compiler and command language are not the only parts of the MAPSE. As more tools are added, the MAPSE becomes more nearly complete and, at some point, becomes a full APSE. The sort of tools that will be provided as part of the APSE are

- Editors
- Automated requirements tools
- Automated design tools
- Assemblers
- Linker/loader
- Static test tools (structure trees, set/use analyzer, code analyzer)
- Dynamic test tools (time and frequency analyzer, decision path coverage, test case generator)
- Text formatters (word processing, pretty-printing)
- File administration tools
- Debuggers
- Configuration control tools

*UNIX is a trademark of the Bell System.

The last set of tools is of particular importance. Stoneman calls for considerable support for configuration management. Large systems built by large teams of programmers over long periods of time are difficult to control. Effective configuration management tools can provide good project control and project team support. Proper management of software as it moves from requirements, to top-level and detailed design, to code, to various levels of test, and to delivery and maintenance is important. For large software systems it is essential. Proper management of such systems requires tools to provide access control over the multiple versions, variations, and releases of software generated throughout the life cycle. Control of the source code, a history of changes, automatic system generation for each release or version, and similar capabilities are some of the tools necessary for long-lived embedded computer systems.

DoD intends to develop several Ada environments, on different hosts and for a variety of target processors. These environments will be available to developers of embedded computer systems. The widespread use of a sophisticated environment will increase programmer productivity and increase the use of the Ada language. The standardization of the environments, though limited at first, will allow programmers to move among projects more easily and reduce or eliminate the poor productivity associated with learning a new environment. In turn, the automation of design methodologies in the APSE could help to spread, and to standardize, design methods and software engineering ideas relevant to Ada. In effect, the widespread use of standard Ada environments should increase the professionalism of programmers, increase overall productivity, and help meet the reliability, cost, and maintainability goals of the Ada program within DoD and real-time commercial environments.

Keys to Understanding

► The APSE is the set of software tools that will be used to design, develop, and maintain Ada programs—the programmer's workbench.
► The APSE is an integral part of the overall Ada effort, and it will do much to enhance the development and maintenance of large software systems.

27

The Ada Compiler
Validation Capability

> Objective: to discuss the Ada Compiler Valida-
> tion Capability (ACVC)

The U.S. DoD intends that Ada be a single, standard language. There are to be no subsets, no supersets. On the other hand DoD does not intend to have a single Ada compiler to be provided to system developers. Anyone may develop an Ada compiler. In order to enforce, and encourage, the necessary standardization, DoD has established a facility to test Ada compilers for their adherence to the standard language definition. The tool used to test and validate candidate compilers is the Ada Compiler Validation Capability (ACVC).

The ACVC consists of the *Ada Compiler Validation Implementers' Guide,* a set of validation tests, and the tools and procedures necessary to effectively test candidate compilers. The tests address only those aspects of a compiler that are relevant to the Ada language standard; characteristics such as efficiency of generated code, compiler execution time, appropriateness of error diagnostics, and so on, are not addressed. The first translator to be validated was the New York University (NYU) Ada/Ed, an interpreter designed to be an executable definition of the language to be used for educational purposes. The first compiler to be validated was developed by the ROLM Corporation.

27.1 *THE IMPLEMENTERS' GUIDE*

The Implementers' Guide (IG) is designed to assist implementers of Ada compilers to adhere to the standard. It is an important part of the DoD's use of the ACVC to encourage compliance and create commonality among Ada compilers built by different organizations. The IG clarifies language issues, discusses the implications of the language standard, addresses features that are likely to pose difficulties in implementation, and serves as a basis for the ACVC tests.

The IG describes each of the tests, actual Ada programs to be submitted to the candidate compilers. It explains the purpose of each test, relates it to the language standard, points out ambiguities and potential problems, and specifies checks for subsets and supersets.

The IG follows the outline of the Ada standard and provides additional information about each feature or section. It addresses the following points:

- Semantic ramifications: nonobvious implications, examples, and additional explanations of features and combinations of features.
- Compile-time restrictions: additional legality restrictions, implied by context, that must be enforced by a conforming compiler.
- Exception conditions: situations requiring that an exception be raised.
- Test objectives: the goal of each test and a guide for design of the test; a test specification.
- Gaps: inconsistencies and ambiguities in the Ada standard. The IG does not attempt to resolve the problem but does specify tests to determine the approach adopted by the candidate compiler.

Each of these discussions serves two purposes: it specifies validation tests, including tests for the language features that interact in subtle ways, and it provides guidance for compiler implementers. Both the IG and the tests themselves have been made widely available to implementers.

27.2 *THE ACVC TESTS*

The ACVC tests are Ada programs. Some are legal programs, intended to be compiled and executed. Others are illegal programs that must be rejected by a conforming compiler. The tests are designed to check for subsets, to ensure that a compiler handles all required features of the language, and to detect supersets. Superset detection is difficult since the test designers must anticipate what (illegal) features might be allowed by a nonconforming compiler. For example, if the standard specifies a comma (",") between parameters of a procedure call, it would be incorrect and nonconforming for a compiler to also allow a semicolon (";") to be used.

The approach taken toward test development has been to prepare many small tests, over 1700 of them, to test specific features and combinations of features. Each test attempts to use as little of Ada as possible, outside of its test objective, to isolate the cause of failure. This approach of having a large number of small tests is of particular value in that, despite standardization, certain features of Ada are optional for conforming compilers. The optional features often depend on the capabilities provided by the hardware of the target machine. Having many small tests helps isolate these features. The difficulty with having many small tests, rather than a few large ones, is that conducting the testing is more difficult. The ACVC includes test tools to help automate the testing process and make testing easier to conduct.

The tests themselves are based on the design guidelines and objectives established in the Implementers' Guide. They therefore focus on specific goals, and an implementer may use a test failure to determine how to modify the compiler to make it conform to the language standard. Indeed, since the tests are widely available, implementers will use them to determine their own progress and to assist in the compiler development.

The breadth of test coverage is shown by the types of programs constituting six classes of tests. The classes are

- Class A: legal Ada programs. Passed if the compiler indicates no errors.
- Class B: illegal programs. Passed if all errors are detected and no legal statements are indicated as errors at compile time.
- Class L: illegal programs. The errors need not be detected until link time. Passed if errors are indicated prior to execution.
- Class C: executable Ada programs. The tests are self-checking. Passed if successfully executed.
- Class D: capacity tests. The tests provide general information about the implementation. No clear pass/fail criteria.
- Class E: ambiguity tests. The tests determine the interpretation of an ambiguous part of the standard. No pass/fail criteria. Useful for determining how implementers are interpreting the standard.

The ACVC provides the DoD with the ability to have a number of competing, but standard, Ada compilers. Allowing compilers to be developed commercially, not just by DoD, will make Ada use more widespread. Ada programs, perhaps using packages originally developed for DoD systems, are likely to be developed for commercial real-time systems. Components of those commercial systems, and other packages of software developed as part of a general-purpose software components industry, are likely to find use in later DoD systems.

By assisting compiler implementers, the ACVC will encourage (and ultimately enforce) Ada standardization. This will promote widespread use of Ada and help bring about a practical software components industry.

Keys to Understanding

▶ The ACVC is a set of Ada programs, both correct and incorrect, that will be used to check Ada compilers for conformance to the standard. It also provides additional information about Ada in order to assist implementers of Ada compilers to adhere to the standard.

▶ Only compilers validated through use of the ACVC will be eligible for use on DoD projects.

28

Twelve Items to Remember

Objective:	to summarize all the material presented, under twelve specific points in two general areas

This chapter provides a summary, in structured form, of the material you need to remember about Ada. The requirement for the chapter and the manner in which it is structured stem from my experience in teaching two-day intensive seminars in Ada for technical managers. These seminars covered a great deal of material. At the end the students always had an enormous amount of information, but it never seemed to be cataloged sufficiently. This is a bit like the story of the fellow who learned to speed read at 4000 words per minute. He then found that he could double his speed, by holding the pages to the light and reading both sides at the same time! One evening he applied this technique to Tolstoy's *War and Peace* and proudly announced the next day at work that he had read the mammoth novel in one evening. His colleagues found this interesting and asked, "What was the novel about?" His only response was a stuttered, "Well, ah, let's see, well, it was about Russia!"

Well, I was concerned that if someone asked my students "What was the seminar about?" the response would be a stuttered, "Well, ah, let's see, well, it was about Ada!" To help them respond to such a question, I suggested that they commit to memory twelve points. These twelve points, presented in figure 28-1, summarize the main topics I covered in my seminars. I have grouped them into two categories:

ADA GENERAL KNOWLEDGE

- Requirement for Ada
- Development of Ada
- General nature of Ada
- Ada Programming Support Environment
- Ada Compiler Validation Capability
- Current status of Ada

ADA LANGUAGE FEATURES

- Pascal-like characteristics
- Strong typing
- Encapsulation
- Generic units
- Exceptions
- Tasks

Figure 28-1   Twelve Items to Remember

• General knowledge: six topics related to issues surrounding Ada development and use.

• Language features: six topics related to the language itself and its key technical features.

I hope these topics also prove useful in summarizing this book. Knowing them should help you in understanding Ada.

28.1 ADA GENERAL KNOWLEDGE

The six topics you should remember that concern Ada general knowledge follow. Each topic is first presented as a set of key ideas or phrases and then by a summary statement.

1. Requirement for Ada

- DoD spends billions of dollars on software
- Embedded computer systems
- Maintenance of long-lived programs
- Wasteful to have many languages
- Ada to be standard

Most of the billions of dollars the DoD spends on software is committed to embedded computer systems, much of it for maintenance of these large,

long-lived programs. The use of many different languages and support environments, and use of assembly language for lack of a suitable high-level language
for systems programming, is wasteful. Ada will be the standard language for
developing embedded computer systems.

DoD NEEDS A STANDARD LANGUAGE

2. Development of Ada

- Major effort over five-year period
- Requirements: Strawman . . . Steelman
- Language evaluations
- Four designs: Red, Blue, Yellow, Green
- Test and evaluation of preliminary Ada
- DARPA/HOLWG

Ada was specified and designed over a period of five years and involved
hundreds of people in government, industry, and academia. There were requirements documents (Strawman to Steelman), extensive language evaluations,
four competing designs (Red, Blue, Yellow, Green), and a test and evaluation
phase to ensure language suitability. The process was managed by the Defense
Advanced Research Projects Agency (DARPA) and coordinated by the High
Order Language Working Group (HOLWG).

ADA UNDERWENT AN INTENSIVE FIVE-YEAR DEVELOPMENT

3. General Nature of Ada

- Classical, strongly typed language
- Embedded computer systems
- Reliability and maintainability
- Systems programming
- Real-time programming
    - Parallel tasks
    - Exceptions

Ada is a classical, strongly typed, high-level programming language designed to support development of large embedded computer system applications. It promotes development of reliable and maintainable programs, provides for systems programming applications, and supports real-time programming with facilities to model parallel tasks and handle exceptions.

> **ADA IS A MODERN LANGUAGE FOR DEVELOPING EMBEDDED COMPUTER SYSTEMS**

4. The Ada Programming Support Environment (APSE)

- Ada software development environment
- Compiler, linker/loader, editor, and so on
- APSE/MAPSE/KAPSE

The APSE is the environment in which Ada programs will be developed. It includes the compiler, linker/loader, editor, debugger, and configuration manager. A Minimal APSE (MAPSE) supports programmer transportability and a machine-dependent Kernal APSE (KAPSE) supports system and tool transportability. The APSE is based on a series of requirements documents culminating in Stoneman.

> **THE APSE PROVIDES ALL TOOLS NECESSARY TO DEVELOP ADA PROGRAMS**

5. Ada Compiler Validation Capability (ACVC)

- Set of tests, Ada programs
- Enforce Ada standard
- Illegal programs and executable programs
- Subsets and supersets
- Implementers' Guide

The ACVC consists of a set of tests (Ada programs) to enforce and encourage correct implementations of Ada. Some tests are illegal programs that must be detected; others are legal programs that must execute successfully. The tests are designed to detect both supersets and subsets of Ada, which are prohibited under current policy. A unique feature of the effort is the Ada

Compiler Validation Implementers' Guide, which discusses implications of the Ada standard.

THE ACVC TESTS ADA COMPILERS

6. Current Status of Ada

- July 1980, LRM. MIL-STD-1815, December 10, 1980. 1982 update
- January 22, 1983, ANSI/MIL-STD-1815A, ANSI approval February 17, 1983
- Army and Air Force developments
- Army ALS, 1984
- Test and subset translators
- Commercial activity

A July 1980 reference manual defines the language. It became MIL-STD-1815 on December 10, 1983. Some clarifications and changes were made as part of the ANSI process, and the reference was updated in 1982. A final version was published as ANSI/MIL-STD 1815A of January 22, 1983. It was approved by ANSI on February 17, 1983. A number of tutorial books have already been published. International standardization procedures have been initiated. The Army and Air Force are proceeding with Ada developments. A number of compilers have been completed, both for the government and as commercial ventures. There is significant overseas and commercial activity.

ADA STANDARDIZATION IS WELL UNDERWAY

28.2 ADA LANGUAGE FEATURES

The six items you should remember that concern Ada language features are:

1. Pascal-like Characteristics

- Some similarity to Algol and Pascal
- Embedded computer systems

- Major new features
  Packages
  Separate compilation
  Generic units
  Exception handling
  Tasks

Ada is generally Algol- or Pascal-like in its syntax, data structures, block structure, and definition of types. It has added features to make it a production-quality language for real-time embedded computer systems. Major new features are packages, separate compilation, exception handling, generic units, tasks, and the notion of the APSE.

> **ADA HAS SOME SIMILARITY TO PASCAL BUT INCLUDES MANY ENHANCEMENTS AND MAJOR ADDITIONS**

2. Strong Typing

- New type definitions
- Each type defines a set of values and allowable operations
- Compile-time consistency checks
- Aids in detecting logical errors

A strongly typed language allows the definition of new types of objects (even if they have the identical machine representation) and forbids compile-time inconsistencies in their usage. Strong typing allows the detection of logical errors by the compiler. It has been found to be a powerful aid in the creation of reliable and maintainable programs.

> **ENFORCING TYPE CONSISTENCY CAN HELP DETECT LOGICAL ERRORS**

3. Encapsulation

- Encapsulates data and programs
- Visibility of names

- Separate compilation
    top-down
    bottom-up
- Private types
- Data abstraction

Ada provides superior capability to encapsulate data and subprograms or tasks providing access to that data. It provides facilities for restricting and opening the visibility of names, and provides for separate compilation with either top-down or bottom-up development. These facilities allow a high degree of data abstraction, that is, the separation of abstract properties from implementation or machine representation.

> **ADA EFFECTIVELY PACKAGES DATA AND RELATED PROCEDURES**

4. Generic Units

- Easy-to-use standard programs
- Template: parameters of object, type, and subprogram
- Instantiation
- Software maintenance

The underlying purpose of generic units is to write a piece of code once that will be used many times. A generic unit is a *template,* with parameters of objects, types, and subprograms. Instantiation (making of copies) occurs only at compile time. Generic methods are likely to have their greatest benefit for maintenance of long-lived software.

> **GENERIC UNITS ARE TEMPLATES WITH PARAMETERS**

5. Exceptions

- Exceptional occurrence
    typically an error
    handler replaces remainder of program unit
- Dynamic propagation
- Encourages defensive programming

An exception is an error, or other unusual/exceptional occurrence, processed by an exception handler. The exception handler replaces the code following the exception. Rules are defined for the propagation of exceptions when no handler exists within the scope of the exception occurrence. The exception handling process is designed to encourage fault-tolerant programming.

EXCEPTION CAPABILITIES ENCOURAGE DEFENSIVE PROGRAMMING

---

6. Tasks

- Tasks allow multiple threads of control
- Rendezvous for synchronization
- Asymmetric

Tasks allow multiple threads of control: real or apparent concurrency. A novel idea is that of using the rendezvous to synchronize and exchange information between tasks. An entry of a task is called by any other task. Hence the rendezvous is asymmetric. Methods are provided to select among alternative entries or to accept alternative entry calls.

TASKS EXECUTE CONCURRENTLY

Keys to Understanding

► Ada general knowledge: *requirement, development,* and *nature* of Ada, and *APSE, ACVC,* current status.
► Ada language features: *Pascal-like, strong typing, encapsulation, generic units, exceptions, tasks.*

29

Conclusions

```
┌─────────────────────────────────────────────────┐
│  Objective:   to present the author's view of Ada │
│               and the Ada community              │
└─────────────────────────────────────────────────┘
```

Since the preceding chapter served to summarize and review the earlier material, I am reserving this final chapter for a few personal comments on Ada and the growing Ada community.

I believe that Ada is a fine language and will be used successfully for the design and implementation of DoD embedded computer systems. As a consequence of DoD use and of the fact that standardization will be enforced, Ada will be widely used in the United States and abroad in commercial scientific and real-time applications. It has great potential to encourage software publishing and to generate a software components industry.

Ada is complex, but not as complex as it sometimes appears to be, and only as complex as it needs to be to fulfill its requirements. Programmers who approach Ada from a FORTRAN or assembly-language background need to become familiar with those parts of Ada that are similar to Pascal. In *Understanding Ada* we have tried to foster and encourage that familiarity. The complexity of the advanced features remains, but these features need be considered only for solving complex problems. The parts of Ada that are difficult to understand are not needed for many applications and will not interfere with the adoption of the language. As more programmers become familiar with Ada's features, as we better understand how to teach the language, and as we learn how to effectively use the tools and capabilities the language provides, Ada will seem far less intimidating.

The other major factor that will emerge through extensive Ada use will be its importance as a design language. The fact that it provides features for the application of modern design concepts, and that it allows the same medium of communication to be used for both the design and programming phases of development, will be better and better appreciated. We do not yet have sufficient experience in using Ada to lay down specific design guidelines. After several large systems have been implemented, and especially after we have implemented major upgrades to operational systems, we will have greater insight into how to use the language effectively to meet its objectives of reliability and maintainability.

Ada is a language for the design of large, long-lived, embedded computer systems. In this way it differs from most modern languages: Pascal, FOR-TRAN, Algol, "C," COBOL, and so on. Because of the capabilities provided by the Ada **package,** Ada is likely to profoundly affect the way in which large software systems are designed. However, it is difficult at this time to determine exactly what design changes will be effected or what the preferred design methodologies will be.

The design methods most discussed are those concerned with the principle of *information hiding,* commonly associated with David Parnas. The basic idea is that large systems should be constructed by partitioning the system into modules based on major design decisions. Using the information-hiding principle, the structure of data is *hidden* from most of the system, while the data itself is provided via procedures that access and manipulate the encapsulated data structures. *Object-oriented design,* popularized in the Ada literature by Grady Booch, builds on notions of information hiding. Object-oriented design uses a strategy in which the problem is stated carefully with verbs that become operations and nouns that become objects to be processed. The objects are the focus of the design and become encapsulated in packages, along with associated operations.

The overall theme of information-hiding and object-oriented design is that of *data abstraction.* By thinking of a problem in terms of data abstractions, the *allowable values* and the *operations on those values* become defined. The design of the software then becomes a process of encapsulating the data and designing the procedures that implement the operation. The approach is similar to that of stepwise refinement, which guides much current thinking on design of systems. But object-oriented methods focus on the data (the objects) rather than on the processes to be performed.

The advantages of information-hiding and object-oriented design over conventional methods of design have not been firmly established, although these two methods show promise. Ada can support data abstraction but does not contradict or disallow conventional methods. Chapters 4 and 21 illustrated some ways in which use of Ada could result in more reliable designs. However, there is no current consensus on how to best use Ada for design. The DoD is currently attempting to develop such a methodology, including an effort popularly called METHODMAN. Similarly, attention is being focused on the issue of how to best teach Ada. The product of this effort is called FRESHMAN. However, development of a comprehensive methodology must wait for Ada to be used in the actual design, implementation, and maintenance of several large systems. Experimental or toy systems, small projects, or anything short of actual operation and modification in response to operational requirements will not serve to illustrate the power—or the problems—of Ada. Ada is intended to be a language for the design of large, long-lived systems. Until we have designed and implemented a large system in Ada, actually used the system, and modified the software in a typical maintenance environment, we will not understand how to best use Ada for design.

The people who will use Ada, who will gain the insights into better use, and who will build and maintain Ada embedded computer systems are those whose primary business is the building of systems applications programs. The emphasis of the Ada community is thus beginning to shift toward Ada *users* rather than Ada *implementers.* So far the Ada community has been, naturally enough, dominated by those involved in language design issues and in development of Ada compilers and environments. The most important organization for those who have an interest in Ada is SIGAda.* It is an outgrowth of AdaTEC, which developed from the informally organized Ada Implementers' Group. SIGAda has User, Design, and Education subcommittees that are beginning to focus on engineering-oriented Ada applications. Over the next several years the large aerospace companies whose primary focus is on building embedded computer systems will have greater influence in Ada affairs and will blend Ada into an engineering discipline for development of large software systems.

Ada will open the eyes of many to the features of modern, strongly typed languages. It will do even more to spread the use of new and effective design methods and principles. Ada is the result of an industry-academia partnership,

---

*The Special Interest Group on Ada, of the Association for Computing Machinery (ACM).

brought together and fostered by effective government leadership. It brings a computer science approch to the solution of difficult engineering problems and has the potential to blend the best of academic thought and industrial experience. It should usher in an exciting and important era in software development.

Keys to Understanding

▶ Ada is complex, but it needs to be so. The proper way to approach the complexity of Ada is to first understand its Pascal-like features.
▶ Use of Ada is likely to lead to use of new design concepts for large systems, but what these concepts will be is not yet clear.
▶ The focus of the Ada community must move from implementers to users/application developers.
▶ Ada, its APSE, and its new concepts of design will provide a superior environment for the development of large software systems. Ada will become widely used both inside the DoD and in commercial environments.

Appendix A: Glossary

This appendix is informative and is not part of the standard definition of the Ada programming language. Italicized terms in the abbreviated descriptions below either have glossary entries themselves or are described in entries for related terms.

Accept statement. See *entry*.

Access type. A value of an access type (an *access value*) is either a null value, or a value that *designates* and *object* created by an *allocator*. The designated object can be read and updated via the access value. The definition of an access type specifies the type of the objects designated by values of the access type. See also *collection*.

Actual parameter. See *parameter*.

Aggregate. The evaluation of an aggregate yields a value of a *composite type*. The value is specified by giving the value of each of the *components*. Either *positional association* or *named association* may be used to indicate which value is associated with which component.

Allocator. The evaluation of an allocator creates an *object* and returns a new *access value* which *designates* the object.

Array type. A value of an array type consists of *components* which are all of the same *subtype* (and hence, of the same type). Each component is uniquely distinguished by an *index* (for a one-dimensional array) or by a sequence of indices (for a multidimensional array). Each index must be a value of a *discrete type* and must lie in the correct index *range*.

Assignment. Assignment is the *operation* that replaces the current value of a *variable* by a new value. An *assignment statement* specifies a variable on the left, and on the right, an *expression* whose value is to be the new value of the variable.

Attribute. The evaluation of an attribute yields a predefined characteristic of a named entity; some attributes are *functions*.

Block statement. A block statement is a single statement that may contain a sequence of statements. It may also include a *declarative part*, and *exception handlers*; their effects are local to the block statement.

Body. A body defines the execution of a *subprogram, package,* or *task*. A *body stub* is a form of body that indicates that this execution is defined in a separately compiled *subunit*.

Collection. A collection is the entire set of *objects* created by evaluation of *allocators* for an *access type*.

Compilation unit. A compilation unit is the *declaration* or the *body* of a *program unit*, presented for compilation as an independent text. It is optionally preceded by a *context clause*, naming other compilation units upon which it depends by means of one more *with clauses*.

Component. A component is a value that is a part of a larger value, or an *object* that is part of a larger object.

Composite type. A composite type is one whose

339

values have *components*. There are two kinds of composite type: *array types* and *record types*.

Constant. See *object*.

Constraint. A constraint determines a subset of the values of a *type*. A value in that subset *satisfies* the constraint.

Context clause. See *compilation unit*.

Declaration. A declaration associates an identifier (or some other notation) with an entity. This association is in effect within a region of text called the *scope* of the declaration. Within the scope of a declaration, there are places where it is possible to use the identifier to refer to the associated declared entity. At such places the identifier is said to be a *simple name* of the entity; the *name* is said to *denote* the associated entity.

Declarative Part. A declarative part is a sequence of *declarations*. It may also contain related information such as *subprogram bodies* and *representation clauses*.

Denote. See *declaration*.

Derived Type. A derived type is a *type* whose operations and values are replicas of those of an existing type. The existing type is called the *parent type* of the derived type.

Designate. See *access type, task*.

Direct visibility. See *visibility*.

Discrete Type. A discrete type is a *type* which has an ordered set of distinct values. The discrete types are the *enumeration* and *integer types*. Discrete types are used for indexing and iteration, and for choices in case statements and record *variants*.

Discriminant. A discriminant is a distinguished *component* of an *object* or value of a *record type*. The *subtypes* of other components, or even their presence or absence, may depend on the value of the discriminant.

Discriminant constraint. A discriminant constraint on a *record type* or *private type* specifies a value for each *discriminant* of the *type*.

Elaboration. The elaboration of a *declaration* is the process by which the declaration achieves its effect (such as creating an *object*); this process occurs during program execution.

Entry. An entry is used for communication between *tasks*. Externally, an entry is called just as a *subprogram* is called; its internal behavior is specified by one or more *accept statements* specifying the actions to be performed when the entry is called.

Enumeration type. An enumeration type is a *discrete type* whose values are represented by enumeration literals which are given explicitly in the *type declaration*. These enumeration literals are either *identifiers* or *character literals*.

Evaluation. The evaluation of an *expression* is the process by which the value of the expression is computed. This process occurs during program execution.

Exception. An exception is an error situation which may arise during program execution. To *raise* an exception is to abandon normal program execution so as to signal that the error has taken place. An *exception handler* is a portion of program text specifying a response to the exception. Execution of such a program text is called *handling* the exception.

Expanded name. An expanded name *denotes* an entity which is *declared* immediately within some construct. An expanded name has the form of a *selected component*: the *prefix* denotes the construct (a *program unit;* or a *block,* loop, or *accept statement*); the *selector* is the *simple name* of the entity.

Expression. An expression defines the computation of a value.

Fixed point type. See *real type*.

Floating point type. See *real type*.

Formal parameter. See *parameter*.

Function. See *subprogram*.

Generic unit. A generic unit is a template either for a set of *subprograms* or for a set of *packages*. A subprogram or package created using the template is called an *instance* of the generic unit. A *generic instantiation* is the kind of *declaration* that creates an instance. A generic unit is written as a subprogram or package but with the specification prefixed by a *generic formal part* which may declare *generic formal parameters*. A generic formal parameter is either a *type,* a *subprogram,* or an *object*. A generic unit is one of the kinds of *program unit*.

Handler. See *exception*.

Index. See *array type*.

Index constraint. An index constraint for an *array type* specifies the lower and upper bounds for each index *range* of the array type.

Indexed component. An indexed component *denotes* a *component* in an *array*. It is a form of *name* containing *expressions* which specify the values of the *indices* of the array component. An indexed component may also denote an *entry* in a family of entries.

Instance. See *generic unit*.

Integer type. An integer type is a *discrete type* whose values represent all integer numbers within a specific *range.*

Lexical element. A lexical element is an identifier, a *literal,* a delimiter, or a comment.

Limited type. A limited type is a *type* for which neither assignment nor the predefined comparison for equality is implicitly declared. All *task* types are limited. A *private type* can be defined to be limited. An equality operator can be explicitly declared for a limited type.

Literal. A literal represents a value literally, that is, by means of letters and other characters. A literal is either a numeric literal, an enumeration literal, a character literal, or a string literal.

Mode. See *parameter.*

Model number. A model number is an exactly representable value of a *real type. Operations* of a real type are defined in terms of operations on the model numbers of the type. The properties of the model numbers and of their operations are the minimal properties preserved by all implementations of the real type.

Name. A name is a construct that stands for an entity: it is said that the name *denotes* the entity, and that the entity is the meaning of the name. See also *declaration, prefix.*

Named association. A named association specifies the association of an item with one or more positions in a list, by naming the positions.

Object. An object contains a value. A program creates an object either by *elaborating* an *object declaration* or by *evaluating* an *allocator.* The declaration or allocator specifies a *type* for the object: the object can only contain values of that type.

Operation. An operation is an elementary action associated with one or more *types.* It is either implicitly declared by the *declaration* of the type, or it is a *subprogram* that has a *parameter* or *result* of the type.

Operator. An operator is an operation which has one or two operands. A unary operator is written before an operand; a binary operator is written between two operands. This notation is a special kind of *function call.* An operator can be declared as a function. Many operators are implicitly declared by the *declaration* of a *type* (for example, most type declarations imply the declaration of the equality operator for values of the type).

Overloading. An identifier can have several alter-native meanings at a given point in the program text: this property is called *overloading.* For example, an overloaded enumeration literal can be an identifier that appears in the definitions of two or more *enumeration types.* The effective meaning of an overloaded identifier is determined by the context. *Subprograms, aggregates, allocators,* and string *literals* can also be overloaded.

Package. A package specifies a group of logically related entities, such as *types, objects* of those types, and *subprograms* with *parameters* of those types. It is written as a *package declaration* and a *package body.* The package declaration has a *visible part,* containing the *declarations* of all entities that can be explicitly used outside the package. It may also have a *private part* containing structural details that complete the specification of the visible entities, but which are irrelevant to the user of the package. The *package body* contains implementations of *subprograms* (and possibly *tasks* as other *packages*) that have been specified in the package declaration. A package is one of the kinds of *program unit.*

Parameter. A parameter is one of the named entities associated with a *subprogram, entry,* or *generic unit,* and used to communicate with the corresponding subprogram body, *accept statement* or generic body. A *formal parameter* is an identifier used to denote the named entity within the body. An *actual parameter* is the particular entity associated with the corresponding formal parameter by a *subprogram call, entry call,* or *generic instantiation.* The *mode* of a formal parameter specifies whether the associated actual parameter supplies a value for the formal parameter, or the formal supplies a value for the actual parameter, or both. The association of actual parameters with formal parameters can be specified by *named associations,* by *positional associations,* or by a combination of these.

Parent type. See *derived type.*

Positional association. A positional association specifies the association of an item with a position in a list, by using the same position in the text to specify the item.

Pragma. A pragma conveys information to the compiler.

Prefix. A prefix is used as the first part of certain kinds of name. A prefix is either a *function call* or a *name.*

Private part. See *package.*

Private type. A private type is a *type* whose structure and set of values are clearly defined, but not directly available to the user of the type. A private type is known only by its *discriminants* (if any) and by the set of *operations* defined for it. A private type and its applicable operations are defined in the *visible part* of a *package,* or in a *generic formal part. Assignment,* equality, and inequality are also defined for private types, unless the private type is *limited.*

Procedure. See *subprogram.*

Program. A program is composed of a number of *compilation units,* one of which is a *subprogram* called the *main program.* Execution of the program consists of execution of the main program, which may invoke subprograms declared in the other compilation units of the program.

Program unit. A program unit is any one of a *generic unit, package, subprogram,* or *task unit.*

Qualified expression. A qualified expression is an *expression* preceded by an indication of its *type* or *subtype.* Such qualification is used when, in its absence, the expression might be ambiguous (for example as a consequence of *overloading*).

Raising an exception. See *exception.*

Range. A range is a contiguous set of values of a *scalar type.* A range is specified by giving the lower and upper bounds for the values. A value in the range is said to *belong* to the range.

Range constraint. A range constraint of a *type* specifies a *range,* and thereby determines the subset of the values of the type that *belong* to the range.

Real type. A real type is a *type* whose values represent approximations to the real numbers. There are two kinds of real type: *fixed point types* are specified by absolute error bound; *floating point types* are specified by a relative error bound expressed as a number of significant decimal digits.

Record type. A value of a record type consists of *components* which are usually of different *types* or *subtypes.* For each component of a record value or record *object,* the definition of the record type specifies an identifier that uniquely determines the component within the record.

Renaming declaration. A renaming declaration declares another *name* for an entity.

Rendezvous. A rendezvous is the interaction that occurs between two parallel *tasks* when one task has called an *entry* of the other task, and a corresponding

accept statement is being executed by the other task on behalf of the calling task.

Representation clause. A representation clause directs the compiler in the selection of the mapping of a *type,* an *object,* or a *task* onto features of the underlying machine that executes a program. In some cases, representation clauses completely specify the mapping; in other cases, they provide criteria for choosing a mapping.

Satisfy. See *constraint, subtype.*

Scalar type. An *object* or value of a scalar *type* does not have *components.* A scalar type is either a *discrete type* or a *real type.* The values of a scalar type are ordered.

Scope. See *declaration.*

Selected component. A selected component is a *name* consisting of a *prefix* and of an identifier called the *selector.* Selected components are used to denote record components, *entries,* and *objects* designated by access values; they are also used as *expanded names.*

Selector. See *selected component.*

Simple name. See *declaration, name.*

Statement. A statement specifies one or more actions to be performed during the execution of a *program.*

Subcomponent. A subcomponent is either a *component,* or a component of another subcomponent.

Subprogram. A subprogram is either a *procedure* or a *function.* A procedure specifies a sequence of actions and is invoked by a *procedure call* statement. A function specifies a sequence of actions and also returns a value called the *result,* and so a *function call* is an *expression.* A subprogram is written as a *subprogram declaration,* which specifies its *name, formal parameters,* and (for a function) its result; and a *subprogram body* which specifies the sequence of actions. The subprogram call specifies the *actual parameters* that are to be associated with the formal parameters. A subprogram is one of the kinds of *program unit.*

Subtype. A subtype of a *type* characterizes a subset of the values of the type. The subset is determined by a *constraint* on the type. Each value in the set of values of the subtype *belongs* to the subtype and *satisfies* the constraint determining the subtype.

Subunit. See *body.*

Task. A task operates in parallel with other parts of the program. It is written as a *task specification* (which specifies the *name* of the task and the names and *formal parameters* of its entries), and a *task body* which defines its execution. A *task unit* is one of the kinds of *program unit*. A *task type* is a *type* that permits the subsequent *declaration* of any number of similar tasks of the type. A value of a task type is said to *designate* a task.

Type. A type characterizes both a set of values, and a set of *operations* applicable to those values. A *type definition* is a language construct that defines a type. A particular type is either an *access type,* an *array type,* a *private type,* a *record type,* a *scalar type,* or a *task type.*

Use clause. A use clause achieves *direct visibility* of *declarations* that appear in the *visible parts* of named *packages.*

Variable. See *object.*

Variant part. A variant part of a *record* specifies alternative record *components,* depending on a *discriminant* of the record. Each value of the discriminant establishes a particular alternative of the variant part.

Visibility. At a given point in a program text, the *declaration* of an entity with a certain identifier is said to be *visible* if the entity is an acceptable meaning for an occurrence at that point of the identifier. The declaration is *visible* by *selection* at the place of the *selector* in a *selected component* or at the place of the name in a *named association.* Otherwise, the declaration is *directly visible,* that is, if the identifier alone has that meaning.

Visible part. See *package.*

With clause. See *compilation unit.*

Appendix B:
Syntax Summary

```
graphic_character ::= basic_graphic_character
  | lower_case_letter | other_special_character

basic_graphic_character ::=
    upper_case_letter | digit
  | special_character | space_character

basic_character ::=
    basic_graphic_character | format_effector
```

2.3

```
identifier ::=
  letter {[underline] letter_or_digit}

letter_or_digit ::= letter | digit

letter ::= upper_case_letter | lower_case_letter
```

2.4

```
numeric_literal ::= decimal_literal | based_literal
```

2.4.1

```
decimal_literal ::= integer [.integer] [exponent]

integer ::= digit {[underline] digit}

exponent ::= E [+] integer | E - integer
```

2.4.2

```
based_literal ::=
  base # based_integer [.based_integer] # [exponent]

base ::= integer

based_integer ::=
  extended_digit {[underline] extended_digit}

extended_digit ::= digit | letter
```

2.5

```
character_literal ::= 'graphic_character'
```

2.6

```
string_literal ::= "{graphic_character}"
```

2.8

```
pragma ::=
  pragma identifier [(argument_association
                    {, argument_association})];

argument_association ::=
    [argument_identifier =>] name
  | [argument_identifier =>] expression
```

3.1

```
basic_declaration ::=
    object_declaration       | number_declaration
  | type_declaration         | subtype_declaration
  | subprogram_declaration   | package_declaration
  | task_declaration         | generic_declaration
  | exception_declaration    | generic_instantiation
  | renaming_declaration     | deferred_constant_declaration
```

3.2

```
object_declaration ::=
    identifier_list : [constant] subtype_indication [:= expression];
  | identifier_list : [constant] constrained_array_definition
                                        [:= expression];

number_declaration ::=
    identifier_list : constant := universal_static_expression;

identifier_list ::= identifier {, identifier}
```

3.3.1

```
type_declaration ::= full_type_declaration
  | incomplete_type_declaration | private_type_declaration

full_type_declaration ::=
  type identifier [discriminant_part] is type_definition;

type_definition ::=
    enumeration_type_definition | integer_type_definition
  | real_type_definition       | array_type_definition
  | record_type_definition     | access_type_definition
  | derived_type_definition
```

3.3.2

```
subtype_declaration ::=
  subtype identifier is subtype_indication;

subtype_indication ::= type_mark [constraint]

type_mark ::= type_name | subtype_name

constraint ::=
    range_constraint        | floating_point_constraint
  | fixed_point_constraint  | index_constraint
  | discriminant_constraint
```

3.4

```
derived_type_definition ::= new subtype_indication
```

3.5

```
range_constraint ::= range range

range ::= range_attribute
  | simple_expression .. simple_expression
```

3.5.1

```
enumeration_type_definition ::=
   (enumeration_literal_specification
     {, enumeration_literal_specification})

enumeration_literal_specification ::=   enumeration_literal

enumeration_literal ::=   identifier | character_literal
```

3.5.4

```
integer_type_definition ::=   range_constraint
```

3.5.6

```
real_type_definition ::=
   floating_point_constraint | fixed_point_constraint
```

3.5.7

```
floating_point_constraint ::=
   floating_accuracy_definition [range_constraint]

floating_accuracy_definition ::=
   digits static_simple_expression
```

3.5.9

```
fixed_point_constraint ::=
   fixed_accuracy_definition [range_constraint]

fixed_accuracy_definition ::=
   delta static_simple_expression
```

3.6

```
array_type_definition ::=
   unconstrained_array_definition | constrained_array_definition

unconstrained_array_definition ::=
   array(index_subtype_definition {, index_subtype_definition}) of
        component_subtype_indication

constrained_array_definition ::=
   array index_constraint of component_subtype_indication

index_subtype_definition ::= type_mark range <>

index_constraint ::=   (discrete_range {, discrete_range})

discrete_range ::= discrete_subtype_indication | range
```

3.7

```
record_type_definition ::=
   record
      component_list
   end record

component_list ::=
      component_declaration {component_declaration}
   | {component_declaration} variant_part
   | null;

component_declaration ::=
   identifier_list : component_subtype_definition [:= expression];

component_subtype_definition ::=   subtype_indication
```

-3.7.1

```
discriminant_part ::=
   (discriminant_specification {; discriminant_specification})

discriminant_specification ::=
   identifier_list : type_mark [:= expression]
```

3.7.2

```
discriminant_constraint ::=
   (discriminant_association {, discriminant_association})

discriminant_association ::=
   [discriminant_simple_name {| discriminant_simple_name} =>]
        expression
```

3.7.3

```
variant_part ::=
   case discriminant_simple_name is
         variant
        {variant}
   end case;

variant ::=
   when choice {| choice} =>
      component_list

choice ::= simple_expression
   | discrete_range | others | component_simple_name
```

3.8

```
access_type_definition ::= access subtype_indication
```

3.8.1

```
incomplete_type_declaration ::=
   type identifier [discriminant_part];
```

3.9

```
declarative_part ::=
   {basic_declarative_item} {later_declarative_item}

basic_declarative_item ::= basic_declaration
   | representation_clause | use_clause

later_declarative_item ::= body
   | subprogram_declaration | package_declaration
   | task_declaration        | generic_declaration
   | use_clause              | generic_instantiation

body ::= proper_body | body_stub

proper_body ::=
   subprogram_body | package_body | task_body
```

4.1

```
name ::= simple_name
    | character_literal        | operator_symbol
    | indexed_component        | slice
    | selected_component       | attribute

simple_name ::= identifier

prefix ::= name | function_call
```

4.1.1

```
indexed_component ::= prefix(expression {, expression})
```

4.1.2

```
slice ::= prefix(discrete_range)
```

4.1.3

```
selected_component ::= prefix.selector

selector ::= simple_name
    | character_literal | operator_symbol | all
```

4.1.4

```
attribute ::= prefix'attribute_designator

attribute_designator ::=
    simple_name [(universal_static_expression)]
```

4.3

```
aggregate ::=
    (component_association {, component_association})

component_association ::=
    [choice {| choice} => ] expression
```

4.4

```
expression ::=
    relation {and relation}  | relation {and then relation}
    | relation {or relation}  | relation {or else relation}
    | relation {xor relation}

relation ::=
    simple_expression [relational_operator simple_expression]
    | simple_expression [not] in range
    | simple_expression [not] in type_mark

simple_expression ::=
    [unary_adding_operator] term {binary_adding_operator term}

term ::= factor {multiplying_operator factor}

factor ::= primary [** primary] | abs primary | not primary

primary ::=
    numeric_literal | null | aggregate | string_literal
    | name | allocator | function_call | type_conversion
    | qualified_expression | (expression)
```

4.5

```
logical_operator    ::=  and | or | xor

relational_operator    ::=  = | /= | < | <= | > | >=

binary_adding_operator    ::=  + | - | &

unary_adding_operator    ::=  + | -

multiplying_operator    ::=  * | / | mod | rem

highest_precedence_operator    ::=  ** | abs | not
```

4.6

```
type_conversion ::= type_mark(expression)
```

4.7

```
qualified_expression ::=
    type_mark'(expression) | type_mark'aggregate
```

4.8

```
allocator ::=
    new subtype_indication | new qualified_expression
```

5.1

```
sequence_of_statements ::= statement {statement}

statement ::=
    {label} simple_statement | {label} compound_statement

simple_statement ::= null_statement
    | assignment_statement    | procedure_call_statement
    | exit_statement          | return_statement
    | goto_statement          | entry_call_statement
    | delay_statement         | abort_statement
    | raise_statement         | code_statement

compound_statement ::=
    if_statement      | case_statement
    | loop_statement   | block_statement
    | accept_statement | select_statement

label ::= <<label_simple_name>>

null_statement ::= null;
```

5.2

```
assignment_statement ::=
    variable_name := expression;
```

5.3

```
if_statement ::=
    if condition then
        sequence_of_statements
    {elsif condition then
        sequence_of_statements}
    [else
        sequence_of_statements]
    end if;

condition ::= boolean_expression
```

5.4

```
case_statement ::=
   case expression is
      case_statement_alternative
      { case_statement_alternative}
   end case;

case_statement_alternative ::=
   when choice {| choice } =>
      sequence_of_statements
```

5.5

```
loop_statement ::=
   [loop_simple_name:]
      [iteration_scheme] loop
         sequence_of_statements
      end loop [loop_simple_name];

iteration_scheme ::= while condition
   | for loop_parameter_specification

loop_parameter_specification ::=
   identifier in [reverse] discrete_range
```

5.6

```
block_statement ::=
   [block_simple_name:]
      [ declare
            declarative_part]
      begin
            sequence_of_statements
      [ exception
            exception_handler
            { exception_handler}]
      end [block_simple_name];
```

5.7

```
exit_statement ::=
   exit [loop_name] [when condition];
```

5.8

```
return_statement ::= return [expression];
```

5.9

```
goto_statement ::= goto label_name;
```

6.1

```
subprogram_declaration ::= subprogram_specification;

subprogram_specification ::=
      procedure identifier [formal_part]
   | function designator [formal_part] return type_mark

designator ::= identifier | operator_symbol

operator_symbol ::= string_literal

formal_part ::=
   (parameter_specification {; parameter_specification})

parameter_specification ::=
   identifier_list : mode type_mark [:= expression]

mode ::= [in] | in out | out
```

6.3

```
subprogram_body ::=
      subprogram_specification is
         [ declarative_part]
      begin
            sequence_of_statements
      [ exception
            exception_handler
            { exception_handler}]
      end [designator];
```

6.4

```
procedure_call_statement ::=
   procedure_name [actual_parameter_part];

function_call ::=
   function_name [actual_parameter_part]

actual_parameter_part ::=
   (parameter_association {, parameter_association})

parameter_association ::=
   [ formal_parameter =>] actual_parameter

formal_parameter ::= parameter_simple_name

actual_parameter ::=
   expression | variable_name | type_mark(variable_name)
```

7.1

```
package_declaration ::= package_specification;

package_specification ::=
      package identifier is
         {basic_declarative_item}
      [ private
         {basic_declarative_item}]
      end [package_simple_name]

package_body ::=
      package body package_simple_name is
         [ declarative_part]
      [ begin
            sequence_of_statements
      [ exception
            exception_handler
            {exception_handler}]]
      end [package_simple_name];
```

7.4

```
private_type_declaration ::=
   type identifier [discriminant_part] is [limited] private;

deferred_constant_declaration ::=
   identifier_list : constant type_mark;
```

8.4

```
use_clause ::= use package_name {, package_name};
```

8.5

```
renaming_declaration ::=
      identifier : type_mark       renames object_name;
   | identifier : exception        renames exception_name;
   | package identifier            renames package_name;
   | subprogram_specification      renames
                                   subprogram_or_entry_name;
```

9.1

task_declaration ::= task_specification;

task_specification ::=
   task [**type**] identifier [**is**
     {entry_declaration}
     {representation_clause}
   end [*task*_simple_name]]

task_body ::=
   task body *task*_simple_name **is**
     [declarative_part]
   begin
     sequence_of_statements
  [**exception**
     exception_handler
     {exception_handler}]
   end [*task*_simple_name];

9.5

entry_declaration ::=
   entry identifier [(discrete_range)] [formal_part];

entry_call_statement ::=
   *entry*_name [actual_parameter_part];

accept_statement ::=
   accept *entry*_simple_name [(entry_index)] [formal_part] [**do**
     sequence_of_statements
   end [*entry*_simple_name]];

entry_index ::= expression

9.6

delay_statement ::= **delay** simple_expression;

9.7

select_statement ::= selective_wait
   | conditional_entry_call | timed_entry_call

9.7.1

selective_wait ::=
   select
    select_alternative
  { **or**
    select_alternative}
  [**else**
    sequence_of_statements]
   end select;

select_alternative ::=
  [**when** condition =>]
    selective_wait_alternative

selective_wait_alternative ::= accept_alternative
   | delay_alternative | terminate_alternative

accept_alternative   ::=
   accept_statement [sequence_of_statements]

delay_alternative   ::=
   delay_statement [sequence_of_statements]

terminate_alternative ::= **terminate**;

9.7.2

conditional_entry_call ::=
   select
    entry_call_statement
    [sequence_of_statements]
   else
    sequence_of_statements
   end select;

9.7.3

timed_entry_call ::=
   select
    entry_call_statement
    [sequence_of_statements]
   or
    delay_alternative
   end select;

9.10

abort_statement ::= **abort** *task*_name {, *task*_name};

10.1

compilation ::= {compilation_unit}

compilation_unit ::=
   context_clause library_unit
  | context_clause secondary_unit

library_unit ::=
   subprogram_declaration | package_declaration
  | generic_declaration | generic_instantiation
  | subprogram_body

secondary_unit ::= library_unit_body | subunit

library_unit_body ::= subprogram_body | package_body

10.1.1

context_clause ::= {with_clause {use_clause}}

with_clause ::=
   with *unit*_simple_name {, *unit*_simple_name};

10.2

body_stub ::=
   subprogram_specification **is separate**;
  | **package body** *package*_simple_name **is separate**;
  | **task body** *task*_simple_name **is separate**;

subunit ::= **separate** (*parent_unit*_name) proper_body

11.1

exception_declaration ::= identifier_list : **exception**;

11.2

exception_handler ::=
   when exception_choice {| exception_choice} =>
    sequence_of_statements

exception_choice ::= *exception*_name | **others**

11.3

raise_statement ::= **raise** [*exception*_name];

12.1

generic_declaration ::= generic_specification;

generic_specification ::=
      generic_formal_part subprogram_specification
    | generic_formal_part package_specification

generic_formal_part ::= **generic** {generic_parameter_declaration}

generic_parameter_declaration ::=
      identifier_list : [in [out]] type_mark [:= expression];
    | **type** identifier **is** generic_type_definition;
    | private_type_declaration
    | **with** subprogram_specification [**is** name];
    | **with** subprogram_specification [**is** <>];

generic_type_definition ::=
      (<>) | **range** <> | **digits** <> | **delta** <>
    | array_type_definition | access_type_definition

12.3

generic_instantiation ::=
      package identifier **is**
          new *generic_package*_name [generic_actual_part];
    | **procedure** identifier **is**
          new *generic_procedure*_name [generic_actual_part];
    | **function** designator **is**
          new *generic_function*_name [generic_actual_part];

generic_actual_part ::=
    (generic_association {, generic_association})

generic_association ::=
    [generic_formal_parameter =>] generic_actual_parameter

generic_formal_parameter ::=
    *parameter*_simple_name | operator_symbol

generic_actual_parameter ::= expression | *variable*_name
    | *subprogram*_name | *entry*_name | type_mark

13.1

representation_clause ::=
      type_representation_clause | address_clause

type_representation_clause ::= length_clause
    | enumeration_representation_clause
    | record_representation_clause

13.2

length_clause ::= **for** attribute **use** simple_expression;

13.3

enumeration_representation_clause ::=
    for *type*_simple_name **use** aggregate;

13.4

record_representation_clause ::=
    for *type*_simple_name **use**
      record [alignment_clause]
          {component_clause}
      end record;

alignment_clause ::= **at mod** *static*_simple_expression;

component_clause ::=
    *component*_name **at** *static*_simple_expression
                        range *static*_range;

13.5

address_clause ::=
    for simple_name **use at** simple_expression;

13.8

code_statement ::= type_mark'*record*_aggregate;

Syntax Cross Reference

In the list given below each syntactic category is followed by the section number where it is defined. For example:

adding_operator   4.5

In addition, each syntactic category is followed by the names of other categories in whose definition it appears. For example, adding_operator appears in the definition of simple_expression:

adding_operator   4.5
    simple_expression   4.4

An ellipsis (...) is used when the syntactic category is not defined by a syntax rule. For example:

lower_case_letter   ...

All uses of parentheses are combined in the term "()". The italicized prefixes used with some terms have been deleted here.

Appendix C:
Predefined Language Environment

This annex outlines the specification of the package STANDARD containing all predefined identifiers in the language. The corresponding package body is implementation-defined and is not shown.   1

The operators that are predefined for the types declared in the package STANDARD are given in comments since they are implicitly declared. Italics are used for pseudo-names of anonymous types (such as *universal__real*) and for undefined information (such as *implementation__defined* and *any__fixed__point__type*).   2

package STANDARD **is**   3

    type BOOLEAN **is** (FALSE, TRUE);   4

    -- The predefined relational operators for this type are as follows:

    -- **function** " ="   (LEFT, RIGHT : BOOLEAN) **return** BOOLEAN;
    -- **function** "/ ="   (LEFT, RIGHT : BOOLEAN) **return** BOOLEAN;
    -- **function** " <"   (LEFT, RIGHT : BOOLEAN) **return** BOOLEAN;
    -- **function** " < ="   (LEFT, RIGHT : BOOLEAN) **return** BOOLEAN;
    -- **function** " >"   (LEFT, RIGHT : BOOLEAN) **return** BOOLEAN;
    -- **function** " > ="   (LEFT, RIGHT : BOOLEAN) **return** BOOLEAN;

    -- The predefined logical operators and the predefined logical negation operator are as follows:

    -- **function** "and"   (LEFT, RIGHT : BOOLEAN) **return** BOOLEAN;
    -- **function** "or"   (LEFT, RIGHT : BOOLEAN) **return** BOOLEAN;
    -- **function** "xor"   (LEFT, RIGHT : BOOLEAN) **return** BOOLEAN;

    -- **function** "not"   (RIGHT : BOOLEAN) **return** BOOLEAN;

    -- The universal type *universal__integer* is predefined.   5

6   **type** INTEGER **is** *implementation__defined;*

-- The predefined operators for this type are as follows:

-- **function** "="   (LEFT, RIGHT : INTEGER) **return** BOOLEAN;
-- **function** "/="   (LEFT, RIGHT : INTEGER) **return** BOOLEAN;
-- **function** "<"   (LEFT, RIGHT : INTEGER) **return** BOOLEAN;
-- **function** "<="   (LEFT, RIGHT : INTEGER) **return** BOOLEAN;
-- **function** ">"   (LEFT, RIGHT : INTEGER) **return** BOOLEAN;
-- **function** ">="   (LEFT, RIGHT : INTEGER) **return** BOOLEAN;
-- **function** "+"   (RIGHT : INTEGER) **return** INTEGER;
-- **function** "−"   (RIGHT : INTEGER) **return** INTEGER;
-- **function** "abs"   (RIGHT : INTEGER) **return** INTEGER;

-- **function** "+"   (LEFT, RIGHT : INTEGER) **return** INTEGER;
-- **function** "−"   (LEFT, RIGHT : INTEGER) **return** INTEGER;
-- **function** "*"   (LEFT, RIGHT : INTEGER) **return** INTEGER;
-- **function** "/"   (LEFT, RIGHT : INTEGER) **return** INTEGER;
-- **function** "rem"   (LEFT, RIGHT : INTEGER) **return** INTEGER;
-- **function** "mod" (LEFT, RIGHT : INTEGER) **return** INTEGER;

-- **function** "**"   (LEFT : INTEGER; RIGHT : INTEGER) **return** INTEGER;

7   -- An implementation may provide additional predefined integer types. It is recommended that the
-- names of such additional types end with INTEGER as in SHORT__INTEGER or LONG__INTE-
-- GER. The specification of each operator for the type *universal__integer,* or for any additional
-- predefined integer type, is obtained by replacing INTEGER by the name of the type in the
-- specification of the corresponding operator of the type INTEGER, except for the right operand
-- of the exponentiating operator.

8   -- The universal type *universal__real* is predefined.

9   **type** FLOAT **is** *implementation__defined;*

-- The predefined operators for this type are as follows:

-- **function** "="   (LEFT, RIGHT : FLOAT) **return** BOOLEAN;
-- **function** "/="   (LEFT, RIGHT : FLOAT) **return** BOOLEAN;
-- **function** "<"   (LEFT, RIGHT : FLOAT) **return** BOOLEAN;
-- **function** "<="   (LEFT, RIGHT : FLOAT) **return** BOOLEAN;
-- **function** ">"   (LEFT, RIGHT : FLOAT) **return** BOOLEAN;
-- **function** ">="   (LEFT, RIGHT : FLOAT) **return** BOOLEAN;

-- **function** "+"   (RIGHT : FLOAT) **return** FLOAT;
-- **function** "−"   (RIGHT : FLOAT) **return** FLOAT;
-- **function** "abs"   (RIGHT : FLOAT) **return** FLOAT;

```
-- function "+"        (LEFT, RIGHT : FLOAT) return FLOAT;
-- function "−"        (LEFT, RIGHT : FLOAT) return FLOAT;
-- function "*"        (LEFT, RIGHT : FLOAT) return FLOAT;
-- function "/"        (LEFT, RIGHT : FLOAT) return FLOAT;

-- function "**"       (LEFT : FLOAT; RIGHT : INTEGER) return FLOAT;
```

-- An implementation may provide additional predefined floating point types. It is recommended that   10
-- the names of such additional types end with FLOAT as in SHORT_FLOAT or LONG_FLOAT.
-- The specification of each operator for the type *universal_real,* or for any additional predefined
-- floating point type, is obtained by replacing FLOAT by the name of the type in the specification
-- of the corresponding operator of the type FLOAT.

-- In addition, the following operators are predefined for universal types: 11

```
-- function "*" (LEFT : universal_integer; RIGHT : universal_real)    return universal_real;
-- function "*" (LEFT : universal_real;    RIGHT : universal_integer) return universal_real;
-- function "/" (LEFT : universal_real;    RIGHT : universal_integer) return universal_real;
```

-- The type *universal_fixed* is predefined. The only operators declared for this type are

```
-- function "*"   (LEFT : any_fixed_point_type; RIGHT : any_fixed_point_type) return
-- universal_fixed;
-- function "/"   (LEFT : any_fixed_point_type; RIGHT : any_fixed_point_type) return
-- universal_fixed;
```

-- The following characters from the standard ASCII character set. Character literals corresponding   12
-- to control characters are not identifiers; they are indicated in italics in this definition.

type CHARACTER **is**   13

(nul,	*soh,*	*stx,*	*etx,*	*eot,*	*enq,*	*ack,*	*bel,*
bs,	*ht,*	*lf,*	*vt,*	*ff,*	*cr,*	*so,*	*si,*
dle,	*dc1,*	*dc2,*	*dc3,*	*dc4,*	*nak,*	*syn,*	*etb,*
can,	*em,*	*sub,*	*esc,*	*fs,*	*gs,*	*rs,*	*us,*
' ',	'!',	' " ',	'#',	'$',	'%',	'&',	''',
'(',	')',	'*',	'+',	',',	'−',	'.',	'/',
'0',	'1',	'2',	'3',	'4',	'5',	'6',	'7',
'8',	'9',	':',	';',	'<',	'=',	'>',	'?',
'@',	'A',	'B',	'C',	'D',	'E',	'F',	'G',
'H',	'I',	'J',	'K',	'L',	'M',	'N',	'O',
'P',	'Q',	'R',	'S',	'T',	'U',	'V',	'W',
'X',	'Y',	'Z',	'[',	'\',	']',	'^',	'_',

```
'''',      'a',      'b',      'c',              'd',      'e',      'f',      'g',
'h',       'i',      'j',      'k',              'l',      'm',      'n',      'o',
'p',       'q',      'r',      's',              't',      'u',      'v',      'w',
'x',       'y',      'z',      '{',              '|',      '}',      '‿',     del);
```

for CHARACTER use -- 128 ASCII character set without holes (0, 1, 2, 3, 4, 5, . . ., 125, 126, 127);

14   -- The predefined operators for the type CHARACTER are the same as for any enumeration type.

15   **package** ASCII **is**

-- Control characters:

```
NUL    : constant CHARACTER := nul;      SOH    : constant CHARACTER := soh;
STX    : constant CHARACTER := stx;      ETX    : constant CHARACTER := etx;
EOT    : constant CHARACTER := eot;      ENQ    : constant CHARACTER := enq;
ACK    : constant CHARACTER := ack;      BEL    : constant CHARACTER := bel;
BS     : constant CHARACTER := bs;       HT     : constant CHARACTER := ht;
LF     : constant CHARACTER := lf;       VT     : constant CHARACTER := vt;
FF     : constant CHARACTER := ff;       CR     : constant CHARACTER := cr;
SO     : constant CHARACTER := so;       SI     : constant CHARACTER := si;
DLE    : constant CHARACTER := dle;      DC1    : constant CHARACTER := dc1;
DC2    : constant CHARACTER := dc2;      DC3    : constant CHARACTER := dc3;
DC4    : constant CHARACTER := dc4;      NAK    : constant CHARACTER := nak;
SYN    : constant CHARACTER* := syn;     ETB    : constant CHARACTER := etb;
CAN    : constant CHARACTER := can;      EM     : constant CHARACTER := em;
SUB    : constant CHARACTER := sub;      ESC    : constant CHARACTER := esc;
FS     : constant CHARACTER := fs;       GS     : constant CHARACTER := gs;
RS     : constant CHARACTER := rs;       US     : constant CHARACTER := us;
DEL    : constant CHARACTER := del;
```

-- Other characters:

```
EXCLAM      : constant CHARACTER := '!';     QUOTATION    : constant CHARACTER := ' " ';
SHARP       : constant CHARACTER := '#';     DOLLAR       : constant CHARACTER := '$';
PERCENT     : constant CHARACTER := '%';     AMPERSAND    : constant CHARACTER := '&';
COLON       : constant CHARACTER := ':';     SEMICOLON    : constant CHARACTER := ';';
QUERY       : constant CHARACTER := '?';     AT_SIGN      : constant CHARACTER := '@';
L_BRACKET   : constant CHARACTER := '[';     BACK_SLASH   : constant CHARACTER := '\';
R_BRACKET   : constant CHARACTER := ']';     CIRCUMFLEX   : constant CHARACTER := '^';
UNDERLINE   : constant CHARACTER := '_';     GRAVE        : constant CHARACTER := '''';
L_BRACE     : constant CHARACTER := '{';     BAR          : constant CHARACTER := '|';
R_BRACE     : constant CHARACTER := '}';     TILDE        : constant CHARACTER := '‿';
```

-- Lower case letters:

LC__A : **constant** CHARACTER := 'a';
. . .
LC__Z : **constant** CHARACTER := 'z';

end ASCII;

-- Predefined subtypes: 16

subtype NATURAL **is** INTEGER **range** 0 .. INTEGER'LAST;
subtype POSITIVE **is** INTEGER **range** 1 .. INTEGER'LAST;

-- Predefined string type: 17

type STRING **is array**(POSITIVE **range** < >) **of** CHARACTER;

pragma PACK(STRING);

-- The predefined operators for this type are as follows: 18

-- **function** "="   (LEFT, RIGHT : STRING) **return** BOOLEAN;
-- **function** "/="   (LEFT, RIGHT : STRING) **return** BOOLEAN;
-- **function** "<"   (LEFT, RIGHT : STRING) **return** BOOLEAN;
-- **function** "<="   (LEFT, RIGHT : STRING) **return** BOOLEAN;
-- **function** ">"   (LEFT, RIGHT : STRING) **return** BOOLEAN;
-- **function** ">="   (LEFT, RIGHT : STRING) **return** BOOLEAN;

-- **function** "&"   (LEFT : STRING; RIGHT : STRING)   **return** STRING;
-- **function** "&"   (LEFT : CHARACTER; RIGHT : STRING)   **return** STRING;
-- **function** "&"   (LEFT : STRING; RIGHT : CHARACTER)   **return** STRING;
-- **function** "&"   (LEFT : CHARACTER; RIGHT : CHARACTER) **return** STRING;

type DURATION **is delta** *implementation__defined* **range** *implementation__defined;*   19

-- The predefined operators for the type DURATION are the same as for any fixed point type.

-- The predefined exceptions: 20

CONSTRAINT__ERROR   : **exception;**
NUMERIC__ERROR   : **exception;**
PROGRAM__ERROR   : **exception;**
STORAGE__ERROR   : **exception;**
TASKING__ERROR   : **exception;**

end STANDARD;

21   Certain aspects of the predefined entities cannot be completely described in the language itself. For example, although the enumeration type BOOLEAN can be written showing the two enumeration literals FALSE and TRUE, the short-circuit control forms cannot be expressed in the language.

Note:

22   The language definition predefines the following library units:

- The package CALENDAR	(see 9.6)
- The package SYSTEM	(see 13.7)
- The package MACHINE__CODE (if provided)	(see 13.8)
- The generic procedure UNCHECKED__DEALLOCATION	(see 13.10.1)
- The generic function UNCHECKED__CONVERSION	(see 13.10.2)
- The generic package SEQUENTIAL__IO	(see 14.2.3)
- The generic package DIRECT__IO	(see 14.2.5)
- The package TEXT__IO	(see 14.3.10)
- The package IO__EXCEPTIONS	(see 14.5)
- The package LOW__LEVEL__IO	(see 14.6)

Appendix D:
Predefined Language Pragmas

This annex defines the pragmas LIST, PAGE, and OPTIMIZE, and summarizes the definitions given elsewhere of the remaining language-defined pragmas.   1

Pragma	Meaning

Pragma   *Meaning*

CONTROLLED   Takes the simple name of an access type as the single argument. This pragma is only   2
allowed immediately within the declarative part of package specification that contains the declaration of the access type; the declaration must occur before the pragma. This pragma is not allowed for a derived type. This pragma specifies that automatic storage reclamation must not be performed for objects designated by values of the access type, except upon leaving the innermost block statement, subprogram body, or task body that encloses the access type declaration, or after leaving the main program (see 4.8).

ELABORATE   Takes one or more simple names denoting library units as arguments. This pragma is   3
only allowed immediately after the context clause of a compilation unit (before the subsequent library unit or secondary unit). Each argument must be the simple name of a library unit mentioned by the context clause. This pragma specifies that the corresponding library unit body must be elaborated before the given compilation unit. If the given compilation unit is a subunit, the library unit body must be elaborated before the body of the ancestor library unit of the subunit (see 10.5).

INLINE   Takes one or more names as arguments; each name is either the name of a subprogram   4
or the name of a generic subprogram. This pragma is only allowed at the place of a declarative item in a declarative part or package specification, or after a library unit in a compilation, but before any subsequent compilation unit. This pragma specifies that the subprogram bodies should be expanded inline at each call whenever possible; in the case of a generic subprogram, the pragma applies to calls of its instantiations (see 6.3.2).

INTERFACE   Takes a language name and a subprogram name as arguments. This pragma is allowed   5
at the place of a declarative item, and must apply in this case to a subprogram declared

by an earlier declarative item of the same declarative part or package specification. This pragma is also allowed for a library unit; in this case the pragma must appear after the subprogram declaration, and before any subsequent compilation unit. This pragma specifies the other language (and thereby the calling conventions) and informs the compiler that an object module will be supplied for the corresponding subprogram (see 13.9).

6   LIST   Takes one of the identifiers ON or OFF as the single argument. This pragma is allowed anywhere a pragma is allowed. It specifies that listing of the compilation is to be continued or suspended until a LIST pragma with the opposite argument is given within the same compilation. The pragma itself is always listed if the compiler is producing a listing.

7   MEMORY__SIZE   Takes a numeric literal as the single argument. This pragma is only allowed at the start of a compilation, before the first compilation unit (if any) of the compilation. The effect of this pragma is to use the value of the specified numeric literal for the definition of the named number MEMORY__SIZE (see 13.7).

8   OPTIMIZE   Takes one of the identifiers TIME or SPACE as the single argument. This pragma is only allowed within a declarative part and it applies to the block or body enclosing the declarative part. It specifies whether time or space is the primary optimization criterion.

9   PACK   Takes the simple name of a record or array type as the single argument. The allowed positions for this pragma, and the restrictions on the named type, are governed by the same rules as for a representation clause. The pragma specifies that storage minimization should be the main criterion when selecting the representation of the given type (see 13.1).

10   PAGE   This pragma has no argument, and is allowed anywhere a pragma is allowed. It specifies that the program text which follows the pragma should start on a new page (if the compiler is currently producing a listing).

11   PRIORITY   Takes a static expression of the predefined integer subtype PRIORITY as the single argument. This pragma is only allowed within the specification of a task unit or immediately within the outermost declarative part of a main program. It specifies the priority of the task (or tasks of the task type) or the priority of the main program (see 9.8).

12   SHARED   Takes the simple name of a variable as the single argument. This pragma is allowed only for a variable declared by an object declaration and whose type is a scalar or access type; the variable declaration and the pragma must both occur (in this order) immediately within the same declarative part or package specification. This pragma specifies that every read or update of the variable is a synchronization point for that variable. An implementation must restrict the objects for which this pragma is allowed to objects for which each of direct reading and direct updating is implemented as an indivisible operation (see 9.11).

13   STORAGE__UNIT   Takes a numeric literal as the single argument. This pragma is only allowed at the start of a compilation, before the first compilation unit (if any) of the compilation. The effect of this pragma is to use the value of the specified numeric literal for the definition of the named number STORAGE__UNIT (see 13.7).

SUPPRESS

Takes as arguments the identifier of a check and optionally also the name of either an   14
object, a type or subtype, a subprogram, a task unit, or a generic unit. This pragma is
only allowed either immediately within a declarative part of immediately within a
package specification. In the latter case, the only allowed form is with a name that
denotes an entity (or several overloaded subprograms) declared immediately within the
package specification. The permission to omit the given check extends from the place
of the pragma to the end of the declarative region associated with the innermost
enclosing block statement or program unit. For a pragma given in a package specification, the permission extends to the end of the scope of the named entity.

If the pragma includes a name, the permission to omit the given check is further
restricted: it is given only for operations on the named object or on all objects of the
base type of a named type or subtype; for calls of a named subprogram; for activations
of tasks of the named task type; or for instantiations of the given generic unit (see 11.7).

SYSTEM_NAME

Takes an enumeration literal as the single argument. This pragma is only allowed at the   15
start of a compilation, before the first compilation unit (if any) of the compilation. The
effect of this pragma is to use the enumeration literal with the specified identifier for
the definition of the constant SYSTEM_NAME. This pragma is only allowed if the
specified identifier corresponds to one of the literals of the type NAME declared in the
package SYSTEM (see 13.7).

Appendix E:
Predefined Language Attributes

This annex summarizes the definitions given elsewhere of the predefined language attributes. 1

P'ADDRESS

For a prefix P that denotes an object, a program unit, a label, or an entry: 2

Yields the address of the first of the storage units allocated to P. For a subprogram, package, task unit, or label, this value refers to the machine code associated with the corresponding body or statement. For an entry for which an address clause has been given, the value refers to the corresponding hardware interrupt. The value of this attribute is of the type ADDRESS defined in the package SYSTEM. (See 13.7.2.)

P'AFT

For a prefix P that denotes a fixed point subtype: 3

Yields the number of decimal digits needed after the point to accommodate the precision of the subtype P, unless the delta of the subtype P is greater than 0.1, in which case the attribute yields the value one. (P'AFT is the smallest positive integer N for which $(10**N)*P'DELTA$ is greater than or equal to one.) The value of this attribute is of the type *universal_integer*. (See 3.5.10.)

P'BASE

For a prefix P that denotes a type or subtype: 4

This attribute denotes the base type of P. It is only allowed as the prefix of the name of another attribute: for example, P'BASE'FIRST. (See 3.3.3.)

P'CALLABLE

For a prefix P that is appropriate for a task type: 5

Yields the value FALSE when the execution of the task P is either completed or terminated, or when the task is abnormal; yields the value TRUE otherwise. The value of this attribute is of the predefined type BOOLEAN. (See 9.9.)

P'CONSTRAINED

For a prefix P that denotes an object of a type with discriminants: 6

Yields the value TRUE if a discriminant constraint applies to the object P, or if the object is a constant (including a formal parameter or generic formal parameter of mode **in**); yields the value FALSE otherwise. If P is a generic formal parameter of mode **in out,** or if P is a formal parameter of mode **in out** or **out** and the type mark given in the corresponding parameter specification denotes an unconstrained type with discriminants, then the value of this attribute is obtained from that of the corresponding actual parameter. The value of this attribute is of the predefined type BOOLEAN. (See 3.7.4.)

7   P'CONSTRAINED

For a prefix P that denotes a private type or subtype:

Yields the value FALSE if P denotes an unconstrained nonformal private type with discriminants; also yields the value FALSE if P denotes a generic formal private type and the associated actual subtype is either an unconstrained type with discriminants or an unconstrained array type; yields the value TRUE otherwise. The value of this attribute is of the predefined type BOOLEAN. (See 7.4.2.)

8   P'COUNT

For a prefix P that denotes an entry of a task unit:

Yields the number of entry calls presently queued on the entry (if the attribute is evaluated within an accept statement for the entry P, the count does not include the calling task). The value of this attribute is of the type *universal _integer.* (See 9.9.)

9   P'DELTA

For a prefix P that denotes a fixed point subtype:

Yields the value of the delta specified in the fixed accuracy definition for the subtype P. The value of this attribute is of the type *universal_real.* (See 3.5.10.)

10   P'DIGITS

For a prefix P that denotes a floating point subtype:

Yields the number of decimal digits in the decimal mantissa of model numbers of the subtype P. (This attribute yields the number D of section 3.5.7.) The value of this attribute is of the type *universal_integer.* (See 3.5.8.)

11   P'EMAX

For a prefix P that denotes a floating point subtype:

Yields the largest exponent value in the binary canonical form of model numbers of the subtype P. (This attribute yields the product 4*B of section 3.5.7.) The value of this attribute is of the type *universal_integer.* (See 3.5.8.)

12   P'EPSILON

For a prefix P that denotes a floating point subtype:

Yields the absolute value of the difference between the model number 1.0 and the next model number above, for the subtype P. The value of this attribute is of the type *universal_real.* (See 3.5.8.)

13   P'FIRST

For a prefix P that denotes a scalar type, or a subtype of a scalar type:

Yields the lower bound of P. The value of this attribute has the same type as P. (See 3.5.)

P'FIRST　　For a prefix P that is appropriate for an array type, or that denotes a con- 14
strained array subtype:

Yields the lower bound of the first index range. The value of this attribute has
the same type as this lower bound. (See 3.6.2 and 3.8.2.)

P'FIRST(N)　　For a prefix P that is appropriate for an array type, or that denotes a con- 15
strained array subtype:

Yields the lower bound of the N-th index range. The value of this attribute
has the same type as this lower bound. The argument N must be a static
expression of type *universal_integer*. The value of N must be positive
(nonzero) and no greater than the dimensionality of the array. (See 3.6.2 and
3.8.2.)

P'FIRST_BIT　　For a prefix P that denotes a component of a record object: 16

Yields the offset, from the start of the first of the storage units occupied by
the component, of the first bit occupied by the component. This offset is
measured in bits. The value of this attribute is of the type *universal_integer*.
(See 13.7.2.)

P'FORE　　For a prefix P that denotes a fixed point subtype: 17

Yields the minimum number of characters needed for the integer part of the
decimal representation of any value of the subtype P, assuming that the
representation does not include an exponent, but includes a one-character
prefix that is either a minus sign or a space. (This minimum number does not
include superfluous zeros or underlines, and is at least two.) The value of this
attribute is of the type *universal_integer*. (See 3.5.10.)

P'IMAGE　　For a prefix P that denotes a discrete type or subtype: 18

This attribute is a function with a single parameter. The actual parameter X
must be a value of the base type of P. The result type is the predefined type
STRING. The result is the *image* of the value of X, that is, a sequence of
characters representing the value in display form. The image of an integer
value is the corresponding decimal literal; without underlines, leading zeros,
exponent, or trailing spaces; but with a one character prefix that is either a
minus sign or a space.

The image of an enumeration value is either the corresponding identifier in
upper case or the corresponding character literal (including the two apostrophes); neither leading nor trailing spaces are included. The image of a
character other than a graphic character is implementation-defined. (See
3.5.5.)

P'LARGE　　For a prefix P that denotes a real subtype: 19

The attribute yields the largest positive model number of the subtype P. The
value of this attribute is of the type *universal_real*. (See 3.5.8 and 3.5.10.)

P'LAST　　For a prefix P that denotes a scalar type, or a subtype of a scalar type: 20

Yields the upper bound of P. The value of this attribute has the same type as P. (See 3.5.)

21   P'LAST   For a prefix P that is appropriate for an array type, or that denotes a constrained array subtype:

Yields the upper bound of the first index range. The value of this attribute has the same type as this upper bound. (See 3.6.2 and 3.8.2.)

22   P'LAST(N)   For a prefix P that is appropriate for an array type, or that denotes a constrained array subtype:

Yields the upper bound of the N-th index range. The value of this attribute has the same type as this upper bound. The argument N must be a static expression of type *universal_integer*. The value of N must be positive (nonzero) and no greater than the dimensionality of the array. (See 3.6.2 and 3.8.2.)

23   P'LAST_BIT   For a prefix P that denotes a component of a record object:

Yields the offset, from the start of the first of the storage units occupied by the component, of the last bit occupied by the component. This offset is measured in bits. The value of this attribute is of the type *universal_integer*. (See 13.7.2.)

24   P'LENGTH   For a prefix P that is appropriate for an array type, or that denotes a constrained array subtype:

Yields the number of values of the first index range (zero for a null range). The value of this attribute is of the type *universal_integer*. (See 3.6.2.)

25   P'LENGTH(N)   For a prefix P that is appropriate for an array type, or that denotes a constrained array subtype:

Yields the number of values of the N-th index range (zero for a null range). The value of this attribute is of the type *universal_integer*. The argument N must be a static expression of type *universal_integer*. The value of N must be positive (nonzero) and no greater than the dimensionality of the array. (See 3.6.2 and 3.8.2.)

26   P'MACHINE_EMAX For a prefix P that denotes a floating point type or subtype:

Yields the largest value of *exponent* for the machine representation of the base type of P. The value of this attribute is of the type *universal_integer*. (See 13.7.3.)

27   P'MACHINE_EMIN For a prefix P that denotes a floating point type or subtype:

Yields the smallest (most negative) value of *exponent* for the machine representation of the base type of P. The value of this attribute is of the type *universal_integer*. (See 13.7.3.)

P'MACHINE__MANTISSA   For a prefix P that denotes a floating point type or subtype: 28

Yields the number of digits in the *mantissa* for the machine representation of the base type of P (the digits are extended digits in the range O to P'MACHINE__RADIX − 1). The value of this attribute is of the type *universal __integer*. (See 13.7.3.)

P'MACHINE__OVERFLOWS   For a prefix P that denotes a real type or subtype: 29

Yields the value TRUE if every predefined operation on values of the base type of P either provides a correct result, or raises the exception NUMERIC__ ERROR in overflow situations; yields the value FALSE otherwise. The value of this attribute is of the predefined type BOOLEAN. (See 13.7.3.)

P'MACHINE__RADIX   For a prefix P that denotes a floating point type or subtype: 30

Yields the value of the *radix* used by the machine representation of the base type of P. The value of this attribute is of the type *universal__integer*. (See 13.7.3.)

P'MACHINE__ROUNDS   For a prefix P that denotes a real type or subtype: 31

Yields the value TRUE if every predefined arithmetic operation on values of the base type of P either returns an exact result or performs rounding; yields the value FALSE otherwise. The value of this attribute is of the predefined type BOOLEAN. (See 13.7.3.)

P'MANTISSA   For a prefix P that denotes a real subtype: 32

Yields the number of binary digits in the binary mantissa of model numbers of the subtype P. (This attribute yields the number B of section 3.5.7 for a floating point type, or of section 3.5.9 for a fixed point type.) The value of this attribute is of the type *universal__integer*. (See 3.5.8 and 3.5.10.)

P'POS   For a prefix P that denotes a discrete type or subtype: 33

This attribute is a function with a single parameter. The actual parameter X must be a value of the base type of P. The result type is the type *universal __integer*. The result is the position number of the value of the actual parameter. (See 3.5.5.)

P'POSITION   For a prefix P that denotes a component of a record object: 34

Yields the offset, from the start of the first storage unit occupied by the record, of the first of the storage units occupied by the component. This offset is measured in storage units. The value of this attribute is of the type *universal __integer*. (See 13.7.2.)

P'PRED   For a prefix P that denotes a discrete type or subtype: 35

This attribute is a function with a single parameter. The actual parameter X must be a value of the base type of P. The result type is the base type of P.

| | | The result is the value whose position number is one less than that of X. The exception CONSTRAINT__ERROR is raised if X equals P'BASE'FIRST. (See 3.5.5.) |

36 **P'RANGE**

For a prefix P that is appropriate for an array type, or that denotes a constrained array subtype:

Yields the first index range of P, that is, the range P'FIRST .. P'LAST. (See 3.6.2.)

37 **P'RANGE(N)**

For a prefix P that is appropriate for an array type, or that denotes a constrained array subtype:

Yields the N-th index range of P, that is, the range P'FIRST(N) .. P'LAST(N). (See 3.6.2.)

38 **P'SAFE__EMAX**

For a prefix P that denotes a floating point type or subtype:

Yields the largest exponent value in the binary canonical form of safe numbers of the base type of P. (This attribute yields the number E of section 3.5.7.) The value of this attribute is of the type *universal__integer*. (See 3.5.8.)

39 **P'SAFE__LARGE**

For a prefix P that denotes a real type or subtype:

Yields the largest positive safe number of the base type of P. The value of this attribute is of the type *universal__real*. (See 3.5.8 and 3.5.10.)

40 **P'SAFE__SMALL**

For a prefix P that denotes a real type or subtype:

Yields the smallest positive (nonzero) safe number of the base type of P. The value of this attribute is of the type *universal__real*. (See 3.5.8 and 3.5.10.)

41 **P'SIZE**

For a prefix P that denotes an object:

Yields the number of bits allocated to hold the object. The value of this attribute is of the type *universal__integer*. (See 13.7.2.)

42 **P'SIZE**

For a prefix P that denotes any type or subtype:

Yields the minimum number of bits that is needed by the implementation to hold any possible object of the type or subtype P. The value of this attribute is of the type *universal__integer*. (See 13.7.2.)

43 **P'SMALL**

For a prefix P that denotes a real subtype:

Yields the smallest positive (nonzero) model number of the subtype P. The value of this attribute is of the type *universal__real*. (See 3.5.8 and 3.5.10.)

44 **P'STORAGE__SIZE**

For a prefix P that denotes an access type or subtype:

Yields the total number of storage units reserved for the collection associated with the base type of P. The value of this attribute is of the type *universal __integer*. (See 13.7.2.)

P'STORAGE—SIZE	For a prefix P that denotes a task type or a task object:	45

Yields the number of storage units reserved for each activation of a task of the type P or for the activation of the task object P. The value of this attribute is of the type *universal—integer*. (See 13.7.2.)

P'SUCC	For a prefix P that denotes a discrete type or subtype:	46

This attribute is a function with a single parameter. The actual parameter X must be a value of the base type of P. The result type is the base type of P. The result is the value whose position number is one greater than that of X. The exception CONSTRAINT—ERROR is raised if X equals P'BASE'LAST. (See 3.5.5.)

P'TERMINATED	For a prefix P that is appropriate for a task type:	47

Yields the value TRUE if the task P is terminated; yields the value FALSE otherwise. The value of this attribute is of the predefined type BOOLEAN. (See 9.9.)

P'VAL	For a prefix P that denotes a discrete type or subtype:	48

This attribute is a special function with a single parameter X which can be of any integer type. The result type is the base type of P. The result is the value whose position number is the *universal—integer* value corresponding to X. The exception CONSTRAINT—ERROR is raised if the *universal—integer* value corresponding to X is not in the range P'POS (P'BASE'FIRST) .. P'POS (P'BASE'LAST). (See 3.5.5.)

P'VALUE	For a prefix P that denotes a discrete type or subtype:	49

This attribute is a function with a single parameter. The actual parameter X must be a value of the predefined type STRING. The result type is the base type of P. Any leading and any trailing spaces of the sequence of characters that corresponds to X are ignored.

For an enumeration type, if the sequence of characters has the syntax of an enumeration literal and if this literal exists for the base type of P, the result is the corresponding enumeration value. For an integer type, if the sequence of characters has the syntax of an integer literal, with an optional single leading character that is a plus or minus sign, and if there is a corresponding value in the base type of P, the result is this value. In any other case, the exception CONSTRAINT—ERROR is raised. (See 3.5.5.)

P'WIDTH	For a prefix P that denotes a discrete subtype:	50

Yields the maximum image length over all values of the subtype P (the *image* is the sequence of characters returned by the attribute IMAGE). The value of this attribute is of the type *universal—integer*. (See 3.5.5.)

Index